Law, Society, Policy series

Series Editor: **Rosie Harding**,
University of Birmingham

Law, Society, Policy seeks to offer an outlet for high quality, socio-legal research monographs and edited collections with the potential for policy impact.

Also available in the series:

Deprivation of Liberty in the Shadows of the Institution
By **Lucy Series**

Women, Precarious Work and Care:
The Failure of Family-friendly Rights
By **Emily Grabham**

Pandemic Legalities:
Legal Responses to COVID-19 – Justice and Social Responsibility
Edited by **Dave Cowan** and **Ann Mumford**

Forthcoming:

Egalitarian Digital Privacy:
Image Based Abuse and Beyond
By **Tsachi Keren-Paz**

Intersex Embodiment:
Legal Frameworks Beyond Identity and Patienthood
By **Fae Garland** and **Mitchell Travis**

Polygamy, Policy and Postcolonialism in English Marriage Law:
A Critical Feminist Analysis
By **Zainab Batul Naqv**

D1612783

Find out more at
bristoluniversitypress.co.uk/law-society-policy

Forthcoming:

The Challenge of Legal Gender:
Decertification, Contemporary Feminist Politics, and the Prefiguring of Reform
Edited by **Davina Cooper** and **Flora Renz**

Sex Worker Rights Activism and the Politics of Rights:
Within and against the Law
By **Katie Cruz**

International advisory board:

Find out more at
bristoluniversitypress.co.uk/law-society-policy

DEATH, FAMILY AND THE LAW

The Contemporary Inquest in Context

Edward Kirton-Darling

BRISTOL
UNIVERSITY
PRESS

First published in Great Britain in 2022 by

Bristol University Press
University of Bristol
1-9 Old Park Hill
Bristol
BS2 8BB
UK
t: +44 (0)117 374 6645
e: bup-info@bristol.ac.uk

Details of international sales and distribution partners are available at bristoluniversitypress.co.uk

British Library Cataloguing in Publication Data
A catalogue record for this book is available from the British Library

ISBN 978-1-5292-1245-7 hardcover
ISBN 978-1-5292-1246-4 paperback
ISBN 978-1-5292-1247-1 ePub
ISBN 978-1-5292-1248-8 ePdf

Cover design: Andrew Corbett
Front cover image: Jovana Milanko – Stocksy
Bristol University Press use environmentally responsible print partners
Printed and bound in Great Britain by CMP, Poole

Contents

Acknowledgements

This book is the product of over a decade's engagement with the inquest system, as a practitioner and academic, and there are a huge number of people who have been part of that and to whom I am grateful.

The whole team at Bristol University Press have been uniformly brilliant – helpful, speedy, responsive and understanding. Many thanks to the anonymous reviewers who gave useful feedback, and to Rosie Harding, whose insightful comments on the final draft were invaluable. It goes without saying that any mistakes which remain are my own.

Going further back in my work in this area, I am very fortunate to have had the most engaging, welcoming and challenging group of supervisors and colleagues while in legal practice, and I want to thank all of them, but particularly Jocelyn Cockburn, who continues to be an inspiration. I also want to thank Mike Atkins, Nick Brown, Jesse Nicholls and Anna Thwaites for many insightful conversations arising out of practice in this area, and to acknowledge the individuals and families I was privileged to work for while in legal practice, who taught me a great deal about the meaning of kinship, bereavement and accountability.

I was fortunate to receive funding from the Economic and Social Research Council (ESRC) for the research which forms the basis of this book, and am very grateful for that support.

I would like to acknowledge and thank those Coroners and officers who agreed to take part in my interviews.

I want to thank all my former colleagues at Kent Law School – an intellectual community which I was honoured to be part of as a doctoral student and lecturer. It does not sit well to pick out individuals in that context, but there are a few I need to particularly acknowledge, including Emilie Cloatre for her engagement with my work, Rosemary Hunter and Davina Cooper for training which opened up research possibilities, Didi Herman for her support and encouragement, and above all Helen Carr, who was an outstanding supervisor, with the perfect balance of provocation, critical insight and enthusiasm.

Outside Kent Law School, there are many people to thank across the global socio-legal community, as well as researchers with a particular interest in inquest scholarship. I am grateful for the many conversations I have had with members of the Socio-Legal Studies Association (SLSA) in the UK, as well as with colleagues from other parts of the world, and in this context, I would particularly like to thank David Baker, Brenda Carpenter, Dave Cowan, Maria Fernanda Salcedo Repoles, Sam McIntosh and Marc Trabsky.

I am grateful to James Martel for his reflections on an earlier draft of Chapter 2, as well as the publishers of *Law, Culture and the Humanities* for permitting me to use some material which was previously published with them. I am very grateful to Rebecca Scott Bray for many fascinating conversations, as well as for inviting me to take part in the Critical Death Investigation Research Lab held at the University of Sydney in November 2018. Finally, my thanks must go to Phil Scraton for his generosity and encouragement, but also utmost respect to him and many others, including INQUEST and the Inquest Lawyers Group, who have worked tirelessly to support bereaved people.

I also want to unthank those responsible for not acting on the systemic inequalities which caused so many deaths from the COVID-19 pandemic. This book was finished in the summer and autumn of 2021, just as – we hope – communities, science, logistics, the NHS and many unseen parts of the state were able to find a way through. However, the loss from the pandemic was catastrophic, and the fear is now that we forget and we fail to properly address that loss. It was a mass event which revealed once again the way in which death links to inequality and the intersection of class, race, poverty and state withdrawal. At the same time, every single person who died is a person who was and is loved. I hope we continue to remember them and the circumstances of their deaths.

To my own friends and family – thank you all, and to Dad especially for a lifetime of support. My Mum did not get to see this published, but she was there for the beginning of my studies and – just as with everything I have ever written – I know she would have read this with a loving and simultaneously honest eye. If you find parts of my discussion poorly written, one significant cause is the lack of her critical scrutiny. Sorry Mum.

Finally, to my own little family, Polly and Ivor – this book is dedicated to you, with love.

Series Editor's Preface

The Law, Society, Policy series publishes high-quality, socio-legal research monographs and edited collections with the potential for policy impact. Cutting across the traditional divides of legal scholarship, Law, Society, Policy offers an interdisciplinary, policyengaged approach to socio-legal research which explores law in its social and political contexts with a particular focus on the place of law in everyday life.

The series seeks to take an explicitly society-first view of socio-legal studies, with a focus on the ways that law shapes social life, and the constitutive nature of law and society. International in scope, engaging with domestic, international and global legal and regulatory frameworks, texts in the Law, Society, Policy series engage with the full range of socio-legal topics and themes.

Death, Family and the Law

Introduction

The inquest is characterized by paradox: a legal forum which is simultaneously high profile and unfamiliar, extraordinary and routine. It is a jurisdiction which often appears anachronistic and peripheral to other systems of justice and governance. At the same time, the human stories which the inquest hearing tells, of accident and violence, individual mistake and structural misdeed, fascinate the media, leading bulletins, filling front pages and provoking heated public debate. It is a court hearing but not a trial, presented as a non-adversarial inquiry into facts, in which the bereaved family are at the centre (Thornton 2012a). However, it is also a setting experienced by many as a combative, contested space, obscurely governed by technical legal provisions.

Cultural and anthropological scholarship would suggest these contradictions emerge from our paradoxical relationships with death itself; irresistible and abhorrent, we look at and look away from death, we silence pain and need to hear it. As with the death it is responsible for explaining, the inquest similarly compels and repels, while the grief of those who remain can provoke complex and conflicting public responses.

This all means that inquests are engaging, but this engagement itself is inherently problematic. Sudden unexpected death is dramatic, containing the potential to grab attention and reveal deeper common truths. It also carries risks associated with exploitation and well-meaning but damaging interventions on behalf of those bereaved by death. This includes emphasis on the therapeutic possibilities in a process 'framed as a precondition to achieving closure' (Fincham et al 2011, 65), positing grief as a psychological process to work through.[1] It is a perspective characterized by Butler as

---

[1] See the discussion in Tait and Carpenter (2013b), (2016); Carpenter et al (2015b), and note the emphasis on the limited nature of a therapeutic perspective (for example, Freckelton 2008), resisting paternalism and focusing on the need for the inquest to minimize harm.

invoking 'the Protestant ethic when it comes to loss' (Butler 2006, 21), which approaches bereavement as an injury to be healed rather than as a feature of precariously held life.

It is a system which scholarship has represented as attempting to give death 'a more predictable veneer' (Howarth 2007, 160), transforming death into an inescapable incident, meaning it 'becomes possible to repair and reaffirm culturally dominant assumptions about the "facts of life"' (Langer 2010, 86). Troublingly, however, this framing can hide the ways in which structures of injustice are frequently implicated in death (Razack 2011b and 2015), and is therefore an approach, emphasizing inevitability and tragedy, which risks amplifying that injustice.

In the context of these overlapping paradoxes and tensions, and in a jurisdiction in which increased official attention has been given to the rights and needs of the bereaved family, this book explores the question of what understandings of the role of family, kinship and bereavement tell us about the contemporary inquest. To do so, the discussion focuses on the current jurisdiction and the perspectives of actors within it, but also goes back into the history of the inquest system to uncover the ways in which the contemporary process has emerged. Perhaps most importantly, it is a discussion of accountability, and the ways in which the role of family relates to and reveals forms of accountability in historical, modern and contemporary inquests.

My analysis suggests the inquest can be understood as moving from the historical to the modern form of the inquest through the course of the second half of the 19th and early 20th centuries (see Burney 2000), while the contemporary form of the inquest emerged in the early 21st century. This broad use of periodization is not to suggest a coherent or inevitable progression in the form of the inquest, but instead is oriented towards highlighting the changing nature of accountability in the Coronial system, and provides the basis for a conceptual examination of those changes (and it is not an attempt to minimize contingency and contestation). The book traces some of the ways in which, in the historical inquest, the community played a central role in the construction of a contextual accounting for death, and how this role fell away in the shifts which I characterize as the development of the modern inquest, which focused instead solely on an expert form of accountability. I argue this community form of accountability can be seen to have re-emerged in the contemporary inquest in a changed form – in a framing in which those close to the deceased are understood as central players, in some ways picking up the responsibility of the historical community to reveal and explain death. However, the modernist understanding of an inquiry remains potent – an understanding in which the bereaved have a less significant role, and are involved in order to assist the Coroner in the task of determining the facts of death.

My analysis explores the ways in which the system can shift between these different frames and suggests that, on a given day in the current system, an investigation and inquest may exhibit elements of both the modern and contemporary understandings.

To understand these tensions in the current inquest system is to understand and analyse the ways in which the bereaved are imagined (including who is legitimately seen as entitled to take on the role of 'family') and how they are engaged. This is the focus of this book and it includes a focus on jurisdiction and process and the pre-hearing process in particular. Under-researched and theorized in legal scholarship, understanding that pre-hearing role is vital in analysing the question of the role kin play and the ways in which the contemporary inquest is constructed.

Drawing together these themes of kinship, accountability, jurisdiction and procedure, this book undertakes an extended analysis of the family in the inquest and the ways in which the public process of the inquest reveals, connects and constructs death, family and the law. This introduction provides a framework for that discussion, firstly by providing an initial introduction to the inquest, before moving to explain my research methods. Following this, I provide further elaboration of my themes of kinship, accountability and jurisdiction/procedure, and close with a brief outline of the contents of each chapter in the rest of the book.

A unique forum

The inquest system is required to investigate violent or unnatural death, deaths where the cause is unknown and deaths in custody or state detention.[2] Coroners oversee the system across England and Wales. They are judicial officers responsible for specified Coroner Areas,[3] and are appointed and funded locally.[4] Together they receive reports of over 200,000 deaths every year, and while most investigations are closed after initial inquiries (which might be with or without a post-mortem),[5] those which continue will proceed to a full, public inquest hearing. At this hearing, and in the investigation which precedes it, family members and

---

[2] Coroners and Justice Act 2009 (CJA 2009), s 1(2), and note ss 4 and 6 in relation to discontinuance of investigations and holding a hearing.

[3] See CJA 2009, sch 2. Each Area must have a Senior Coroner, and may also have Area Coroners and Assistant Coroners who work alongside the Senior Coroner; see sch 3 CJA 2009.

[4] Albeit with the consent required of the Lord Chancellor and the Chief Coroner.

[5] In most cases, the investigation will not continue if the cause of death is revealed to be natural causes, although the question of when the cause of death is natural but other factors make the death unnatural 'has been dynamically changing as society develops, and remains poorly articulated' (Matthews 2020, 106) and can be contested, although Coroners have

others involved in the death have rights to be involved,[6] including rights to ask questions of witnesses. When the hearing concludes, legislation provides that the Coroner (or, in some cases, the jury) cannot make any finding of civil or named criminal liability and are directed to answer four questions: who the person was, and how, where and when they died.[7] The decisions of a Coroner (or their failures to decide) are susceptible to the review of the High Court on limited grounds,[8] but there is otherwise no right of appeal to their rulings. Provision to create a Chief Coroner's office with a right to hear appeals was enacted in 2009, but while that appeals process was repealed before it was brought into force,[9] the Chief Coroner post was retained with a responsibility to provide leadership, including guidance, to Coroners.

These inquest hearings can range from the most high profile, where facts are hotly contested and ranks of lawyers represent a wide range of interested organizations (and occasionally lawyers for the bereaved family, in a context in which legal aid is uncommon), to cases where the Coroner sits in a room alone and reads the evidence into the record. Many cases fall somewhere between these two, and as an illustration of the system and the themes I explore later on, I describe one such inquest in particular – the inquiry into the death of Malcolm Burge.

A very quiet and proud man

Malcolm Burge, a 66-year-old former cemetery caretaker from the City of London, died on 28 June 2014 in hospital in Bristol 'having earlier that day set light to himself and his car in a car park in Cheddar Gorge, Somerset' (Courts and Tribunals Judiciary, 2015). His inquest was held in February 2015. It heard evidence that, as a result of an administrative backlog at Newham Council, he had been overpaid £800.69 in benefits and the Council had initiated legal proceedings to recover the money. The Coroner found that 'due to a number of factors in particular his age, lack of mental awareness, inability to both understand and use the internet and modern telephone procedures

---

fairly broad discretion to reach this determination; see, for example, *Canning v County of Northampton Coroner* [2006] EWCA Civ 1225. See also the discussion in Harris 2017a; and Harris and Walker (2019).

[6] See further the discussion in Chapter 6.

[7] As will be discussed further later on, 'how' is extended where the state is in some way implicated in the death to include the circumstances of that death. See CJA 2009, ss 5 and 10. I discuss potential outcomes from an inquest further in this introduction in the 'Forms of accountability' section later on.

[8] Coroners Act 1988, s 13, or under general judicial review principles.

[9] See CJA 2009, s 40, repealed by the Public Bodies Act 2011.

[to] communicate his problems to the Council, [he] took the drastic action that brought about his death' (Courts and Tribunals Judiciary, 2015).

The details of Malcolm Burge's death and inquest were reported by Cahal Milmo in *The Independent* under the headline 'The appalling death of a man caught up in benefits nightmare':

> [Malcolm Burge] had spent all but four years of his life living in the grounds of the City of London cemetery. The imposing Victorian graveyard in Manor Park, east London, is one of the largest in Europe and his father – Mervin – was head groundsman, raising his family in the grey-stone lodge house … [Mr Burge] followed his father into the gardening trade, working at the cemetery and elsewhere in adjoining Wanstead. But when his mother died in 1992 and his father contracted Parkinson's Disease, Mr Burge gave up the work he loved to become Mervin's full-time carer, moving to a smaller property in the grounds of the cemetery. It was to this house that his family came last year in the immediate days after the harrowing events in Cheddar Gorge. (Milmo 2015)

The Coroner understood that Malcolm Burge 'had never before owed money or been in debt', while Milmo describes the legal action by Newham as a 'harsh indignity for a man from a proudly working class background who, according to his family, had a traditional attitude to debt'. The report in *The Independent* also records his family stating that when they visited his home, he had destroyed other documents, but had 'clearly left out his communications with the council. … It was clearly of importance to him' and quotes his sister telling the inquest 'He was a very quiet and proud man. We knew nothing about this until after his death', with his niece adding: 'His pride kept him away from asking us. We would have helped him.'

The account is affecting, a news report which doubles as an obituary and an indictment of failures in social welfare provision. The inquest hearing constructs the 'sad sad sad story'[10] of the death of Malcolm Burge as a victim of bureaucracy, an existence made precarious by digital technology, out of time and place in a world of smartphones and the internet. According to the Coroner, he was

> a tragic tale of a man who had lived all of his life in the city of London being caught up in the changes to the government benefit system. And

---

[10]   As Milmo described it on his Twitter account in a tweet promoting his report, 12:00 on 7 February 2015, https://twitter.com/cahalmilmo/status/563970469607784448 [Accessed 24 January 2022].

while it seems clear to me now that he was a man who needed help and was in distress, unfortunately Newham Borough Council were unable to give it to him. (Milmo 2015)

The report concludes with a final reflection:

For the man who felt he had to travel far from home to end his life, there was at least a return to the place that had provided sanctuary throughout his life. His remains were placed in the memorial garden of the City of London Cemetery, the place he knew best. (Milmo 2015)

It is a story which highlights the ways in which paradoxes cluster around the inquest. Malcolm Burge was a quiet man, who died the most lurid and public of deaths. Appalling and compelling, his was a vivid death, in direct opposition to the banal mundanity of administrative inertia which provoked him to act. These paradoxes prompt engagement with a story which illustrates the contemporary jurisdiction and, in particular, the ways in which forms of accountability can emerge through the process of the investigation and inquest, fundamentally shaped by the involvement of the bereaved family.

Formal outcomes from the inquest into the circumstances surrounding the death of Malcom Burge answered the four questions required by legislation: he was Malcolm Burge, he died on 28 June 2014 in hospital, having set fire to himself and his car in Cheddar Gorge, and he had committed suicide. The other formal outcome was a report from the Coroner to London Borough of Newham. At the hearing, Newham had acknowledged failings in their communications with him and apologized if these failings had contributed to his death in any way. Presumably dissatisfied with their response, and under a duty to act if other deaths could be prevented, the Coroner's report set out action to be taken in relation to communication with individuals in Mr Burge's position, including suggestions to see people in person, offer them assistance or direct them to 'some responsible organisation such as the Citizen's Advice Bureau' (Courts and Tribunals Judiciary, 2015).

At the same time, the inquest also provided an opportunity for other forms of accounting – explanations which focused less on establishing whether the legal threshold for suicide was met or tweaking administrative procedures, and engaged instead with the politics surrounding his death. This included the potent critique from Milmo, which ties his death to wider debates around austerity and suicides associated with benefits cuts. It is an account which simultaneously individualizes Malcolm Burge and the injustices he suffered, and makes his story universal and familiar, connecting to common frustrations with dealing with a faceless system and experiences of cutbacks in state provision.

The effectiveness of Milmo's narrative derives from both the circumstances in which Malcolm Burge died and the story his family were able to tell about him. It is the public space of the inquest, and the account related by Milmo, which provides Burge's sister and niece with an opportunity to tell a story of care, dignity and connection. Their account emphasizes Malcolm Burge as a person, as well as the contingency of what happened and the unjust nature of his treatment, and demonstrates the ways in which the inquest can provide an opportunity for family to be involved in an accounting which contextualizes the deceased, producing a narrative of his life which is not limited to the medico-legal causes of a death. Although he died alone, it is a story which emphasizes Malcolm Burge as part of a loving family and the importance of their role in the hearing into his death.

The importance of establishing a family relationship is the role it plays in determining the possibility for what Judith Butler describes as a 'grievable death' (Butler 2006) – a death which is capable of being grieved, not dismissed and ignored. Her analysis rejects accounts of the privatization of death, arguing that the loss in death is not exclusively composed of the loss of the deceased or the loss felt by the living, but of a relational tie. Grief is not a privatizing practice, but instead 'furnishes a sense of political community of a complex order, and it does this first of all by bringing to the fore the relational ties that have implications for theorising fundamental dependency and ethical responsibility' (Butler 2006, 22). Developing this, Reimers (2011) argues that practices of grieving are kinship practices which can presuppose and reinforce the heteronormative conjugal family, potentially preventing 'other relations and identity positions from being articulated as legitimately in mourning' (Reimers 2011, 259). What matters in these accounts is not formal familial ties, but the relational ties and connections. For an inquest system committed to putting family 'at the heart of the process' (Thornton 2012a), there are clear implications in terms of who 'the family' is who are being put at the heart of the process, and how to respond where there is no family, or no one to represent connection.

These are implications not just for the way in which death is represented at the end of the hearing, but also the way in which it is investigated. As the explanation of what was found in Malcolm Burge's house suggests, the pre-hearing processes, and the involvement of family in those processes, is intimately linked to what emerges in the final public hearing. It was family who visited his home and discovered that while he had destroyed many documents, he had left out those which related to his debt to the Council. The suggestion implied in the account is that his family therefore played a central role in drawing out the story which was eventually crystallized in the conclusions of the hearing. The role of family in this, or how they link to the representation and legitimation of the law of the inquest, has rarely been examined. Unpicking that pre-hearing process, and exploring the procedural

7

techniques which shape it, is an essential part of understanding the inquest. This is why I explore these interlinked themes of family, of accountability and of procedure/jurisdiction in this book, but, before turning to cover each of these in more detail – as this discussion includes some quotes from my interviews – I firstly briefly turn to explain aspects of my research methods.

Researching the inquest

The analysis which is set out in this book emerged through an exploration of a wide range of conceptual materials focused on questions of governance, justice and accountability, followed by research in which I explored historical/archival resources, interviewed a series of Coroners and their officers, and undertook research into a wide range of legal materials. I used that empirical, legal and historical data to reflect back on the conceptual materials – drawing them into 'dialogue' (as Garland puts it) to try to think through 'the interpretative and explanatory puzzles' which the research raised (Garland 2019, 651). This iterative move between materials, bringing them into conversation with each other, was ongoing throughout my research, meaning that, for example, analysis of my interviews led me to go back over and re-explore conceptual and historical questions, which then led me back to re-interrogate my interview material, to seek to develop the themes and links I set out in my narrative.

I chose to interview Coroners and their officers because I was interested in how actors in the system understood the role of kinship and family. Taken together, my interviews provided over 17 hours of discussion, with 8 Senior Coroners and 5 officers interviewed.[11] In relation to Coroners, there are currently 85 Senior Coroners across England and Wales, and so my interviewees represent a significant proportion of that population. The Coroners' experience spanned England (not Wales), from north to south and east to west, and their jurisdictions varied widely, from heavily populated urban districts, to areas incorporating medium-sized towns/suburban areas, to rural areas. The support they received and their place of work varied widely as a result, and I conducted interviews in offices based in police stations, council offices, offices in a solicitor's practice and purpose-built Coroner's courts (a diversity highlighted by Thornton [2014]). I did not seek any personal information from my interviewees and I refer to all interviewees in gender-neutral terms throughout my discussion, but all presented as White British, with five female interviewees (three out of five officers) and eight male (six out of eight Coroners). My interviewees on the whole had

---

[11] The interviews with Coroners each lasted 1 hour and 40 minutes on average, while the interviews with officers lasted an average of 1 hour and 20 minutes.

considerable experience in post: officer interviewees had been in post for an average of five years, while the Coroners I interviewed had an average of 13 years' Coronial experience (both full and part time).[12] Finally, I was initially concerned that the refusal of some interviewees to take part and the social desirability bias of those who did (Grimm 2010) might mean my interviews were skewed towards positive views of the role of the family. In the event, I was able to secure interviews with Coroners and officers with a broad range of approaches to the role of the family (as I believe my quoted excerpts demonstrate).

However, while there was wide variety in my interviews in a range of ways, I do not claim to have produced a systematic or representative sample of the Coroners and Coronial areas across England and Wales (Finch and Mason 1993, 30), and have not sought to produce generalizable results. My methodology draws from ethnographic preference for thickness and richness, and seeks to develop theory rather than purporting to provide an accurate representation of a larger world (drawing on 'theoretically informed ethnography'; see Taylor (2002, 5), drawing on Willis and Trondman). This means I did not seek to explore how common it is for Coroners and officers to respond in a particular way, and I do not suggest in most scenarios how common a particular approach was (although where it is overwhelming, I have made an exception), but rather seek to 'indicate broad patterns and associations' (Hawkins 2002, 453). This approach – combined with a concern to avoid patchwork identification in the context of a small (and in some cases high-profile) group of interviewees – means that I do not denote my interviewees with what would otherwise be a commonplace Coroner A, B and C or rural Coroner, urban Coroner and so on.

I do still make knowledge claims, to the extent that I claim that an individual Coroner or officer made the statements I report. One finding across all of my interviewees was that they considered that the family had achieved greater importance in the contemporary inquest and had more involvement in it, but as with all my findings, this can only be said to be true for those Coroners and officers who agreed to take part in my research. I am also not engaged in establishing the truth or falsity of those claims. In the most basic terms, this means that I was not seeking to establish if family do actually have greater importance or if this impacts on the way in which a particular Coroner actually treats family by testing their account against a review of files (contrast Hawkins 2002, 448), observations or interviews with bereaved participants. Instead, I sought to undercover how the Coroner understood the role of the bereaved family in relation to the inquest process

---

[12] And these averages do not include some examples of lengthy relevant experience before becoming a Coroner or officer.

and to explore how those accounts represent the world. What can be said, however, drawing on Platts (1988, cited in Roseneil and Budgeon 2004, 153), is that if these practices are at least possible in the examples I give, then they are possible in other cases and must be taken into account when thinking about general propositions.

Influenced by the work of Keith Hawkins, my interviews were loosely structured and 'made to seem as much like natural conversations as possible' (Hawkins 2002, 453). Where possible (in all but two interviews), I closed with a discussion of individual vignettes, which were designed to raise questions of legal and cultural definitions of family, and which are discussed in more detail in Chapter 4. In one interview I did not have time to discuss the vignettes at the end, while in another I was told there was little time to conduct the interview and so opened with the vignettes (and the interview in fact went on for an hour and ten minutes). My general approach was to open each interview with scene-setting questions about the experience and background of my interviewee, before moving on to a series of semi-structured questions (Bryman 2012, 468–496) and ending with the vignettes. My decision to end with the vignettes in this way in the majority of my interviews was to avoid foreclosing areas and channelling responses in particular directions (Barter and Renold 1999). The vignettes enabled my interviews to engage more deeply in exploring the meanings my interviewees attributed to particular circumstances in the constitution of family and, ultimately, their role (Barter and Renold 1999).

Family, kin, bereaved, community

'Families at one point could arguably be ignored, they can't be ignored now, they are very powerful.' (Coroner)

To understand what is meant by a powerful family, it is necessary to analyse how the law represents kinship, how the actors in the system understand it and how together this constructs a place for the bereaved. My analysis draws on scholarship which critically analyses the privileging of formal, heteronormative, biological and conjugal ties over alternative forms of kinship (Law Commission of Canada 2001; Weeks et al 2001; Roseneil and Budgeon 2004; Roseneil et al 2013; Weston 2013). My objective is to analyse the meaning and place of family and kinship in the process, resisting the reification of family by focusing on practices of family, but also examining the power of the category of family (Morgan 2011). Feminist scholarship has traced and critiqued legal and administrative reconceptualizations of family and kinship (Smart 2009; Sloan 2011; Cornford, Baines and Wilson 2013) and has called for critical reflection on the theoretical framings in those shifts (Pylkannen 2007; Wilson 2007), including the 'ambivalent gift' of legitimation of relationships (Butler 2002; Barker 2012).

In the inquest, scholarship has described families as helping to 'reach a fair and accurate outcome' (Easton 2020, 139), and in the contemporary inquest, they are represented as 'the focus of this public process' (Thornton 2012a). However, the question of who family is – or, more precisely, who the law and the actors in the system perceive family to be – has rarely been examined. My analysis challenges the obviousness of family, suggesting the need for nuance in suggestions of a hard line between family and non-family (Freckelton 2016), and emphasizes the iterative, potentially productive relationship of the law and kinship in the inquest, with an emphasis on both what family do and who family are. Kinship can be seen to be contingently constructed in the process of the inquest and the law, and those I interviewed emphasize kinship and connection as well as (and sometimes instead of) formality. Crucially, family is perceived to play a central role in wider engagements, bringing in circles of kin beyond the prescribed legal categories.

My focus is on the way in which the system understands the bereaved, not on the experiences of the bereaved, but scholarship, activism and personal stories of the inquest from the perspective of the bereaved have informed my analysis, and particularly those which relate to 'deaths in controversial circumstances' (Scraton 2007, 11). These are accounts of a process which Ryan has described as an 'intricate, archaic, law-drenched and uncertain journey, in which families without expert legal representation are too easily silenced' (Ryan 2018, 151). Her insight into the ways in which the inquest system investigates is not uncommon, as attested to by the evidence collected by INQUEST and other campaigning organizations (Ryan 1996; Coles and Shaw 2006; Shaw and Coles 2007; Speed 2012; IRR 2015) as well as academic scholarship. This scholarly work developed out of critical criminological analysis in the 1970s and 1980s (see Warwick Inquest Group 1985; Scraton and Chadwick 1987; Tweedie and Ward 1989), and has particularly focused on deaths relating to policing and in custody (see Beckett 1999; Pemberton 2008; Martin and Scott Bray 2013; Scraton 2013; Erfani-Ghettani 2015; Baker 2016a and 2016b; Easton 2020; and see also Angiolini 2017). The combination of campaigning work (including legal action) and academic research which has been built up has provided a sustained critique of the workings of the inquest system, including insights into the way in which the inquest system in England and Wales and elsewhere can reinforce hegemonic power through reproduction of structures of race and class (Scraton 2002; Keenan 2009; Antony 2013; Razack 2011a, 2011b, 2015; Carpenter et al 2021) and not only in the context of deaths involving state agents (Carpenter et al, 2015a). From the perspective of the bereaved in such cases, as Leslie Thomas QC puts it, 'the legal process is often brutally traumatic in its own right' (Thomas 2020, 10), and there have been extensive calls for further reforms as a result of these criticisms (Angiolini 2017; Owens 2020; Justice Committee 2021). An understanding of the meanings and roles of kinship can assist in framing such reform – a contention which links closely to the question of how the system frames accountability in the inquest.

Accountability

'There are a range of simple inquests that I could just read, but I feel if an interested person needs to understand an explanation, it is right that they have somebody to ask the questions to, even though I understand it all, because I can't give the answer, and nor can I explain what is down there. Probably the best example is a cot death. In many cases I don't need to call a witness, the pathologist and clinician give the expected results and I could read the whole thing, but how terribly unsatisfactory is that for some families? The family may want to ask questions like, 'did it matter that I put them on their side?' and that is part of closure, so depending on the case I would try to call either the pathologist or the clinician, it depends a bit on the case and circumstances but I would try to have a witness for them to question if the family want. Occasionally the family are too distressed and don't want it. I suppose that increases my backlog doesn't it, because it adds another hour, a bit more work, but I think that is right.' (Coroner)

As the preceding quote from the Coroner illustrates, actors might perceive that the law does not technically require it – the facts could simply be read out – but the inquest can be understood and constructed as a space where explanation is linked to participation. It is this characteristic which underpins my exploration of forms of accountability, with a particular focus on accountability as a communicative process. It is an analysis in which the inquest can be seen to illustrate themes of expertise and neutrality, but it is also a jurisdiction in which the participation of a tacit community can play a central role.

Forms of accountability

Answering the four questions asked in the inquest requires the presentation and examination of facts, and explanations (and sometimes justifications) from those who had some involvement with the deceased before their death, those who examined the body and those who provide other forms of expert insight into the circumstances surrounding the death. It is therefore a process of accountability (Scott 2000, drawing on Normanton), in which both the process (including the public airing of evidence) and the outcomes form part of the accounting for death. However, as Morgan (2006) argues, this is the most basic description of accountability – in her words, 'Spartan' – and says little about institutional design or the values and purposes of any given mode of accountability.

Morgan's analysis examines the ways in which a range of different systems have converged on an approach to accountability which she describes as 'technocratic', in which a neutral actor provides explanation in expert language. She contrasts this with 'convivial' accountability, which she describes as being a participative, non-expert approach to accountability. I adopt Morgan's framework in this book, but relabel this non-technocratic approach as 'community' accountability, with a concern to avoid the potential connotations of good cheer and geniality associated with the word 'convivial'.[13]

These two categories are key in my analysis of the inquest jurisdiction and require further introduction.

Technocratic accountability

Technocratic accountability, Morgan suggests, is based on the basic form of legal accountability, which is a triadic logic in which there is a 'neutral mediator who frames the issues at stake in a purportedly disinterested, objective language' (Morgan 2006, 249). Language and the process of communication is central to Morgan's account, and she suggests that: 'The core of the triadic logic … is its delegation of the communicative processes of revelation, explanation, and justification involved in accountability to an arm's-length, neutral, and independent institution' (Morgan 2006, 246). Her contention is that this process produces justifications, explanations and revelations which are in 'technical abstract languages that apply, or at least purport to apply, in a relatively context-free manner' (Morgan 2006, 247). It is these processes and outcomes which Morgan characterizes as technocratic.

The inquest demonstrates many aspects of the technocratic methods of communicating she describes; it produces outcomes in a context of a significant body of technical law and medical expertise, which are capable of being challenged and quashed if they do not adhere to public law requirements founded in rationality and objectivity, and which are the product of a Coroner or jury sitting at arm's length from those contesting the

---

[13] This is not intended as a critique of Morgan. 'Convivial', from Latin words for feasting and living together, might be appropriate to characterize many community responses to death, but does not sit comfortably with the inquest, and my primary concern is to avoid the potential insensitivity of using the phrase in this particular context.

death. However, at the same time, a technocratic framing does not entirely capture the traditional accountability of the inquest.

Morgan suggests that technocratic approaches are influenced by the geographical scale at which contemporary accountability operates, noting that where justification takes place largely 'between and for actors that are strangers to each other, accountability processes must find a language that bridges social, normative, and geographical space [a process which is] facilitated by technical abstract languages that apply, or at least purport to apply, in a relatively context-free manner' (Morgan 2006, 247). This may be no less true in the inquest, but it is also a process which takes place at a far more local scale than most mechanisms of public accountability, and is a system in which local context is a powerful legitimating narrative. In addition, a distinctive feature of inquests is the wide range of potential outcomes which an individual investigation can produce, in both form and substance. This includes the formal conclusions of the inquest and also the Report to Prevent Future Death (PFD Report). These have both undergone significant development in the contemporary jurisdiction, and these developments will be explained in more detail here.

The results of the inquest are recorded in the 'Record of an inquest',[14] which might include a range of possible 'short-form' conclusions,[15] but the list of potential conclusions is not definitive and it is entirely lawful to reach a different short-form conclusion.[16] In addition, the form notes that 'as an alternative, or in addition to one of the short-form conclusions [the Coroner or jury] may make a brief narrative conclusion' (Chief Coroner 2015; see also Baker 2016b). The contemporary inquest has seen a significant rise in the use of such narrative conclusions, potentially providing a far more 'subtle, contextualised and nuanced' (Freckelton and Ranson 2006, 618) explanation

---

[14] Form 2 contained in sch 1 to the 2013 Rules. This includes the name of the deceased, the medical cause of death, the answer to how, when and where the deceased came by their death, and the conclusion of the Coroner (or jury) as to the death. The inquest also must record some additional facts as required for registration purposes: sex, maiden surname of married woman, date and place of birth, and occupation and usual address.

[15] Including, for example, natural causes, lawful/unlawful killing, suicide, and accident or misadventure.

[16] If there is sufficient evidence to support it and it would be safe to leave the conclusion to the jury – *R (on the Application of Secretary of State for Justice) v HM Deputy Coroner for the Eastern District of West Yorkshire* [2012] EWHC 1634 (Admin). It is notable that legislation provides that no opinion can be expressed on any matter which is not within the answers to these questions, although there is some flexibility here; the courts have held that, for example, a jury adding handwritten notes setting out particular facts on a conclusion and so drawing attention to particular aspects of the evidence is not necessarily unlawful; see *R (Hamilton-Jackson) v HM Assistant Coroner for Mid Kent and Medway* [2016] EWHC 1796, para 66, notably the judgment of the Chief Coroner.

of how the deceased died. However, the possibilities for such conclusions are by no means unlimited. Official guidance has emphasized that in most cases, such conclusions must be 'brief, neutral, factual', not 'express[ing] any judgment or opinion' (Chief Coroner 2015, 7), and as with all conclusions, they are circumscribed by the fundamental principle that the inquest cannot make, or appear to make, findings of criminal liability in respect of a named individual or of civil liability.[17]

Importantly, as the guidance from the Chief Coroner notes: 'By contrast, a conclusion in an Article 2 case may be judgmental' (Chief Coroner 2015, 7). Such inquests, in which the right to life contained in Article 2 of the European Convention on Human Rights (ECHR) is engaged,[18] can reach conclusions which identify failures and inadequacies, as long as they do not use words which suggest civil liability (such as negligence or breach of duty). Appearing as the finest of fine distinctions in an individual case, these are determinations where the role and responsibility of the state in relation to the death can be fiercely contested and which are unlikely to be coherent to a non-technically adept audience (and not always to those immersed in the law). This is the most high-profile way in which human rights law has impacted on the work of the inquest, significantly shaping the scope of the investigation and producing much greater scope for critical conclusions.

The other significant shift has been less litigated, but is central to the way in which the contemporary inquest is represented, and this is a greater emphasis on preventing future deaths. For the first time, in 2009, the longstanding principle that inquests ought to take responsibility for seeking to avoid future deaths was included in primary legislation. Coroners were put under a duty[19] to send a PFD Report which identifies where action should be taken to save life in the future, as happened in the case of Malcolm Burge.[20] Where one is produced, it is a key official outcome from a hearing (Moore 2016).[21] More widely available for the public to view than the Record of Inquest[22] and containing (and potentially expanding on) much of the contextual detail contained in the Record of Inquest, the PFD Report is a vital feature of the contemporary jurisdiction. Some of my interviewees reflected on

---

[17] CJA 2009, s 10.

[18] There is a great deal written on this, and it is a fairly fast-changing area of law, but see, for example, Cross and Garnham (2016, 77–135).

[19] They had previously had a power to do this under secondary legislation.

[20] CJA 2009, sch 5.

[21] Note that a PFD report is the responsibility of the Coroner even where there is a jury, although the jury may have a role in finding facts; see *(Lewis) v HM Coroner for the Mid and North Division of Shropshire* [2009] EWCA Civ 1403.

[22] They are published by the Chief Coroner and so are available online, although see the discussion in Chapter 8 about the efficacy of this public availability.

this and, in particular, on the importance of producing outcomes which are comprehensible:

Coroner: I have always had this tendency to write long reports, but always with good purpose and always to explain why, because unless you tell a story people won't understand why you are making your concerns.

Ed: Do you think it elicits a better response?

Coroner: In practice I think it does, because it is also unarguable, if you have got some vague nonsense, you get vague nonsense back, if you have told the story, it also means that the family know when I have taken so much care and time, that (1) the story has been told and (2) if the responses are inadequate then the families can then challenge and say 'you haven't responded, you haven't adequately dealt with it'.

The contrast between telling a meaningful story and writing 'vague nonsense' is a version of accountability which sits outside a solely technocratic framing. It does not fit neatly into a description of the inquest as an expert inquiry limited to finding facts solely to answer the statutory questions, with Coroners justifying decisions 'that are communicated in an expert language' (Morgan 2006, 246). It instead emphasizes the need for outcomes which are meaningful for non-experts, as well as providing the bereaved with a demonstration of the care and attention which has been given to investigating the case, and with an explicit eye on the possibility that outcomes can provide tools for the bereaved to take further action once the inquest's statutory duties have been fulfilled.

It can also be linked to a long tradition of conclusions being explicitly framed in non-neutral ways, exemplified by the apparently uncivil (at times) 19th-century Coroner Thomas Wakley (discussed in Chapter 2) who described his responsibility as uttering 'unpalatable truths to ears attuned to courteous fictions' (Sharp 2012). In the contemporary jurisdiction it is not insignificant that one of the first pieces of guidance issued by the newly appointed Chief Coroner in 2013 was to direct Coroners that they should employ moderate, neutral, well-tempered language rather than forcefully expressing themselves to be appalled or disgusted (Chief Coroner, Guidance Note 3, 2013).

These unique features of the inquest blur the edges of a technocratic approach, but nevertheless retain the central triadic form: the idea that the Coroner is a neutral expert who delivers accountability to those listening, whether bereaved or not. However, a solely technocratic account – even one adapted to accommodate the unique features of the inquest – would only partly capture how the contemporary inquest system is represented and seen by those who work within it. What this is missing is the communicative function of the inquest which is linked to broader participation and, in particular, connections to the deceased, which can be seen as inherent in Morgan's conception of convivial accountability.

Community accountability

Morgan's key critique of technocratic accountability is the ways in which this approach to accountability

> misses a crucial aspect of social systems – a particular lucidity of discussion, a particular tenor or texture of discourse, a particular set of implicit or tacit shared assumptions, all of which link to a sense of implicit community. Historically, this particular tenor of discourse has been associated with geographic and cultural commonality, revolving around shared identity and custom. (Morgan 2006, 245)

Morgan describes convivial accountability as accountability grounded in social identity and implicit or tacit knowledge, and focused on the importance of revealing, explaining and justifying in ways which are meaningful to those involved in the community. Such accountability is local and contextual, emphasizing connection and community. In the inquest, the connections which are central in making possible this form of accountability are found in bereavement and kinship, which then provide a link to a wider community.

One officer told me a story about a death in which a doctor was not sure about certifying the cause of death:

> 'You need to speak to the next of kin [and] they said, well that is what his father died of, and they thought that it was just a ticking time bomb. [You need to] reassure the family, then seek their opinions with regards to your objectives, and not only are you dealing with their loss, but also gathering from them any information that you think would be supportive of the Coroner's decision, and so their needs are satisfied.'

This was not a case which went to a hearing, as the family helped to establish the medical cause of death, but in the hearing itself, family play a central role in revealing and constructing meaningful explanations, as this officer explained:

> 'The family represent moreover more about the person, rather than just the past medical history … so at least they have an opportunity to say, this guy had worked all his life, up until the age of 75, he was a master builder, he had worked in all sorts of environments, he was a lovely

caring person ... it is representative of the person rather than: Chest infection. Pneumonia. Died.'

Unexpected deaths can raise fears of social failure, requiring the construction of counter narratives emphasizing connectedness (Klinenberg 2001; Kellehear 2009; Fincham et al 2011; Howarth 2007), just as this officer describes, and as can be seen in the public statements of Malcolm Burge's family. Seale (1995) argues that such narratives are key to resisting fears of abandonment and isolation, and are central to strategies to contain death in contemporary society. His argument is in part a response to the contention by Aries (1981, 614) that the modern invisible death is a solitary private affair, separated from the rest of the community and reduced to a medical, institutional event. By contrast, medieval death 'could not be a solitary adventure but had to be a public phenomenon involving the whole community' (Aries 1981, 604), and where community rituals after death had once contained the forces of nature, the modern community, ashamed of death, abdicates its responsibility for death and mourning. Others also contest the Ariesian account, identifying community strategies in, for example, late Victorian England (see Frisby 2015), rejecting a proposed 20th-century disengagement with death through attention to graves and churchyards (Rugg 2013a) or emphasizing the possible agency of elderly individuals who choose to die at home alone (Kellehear 2009). Actors within the inquest system can also see themselves as part of this process, providing a forum in which family, kin and the wider community can take part in producing an account of a person beyond their medical history, creating the possibility of a meaningful, contextual story of life and death (Scott Bray 2010), with emphasis on connections and care. In this framing, the inquest process is not solely directed at establishing causation (Timmermans 2005), but also seeks to engage in a wider construction of meaning, an accountability through meaningful revelation and representation, engaging with family understandings of 'ticking time bombs' and accounting for a person beyond the perfunctory 'Chest infection. Pneumonia. Died'.

The contemporary reformulation of the inquest, including legislative reform and prompts from human rights law, has been critical in opening up a space for this possibility, but it remains deeply contingent (and sometimes fiercely contested) in an individual case. Given this complexity, significant insights can be gained by focusing on the ways in which cases proceed through the inquest system, and the way in which procedure and practice operate in the inquest jurisdiction.

Process, procedure and jurisdiction

There are two interlinked ways in which attention to procedure and process play an important role in my analysis. This is firstly because I argue that the procedural rules and practices in the pre-hearing process shape the final outcome, and focusing solely on the final hearing (or the outcomes from the final hearing) misses the ways in which that hearing and the outcome it produces are made possible. This is particularly true in the context of a contemporary process in which much more is now done before the hearing, and that pre-hearing process is more closely regulated than was the case before the 2009/2013 reforms. Secondly, and building on this focus on the procedural rules which govern the pre-hearing process, it is because I argue that attention to these legal practices enables me to undertake a jurisprudential analysis of the contemporary inquest.

Ten months before those reforms were implemented in the summer of 2013, the then newly appointed first Chief Coroner Peter Thornton set out his perspective on the two fundamental purposes of the inquest system. Second, the system should be focused on preventing future deaths, but first:

> [T]he public, especially the bereaved, family and friends, need to know what happened, how the deceased came by his death. That applies particularly to deaths in custody or at the hands of an agent of the state, where there is a wider duty to protect citizens from the wayward or mistaken actions of the state and to expose wrongdoing and bad practice. But it applies equally to all deaths where there is a real element of uncertainty. The public need to know. They have a right to know. It is natural justice, public justice and justice to be done in public, openly and transparently, for all to see, particularly the family. The family has now become, quite rightly, the focus for this public process, to give them answers, where that is possible. They are at the heart of the process as the Charter for Coroner Services[23] makes clear. (Thornton 2012a)

Family, friends, public and the bereaved are all highlighted, but the focus is family in this account, and the inquest ought to be giving them answers. However, it is also the emphasis Thornton places on process, and the public process, which is of note. This is because the impact of the 2013 reforms was to make the inquest a far less public place (on which see Chapters 6 and 7), and to place far greater emphasis (including greater regulation) on the pre-hearing process and procedure.

In relation to pre-hearing processes, it is productive, particularly following the 2013 reforms, to examine the everyday, procedural and routine decisions taken, as these shape the possibilities which emerge in the final public hearing. My focus is on questions relating to who family is and what they can do,

---

[23] The Charter (part of the Guide to Coroners and Inquests and Charter for Coroner Services 2012) has now been replaced by the Guide to Coroner Services (2014).

and how decisions about their proper place in the process are taken. These are decisions taken not only by Coroners but also their officers, who play a significant role in the investigation. It is therefore necessary to understand the ways in which systems, including typification, routinization and sequential exercises of power, can shape decision making, and also to analyse the ways in which approaches and understandings can shift in a process of decision making (Lukes 1974; Hawkins 2002). This is particularly important because what emerges in the public process (and not just the outcome) is part of accountability. Others have explored the ways in which investigations prior to the inquest shape the process. Atkinson (1978), for example, explored the role that the preconceptions of the Coroner's officer played in the investigations and ultimately the verdicts that the system produced. However, this work pre-dated the contemporary move to regulate the front loading of the process; now much more of the investigation happens before (or even without) any meaningful final hearing. A crucial shift in the contemporary jurisdiction has been the development of greater rights for the bereaved in relation to what happens before the final hearing, including extended rights to be notified about the investigation and to be involved in the pre-hearing process.

The final argument I make focuses on these enhanced rights for the family. Analysis of the ways in which these rights are represented and understood by actors in the system, using conceptual tools drawn from scholarship on jurisdiction, helps to explain the role kinship plays in constructing accountability in the inquest. This is because it provides an alternative way to approach questions of authority.

Broadly understood, the traditional way to approach authority starts with sovereignty and the question of who has the authority to decide a particular question. In the inquest, this is the Coroner. Courts have often described Coroners as having a broad discretion over many aspects of the inquest. An all too obvious example of this for anyone familiar with the process of the inquest is the question of 'scope'. The question of what is required in order to provide legally sound answers to the four questions is a matter of the 'scope' of the inquest; this is a key term of art for the jurisdiction, which does not appear in any legislation, but which the courts have repeatedly approved, emphasizing that it is an issue for the Coroner:

A decision on scope represents a coroner's view about what is necessary, desirable and proportionate by way of investigation to enable the statutory functions to be discharged. These are not hard-edged questions. The decision on scope, just as a decision on which witnesses to call, and the breadth of evidence adduced, is for the coroner.[24]

---

[24] *Coroner for the Birmingham Inquests (1974) v Hambleton and Others* [2018] EWCA Civ 2081, para 48.

Such an approach is understandable from a legal perspective concerned with the questions of when a decision can be open to review by a superior authority. However, from the perspective of an analysis of authority within the inquest, the problem with a framing which starts from the Coroner as exercising a form of sovereign power is that it hides what goes on before the decision and how that decision is shaped. It also obscures the role of implicit and provisional decisions, and those which are not just influenced by but also taken by others, including officers and kin. Furthermore, starting from the question of who has the right to decide makes a central family conceptually impossible, as family become simply another participant in the investigation.

An alternative approach is to start from the beginning of the process and to look at the practices which form a jurisdiction, on the basis that jurisdiction precedes, produces and shapes sovereignty (McVeigh and Padhuja 2010; Matthews 2017). This is an approach which acknowledges that there may be multiple representations of the authority of law, a point that is productively illustrated by the multiple ways in which my Coroner interviewees explained who they were responsible to:

'Do you know, it is a question I have never asked myself. I don't know, anyone who has an interest in the deceased, I suppose is the broad answer.' (Coroner)

'Well, on one level, I have a statutory responsibility to do my job properly as complying with the statute, I am technically responsible to the Chief Coroner and the Lord Chief Justice, and I have got a wider responsibility to the public, to ensure I think that I am doing my job properly, and that I can identify circumstances that if remedied could prevent future deaths. And so I think I have got three comparative layers of responsibility.' (Coroner)

'I suppose the relatives.' (Coroner)

'I see it as a responsibility to society, to do your duty as best you can, as independently as you can, so public service I think is important, that is what I really try to do, it is an independent judicial position, very much with an emphasis on public service.' (Coroner)

'I serve the people of [this area], that is my primary responsibility, I have no problem though in saying that I report to the Chief Coroner. A lot of people think that being appointed by the local authority and being funded by the local authority, yes it is bizarre, but that it is a real problem. I see myself as a local officer, serving the people of [this area].' (Coroner)

'Well the joker answer is God and the Queen. You are responsible for doing your job; I am not answerable to the local authority, I am not answerable to anybody really other than the duty to do my job well and if I am not doing it well I can be judicially reviewed, so I am an independent judicial officer with all that that implies.' (Coroner)

From the pragmatic to the technical legal, and from an emphasis on judicial independence to an office embedded in intensely local foundations, these reflections demonstrate the range of ways in which authority is constructed from the perspective of the Coroner. They are important in two ways. Firstly, they illustrate the thinness and inadequacy of a narrow account of legal authority focused on the power emanating from a sovereign Parliament. Secondly, they are a group of reflections on questions of jurisdiction; questions of who belongs to the law of the inquest and who that law is properly addressed to: from relatives to those with an interest in the deceased, from the local population to a wider public, and ultimately – the joker answer – to God and the Queen. They are about geographical and legal boundaries and the hierarchy in which the inquest exists, and they are bound up with questions of how the law – which the inquest operates within and is also responsible for delivering – is represented. They also illustrate the broad power of an individual Coroner to determine how it ought properly to be represented and, more widely, the authority they have to shape their own jurisdiction, but also the obligations they owe and the ways in which they may be constrained in the exercise of that authority.

Given these competing and simultaneously unreflective accounts ("It is a question I have never asked myself"), an analysis which starts with a focus on practices and on the representation of law enables insights into accounts of legal relationships and legal authority which do not presuppose sovereignty and power and then work downwards. My approach focuses in particular on the ways in which particular practices create jurisdictions, linking people to law and representing that law – practices or legal devices which Dorsett and McVeigh (2012, 54–80) describe as 'technologies of jurisdiction'. I focus on three technologies which aim to produce jurisdiction in particular – three ways of connecting people and things to law and representing law – the declaration of deodand, the notification of next of kin, and the ways in which the family are enabled to participate in the inquest.

Different forms of accountability can be understood as questions of jurisdiction: whether the inquest jurisdiction is perceived as properly extending to combining forms of accountability or whether it ought to be conceived solely as a technocratic process, emphasizing the power of the neutral, independent Coroner to decide. In both understandings of the jurisdiction, kinship and family have an authority which is produced through the inquest process and which shapes the process. This continues to emerge in the contemporary jurisdiction and provides a new foundation for the inquest, one in which a broad understanding of effectively participating kin is part of combining forms of accountability. However, this is not inevitable and remains in tension with understandings of the system as a jurisdiction in which family assist the Coroner in a narrower, technocratic process. This latter approach, falling back on to risk, constraint and technicality, represents a failure on the part of the system to put the bereaved at the centre of the process.

Coverage of the chapters

My core themes – kinship, accountability, procedure and jurisdiction – are developed throughout my discussion, which is divided into seven chapters. Chapter 2 focuses on the historical inquest and, in particular, on accountability and the roles of the community, the jury and the family in that historical jurisdiction. Focusing on the deodand and its abolition, it traces the diminishing role of community forms of accountability in the shift from the historical to the modern inquest. Chapter 3 picks this up and examines the ways in which family emerged in the shift from the modern to the contemporary form of the inquest, arguing that the family are represented as taking on the role of the historical community, with responsibility for meaningful participatory accountability in the investigation. It draws on jurisdictional scholarship in particular to identify notification of family and the encouragement of their participation as central devices in the creation of the contemporary jurisdiction.

The subsequent chapters examine the current jurisdiction. This discussion explores the ways in which the role of the family reveals shifts between an approach which prioritizes endeavours to combine community and technocratic forms of accountability, and a framing in which kin are understood to threaten that technocratic approach, meaning the bereaved need to be constrained and limited. They work through the process of the inquest, from notification of next of kin (Chapter 4), to questions about dignity and the relationship of the family and the dead body (5), to pre-hearing processes (Chapter 6) and to the hearing itself (Chapter 7). Chapter 8 is my conclusion, examining the future, including proposals for reform.

In these chapters I explore the ways in which these forms of accountability can be seen to be understood by those within the system, arguing that different understandings of the role of the family constitute different frames through which decision makers understand accountability in the inquest. Therefore, a key question when it comes to the investigation of each individual death which goes through the contemporary inquest process is: does the system (including the actors within it) see the bereaved as a risk to the proper working of the process, which means that legal rights to be involved must be honoured but family members need to be tightly defined and closely managed, or are they framed in a way which understands them to be co-authors in an explanation for what happened? This latter understanding is that kin are not just central players in terms of reaching a conclusion, but also preceding that, in a process of revelation, explanation and justification of the circumstances of death – crucially, a process of accounting for that death.

2

Accountability and Authority in the Historical Jurisdiction

Introduction

History – and in particular a sense of the inquest as a venerable feature of English justice – plays a vital role in the contemporary jurisdiction. This history buttresses – and, I argue, can potentially disrupt – a system often represented as brought up to date for modern needs, focused on fact finding, aided by expert medical knowledge and tweaked to tie in human rights concerns: flexible, pragmatic and local. In this chapter, I examine that history, focusing in particular on the relations of the community, the jury, the Coroner and the family in the historical jurisdiction. My suggestion is that the role of the community, and the authority of the jury in particular, made possible a form of community accountability for death. Furthermore, it was the notification and the participation of that community which established the law of the inquest. By contrast, family and kinship is harder to find in the historical record. Where it does become clear is in the device of the deodand and, in particular, in the moment of abolition of the deodand.

For centuries in England and Wales, at the end of in an inquest into a death, the jury could declare an animal or inanimate object to be responsible for the death. Such an object was named deodand, a gift to God, and was forfeit to the sovereign, but could be used as a means of compensating bereaved kin. The deodand was abolished in 1846 and was replaced with the first Fatal Accidents Act, allowing bereaved family members to claim compensation following death.

That moment of abolition simultaneously illustrates a slowly diminishing role of the community and jury, and the rising importance of the family. This means that analysis of the deodand enables reflections on the ways in which the construction of accountability shifted, and the way in which family began to emerge as a key part of the inquest process.

This chapter opens with analysis of some of the unique aspects of the contemporary jurisdiction, including the role of history, before moving to examine the historical inquest and, in particular, to reflect on accountability and authority in that historical jurisdiction. It then moves to focus on the deodand; examining the ways in which it operated as a form of accountability, its abolition and the aftermath of that change.

On mish-mash, local identity and history

At one level, the aim of the process of investigation in the contemporary inquest is clear – the requirement to answer the questions of who the person was, and how, where and when they died. During my interviews with Coroners, I asked them about this, and what they thought the inquest was for. One told me:

> 'I don't know, it is a very interesting question isn't it. I think the trouble with Parliament again and again is it does not state its purpose, both under the old law and the new, nowhere does Parliament say "and the purpose of the inquest is…" – all it says is "as an inquest you shall answer these four questions". Yeah, why? What for? What good does it do? No answers.'

This absence of defined purpose enables very different understandings of the inquest process to co-exist (Scott Bray and Martin 2016). These range widely. They include a framing of the inquest as a limited and narrow quasi-administrative process, linked to advancing medical knowledge and ensuring accurate population-wide statistics, and perhaps, in addition, an understanding of the inquest as a back-up for the criminal process as well as other investigative and regulatory systems. They also include a perception that it has a role in providing 'closure' for the bereaved, or the further possibility that the forum might see itself as providing an opportunity for bereaved kin to seek forms of justice, truth and accountability for death.

This flexibility and the way in which the inquest draws together medical and legal knowledge, together with the role of the bereaved, are part of the uniqueness of the system, but there are also other unusual aspects, including its local organization.

As the Chief Coroner notes: 'The coroner service of England and Wales remains essentially a local service. There is no national structure' (Chief Coroner 2020, 7). While I use the term 'system' as shorthand for my discussion of the legal framework and processes, it is not a single national system. Created in 1194 (Hunnisett 1958), fundamentally re-organized in 1887–1888 and subject to further reform in the years since, most notably when the Coroners and Justice Act 2009 was brought into force in 2013, the Coroner remains an office primarily organized on a local rather than a national level. A national service was proposed by Luce (2003, 101), but this was rejected and Coroners continue to be appointed and funded by local authorities. One of my interviewees reflected on this, telling me that

'Parliament in its infinite wisdom, despite the advice of Dame Janet Smith and Tom Luce that it should be a national service, has decided no, it remains a local service, and yet we have got this fudge that it is a local service but with national leadership from the Chief Coroner. Well if it is a local service it is going to serve local needs, quite properly in my view, if they really wanted to make it a national service and we all did it the same way then why didn't you make it a national service? Instead we have got a mish-mash which is perhaps the worst of all worlds.'

The impact is that locality remains a central feature of the office of the Coroner (Scraton and Chadwick 1987; Tait and Carpenter 2013a), as one interviewee told me;

'[This] is a lovely jurisdiction because it is very wide-ranging, a real mixture ... it is quite a nice rural area; we get a lot of people coming out on bikes on Sundays.'

Another expressed enthusiasm for the complex urban area they were Coroner for, telling me this wasn't just anywhere, it was a place with

'really complex difficult cases, lots of difficult custody deaths, complex cases where police cover-ups are involved'.

Another stated that

'this really is a jurisdiction where I have done the death of a homeless person found on the street followed by the death of a member of the aristocracy, it is a place of real extremes, it is a fascinating place to work because of the range of cases'.

This fascination turned to local pride in some cases:

'It may be that some areas of the country are different, but on the whole in my jurisdiction anyway, people are not liars.'

For another Coroner, this connection was key to doing their job:

'I get to understand [this area], so when you are a judge, circuit judge, you move around a lot of different courts, you are just looking at the defendant and his offending record, with here we are looking at why death is occurring in certain parts of [the area], do we need to put fencing up on a bridge over the dual carriageway because people keep jumping off it, that sort of thing, you get to know the community.'

These themes, of local connections and pride, local knowledge and spaces, and local distinctiveness were common themes in my interviews, and are closely linked to another theme which came up in interviews – the importance of the 'ancient and fine heritage' (Thornton 2012b, 1) of the office of the Coroner and the inquest. Longstanding legal commentator Joshua Rozenberg sums up this sentiment in his foreword to a textbook on Coronial law: 'No other institution in our legal system has survived unchanged for so long' (Dorries 2004, vii). Understanding the importance of history is key to understanding the inquest system. One of my interviewees, for example, described the power of a jurisdiction which

'pre-dates the Star Chamber which was the first court in this land, by three hundred years, you have got ancient and very real common law powers. And I think that is a strength of our service, even though I like things to move on, I am not hide bound, but it is our difference that makes us good.'

History works in these accounts of the inquest to situate the jurisdiction as a fundamental part of the English constitution. However, as Scraton and Chadwick (1987, 22) argue, this emphasis on a static institutional account can disguise the dynamic nature of the inquest system and the sometimes controversial role Coroners have played, losing sight of the contingent ways in which the system has developed in response to other pressures. Importantly, history also has the potential to disturb and to provide alternative foundations, which can include disrupting a Coroner-centric account of the system.

The modern view of the historical inquest includes an emphasis on the power of the Coroner at the expense of all others, minimizing or entirely disregarding the ways in which other actors played a central role in the process. Scholars have begun to unpick this in order to examine the ways in which this depiction does not accurately capture the legal relationships in the pre-modern inquest (see, for example, Cawthon 1997; Butler 2014). This chapter takes a similar approach, drawing on a post-foundational theory of history, a position which contends that facts about the past cannot be given outside of contemporary theories and narratives, and, as Bevir suggests, there 'cannot be access to the past outside of our present reconstruction of it' (Bevir 2011, 32). This is not to suggest that facts are manipulated to fit a particular narrative, but rather to contend that modernist endeavours to separate facts and narrative are impossibly flawed.

It is also not to dispute the importance of the 'civic role' (Trabsky 2019, 9) of the Coroner in the inquest, but instead it is an argument that an exclusively Coroner-centric focus misconceives the historical jurisdiction. It is an approach which necessarily includes understanding the place of the historical Coroner and taking seriously an office (Condren 2006; McVeigh 2015) which was constituted through contrasting sources: a knight (or later) landowner who was responsible for the revenue to the Crown, but who was also often an elected magistrate with a 'truly popular characteristic' (Toulmin Smith 1852). However, it is also vital to examine and acknowledge the role of the jury in the process, to understand their authority and role in constructing accountability in the historical jurisdiction, and also to explore the role of the wider community.

The community, the jury and the Coroner: authority and accountability

Until 1926, every inquest was held with a jury, and until 1888 most Coroners were elected. Before the passage of the 1888 Local Government Act, this meant that the local community was not only involved in the historical inquest through acting as jurors, but was also, in the majority of areas, voted to elect the Coroner. These elections could be hard-fought and expensive affairs, with a potentially broader and more flexible franchise than in parliamentary elections.[1]

It is easy to romanticize the relationship between the Coroner and the community in the historical inquest and to focus nostalgically on an elected judicial official presiding over a popularly constituted court, providing a local form of accountability for death. In contrast, there is extensive evidence that historical inquests could be spaces with a striking absence of any form of accountability, with, for example, many Victorian Coroners subject to fierce criticism and accusations of bias towards vested interests. Scraton and Chadwick (1987, 25–28) highlight the ways in which the historical Coroner's role could reinforce 'local power relationships based on wealth and property', as the inquest into the deaths of 95 miners in an explosion at Haswell Colliery in County Durham in 1844 illustrated. W.P. Roberts, a campaigner for improved mine safety, attended the inquest and reported

---

[1]   Nominally 'freeholders', but this was vaguely defined and there were concerns that non-freeholders had also taken part in elections; see Glasgow 2007, 80–82. In America at a similar time, as European settlers spread west 'and the number of Coroners grew, there was no accompanying demand that they possess medical or legal credentials. Political, not professional skills were what was demanded of potential Coroners' (Johnson 1994, 269). For discussions of selected Coronial elections, see Burney (2000, 16–51); Glasgow (2004a), (2004b), (2007); Hurren (2010).

that: 'A stranger coming suddenly into the room might without much difficulty have fallen into the error that the Coroner was the attorney for the coal owners' (Roberts, 1844, 70).

Much depended on the local context, as inquests were local community spaces in which politics, interests and knowledges could be contested, and in which Coroners could exert huge influence and develop their own distinct approach. While there is evidence of earlier inquests examining social conditions,[2] a key example of this is the way in which 'leading' 19th-century Coroners saw themselves as the 'magistrate of the poor' (Sim and Ward 1994) through a focus on social welfare, inequality and public health. As an illustration of the ways in which the office can enable the inquest to bring together popular concerns alongside medical expertise, this development is particularly instructive and worth examining in more detail.

Perhaps the most famous example of the Coroner as social welfare champion is Thomas Wakley: medical doctor, founder of *The Lancet*, radical MP and prominent campaigner on behalf of the six Tolpuddle Martyrs imprisoned for forming a trade union in 1834. Wakley, the 'zealous advocate of the working classes' (Sharp 2012, 379) and 'one of the most fearless, capable and sympathetic Coroners who ever served the public' (Cowburn 1929, 397), had represented at least one bereaved family in an inquest before being elected Coroner for West Middlesex in 1839 (Hempel 2014) and, once elected, his investigations could be high profile and deeply controversial, with significant public interest in their outcomes.

In one example of an investigation overseen by Wakley, in November 1840, a diabetic inmate at Hendon workhouse died after being confined for impertinence in a damp room with only bread and water to sustain him. In the inquest into his death, Reverend Williams, a local magistrate and chairman of the guardians of the workhouse defended the incarceration, arguing that the room was more comfortable than 99 cottages out of every 100 in Hendon. The jury disagreed, finding that this inhumane treatment of an infirm man had caused his death, and Wakley's oversight of the inquest left no question over where his sympathies lay; accounts of the inquest describe him stating that the guardians of the workhouse had shown as much impertinence to him during the inquest as the deceased had shown to them (Sim and Ward 1994).

In another high-profile case in July 1846, Wakley oversaw an inquest into the death of Frederick White, a soldier who had received the lash for indiscipline. He sought a medical opinion from Horatio Grosvenor Day,

---

[2]   See, inter alia, Angell's (2007) review of Ellwood, which refers to 'a Coroner's inquest that resulted in better living conditions for imprisoned Quakers' in the seventeenth century, and contrast Scraton and Chadwick (1987, 29–30).

a surgeon, but after examination of the case, Day disputed any causative medical link between the corporal punishment and White's subsequent death. Wakley disregarded his opinion, insisting on the link between the use of the lash and White's death, and the jury agreed with him. Their verdict found that the 150 lashes White received had caused his death, and furthermore declared themselves unable to 'refrain from expressing their horror and disgust at the existence of any law ... which permits the revolting punishment of flogging to be inflicted upon British soldiers' (Hopkins 1977, 180). The case was credited with stopping corporal punishment in the British Army (Sprigge 1897; Thurston 1969; Hopkins 1977; Sharp 2012), and meanwhile Day was subjected to a very public backlash for refusing to subject his expert opinion to Wakley's cause (Day 1849). At the same time, Wakley was himself subjected to fierce criticism in the House of Lords for 'rejecting the evidence of four [doctors] because it was not such as he wished'.[3] In the light of the controversy over the cause of Frederick White's death, particularly the testimony of Day, and the apparent desire of Wakley and others to use his death as a campaigning tool to stop corporal punishment in the Army, it is incorrect for Pietz to state that: 'Reformers like Wakely [sic] were revaluing the reasons for death within a scientific framework of purely physical causality for which moral considerations were, quite properly, removed' (Pietz 1997, 107). For Wakley, in this case and in many others, moral considerations and physical causality were intimately intertwined; after the verdict, he announced that he had made inquiries and White was insane at the time he was punished, and media reports at the time of the hearing noted that '[t]he worthy Coroner seemed much affected' by the lashing to death of an insane man (Hopkins 1977, 182).

Wakley's high-profile stint from 1839 to 1862 was followed by other Coroners similarly engaged in pushing a public health agenda, including Edward Hussey, the controversial, empathetic and fractious Coroner for Oxford from 1876 to 1894. Hussey's tenure as Coroner was a natural step for a doctor who had held himself out as a campaigner for the poor from early on in his career, and as Coroner he championed causes relating to deprivation and poverty, including child healthcare, infanticide and neglect (Hurren 2010, 226).

Coroners like Wakley and Hussey illustrate the influence a Coroner could have, but whether or not the Coroner overseeing the case focused on social conditions, in all of these cases it was the jury which was responsible for the verdict. And their responsibility was not limited to pronouncing the verdict. One contemporary drawing of an inquest hearing which appears to have taken place in the boardroom of University College Hospital 'records

Wakley's choice of position at the head of the table, the jury seated in equality along each side' (Richardson 2001, 2152). These hearings, usually in a local pub, were 'held by the free-men of the neighbourhood *before* the Coroner and not *by* him' (Wellington, 1905, 9, emphasis in original), and the equality shown in the illustration was key. For example, it was critical that those jury members were entitled to directly question witnesses, as a guide on Coronial practice from 1888 notes:

> After each witness has been examined, the Coroner should inquire whether the jury wish any further questions to be put. This is essential to the administration of justice; the jury living in the neighbourhood being, most probably, acquainted with the circumstances better than the Coroner. (Melsheimer 1888, 35)

Unlike the modern disinterested detached jury, the inquest jurors were framed as active and central participants in the hearing. Furthermore, the jury itself was potentially more diverse than juries in other jurisdictions, as the inquest was the only court in which working-class men could act as jurors (Sim and Ward 1994). In alliance with a campaigning Coroner or in opposition to the Coroner's direction, as in the case of the 'Calthorpe Street' jury that ruled the death in 1833 of a police officer in clashes with protestors a 'justifiable manslaughter' (Scraton and Chadwick 1987, 31), the inquest jury could act to resist powerful factions and produce locally attuned accountability for deaths.[4]

It is because of this central role of the jury that it is necessary to be cautious about reading the authority of the law of the historical inquest solely through a top-down view of the Coroner as the representative of the sovereign. A modern emphasis on an inquest headed by a Coroner with responsibility to direct and manage the jury runs afoul of Hannah Arendt's critique of the historian overlooking what actually happened in an endeavour to find objective meaning, 'independent of the aims and awareness of the actors' (Arendt 2006 [1954], 88). Historical aims and awarenesses were contested, but it is undoubtedly true that analysis of contemporaneous perspectives on the role of the jury undermines an exclusively Coronial perspective on the law of the historical inquest. For example, in one classically liberal mid-19th-century formulation, the Coroner was framed as

> an officer at common law, with a thoroughly constitutional and responsible origin and wide jurisdiction. ... There is no more important thing

---

[4]   Although, like the Calthorpe Street jury, jury decisions which were critical of the powerful could be overturned on appeal.

needed in our day, than to induce the public to know that the common law, instead of being a mystery which they cannot understand, is the sole guarantee of their liberties; and that every man may understand it, and is bound to understand it. Its entire foundation rests upon the principle. … That freemen are not to have so-called 'justice' administered to them by functionaries, but are to adjudge of all matters that concern them for themselves; that every man is to be tried by his peers; that every matter, inquiry into which concerns the welfare or safety of freemen, is to be inquired into by the freemen themselves, and none other; and that the magistrates whom they shall acknowledge as legitimate are those only whom they have themselves, as free men, chosen. (Toulmin Smith 1852)

As with contemporary doctrinal formulations, this opens with the wide jurisdiction of the office holder and places a strong emphasis on the breadth of the Coroner's discretion. However, lawful authority in this account is dispersed. The Coroner's legitimacy is founded in the choice of the free men in the community, and it is that community which both inquires and decides, challenging a thin account of a judicial officer exercising the authority of the sovereign within their jurisdiction, and instead inserting rival constitutive authorities. The Coroner's official authority in the inquest was combined with the principle it was for 'free unofficial men … to declare for the satisfaction and security of all, whether it appears to their plain common sense that the case is free from suspicion' (Toulmin Smith 1852). This framing is echoed by the discussion in Wellington's 1905 history of the role of the Coroner, describing an office holder who 'did not "hear and determine", but *kept* records of all that went on in the county and that in any way concerned the administration of criminal justice' (Wellington 1905, 1, emphasis in original).

This administration included calling the jury together to undertake the inquiry. When the historical Coroner was informed of a suddenly dead body lying within their jurisdiction, the first step they had to take was to call together the community to carry out an inquest. *De Officio Coronatoris* in 1275 provided that the Coroner was 'to go to the place [where the body was] … and shall forthwith command four of the next Towns, or five or six to appear before him in such a place'.[5] Fines were levied on Coroners who did not call the jury, or on community members who did not attend. Earlier statutes ensured that where an inquest is held 'for the Death of Man … all being twelve years of age ought to appear unless they have reasonable cause of absence'.[6] These inquests into the death of man were distinguished from other inquiries into robbery and burnings of houses, from which some

---

[5]   See *De Officio Coronatoris*, AD 1275–1276, 4 Edward I.
[6]   Statute of Malborough, AD 1267, 52 Henry III, c 24.

could be excused. Where a death had occurred, all were obliged to attend, and it was the gathering which initiated the inquest. As Chapter 3 will examine further, notification, and then participation, are essential aspects of the creation of the inquest jurisdiction in an individual case.

That jurisdiction, a public hearing which connected the event of death to law, was focused on accountability; providing explanation and seeking justification, as well as allocating and registering fines which arose from the death. Its ultimate responsibility was making the death legal – public, explicable, irrefutable and official. The joint participation of the community and the Coroner constructed this accounting, with the jury declaring the concluding verdict in each case.

It is therefore a jurisdiction in which law is produced through the Coroner and jury combining their authority. However, deeper analysis is needed to explore the ways in which practices produce this jurisdiction and to identify the role of kin in this, and I therefore turn to explore the deodand and its abolition. Importantly, it makes no sense to conceptualize the deodand as existing through the delegation of sovereign authority to the jury. The deodand is far too open textured to be seen in this way and, indeed, for much of its existence, legal rules followed jury decisions, not the other way round. In contrast, the deodand highlights the ways in which authority comes not from above, but from the practice in each case and the ways in which the inquest was responsible for contextualizing and accounting for death in an individual case. Instead, adopting an approach to legal authority which emphasizes the devices that create and shape jurisdiction, and conceiving the practice of declaring deodand as a practice of jurisdiction highlights the ways in which the inquest was produced as a space of law.

The deodand: flexible, contingent and anti-modern

In London, in late August in the mid-13th century, a jury gathered on a Monday morning to consider the death of William Bonefaunt. They concluded that:

> On the preceding Sunday, at the hour of curfew, the above William, had stood drunk, naked and alone, on the top of a stair in the aforesaid rent for the purpose of relieving nature when by accident he fell head foremost to the ground and forthwith died. The stair appraised at 6d for which William De Brykelworth, one of the Sheriffs, will answer.[7]

---

[7] Sharpe 1913, 194–195, Roll F27. See also a deodand of 12d for a step in the case of William Hamond (at 233, Roll G). Other Coroner's rolls have instances of deodands; see, for example, Hunnisett (1961b).

The stair from which William fell was a deodand, and the value of it was forfeit. 'Any moveable thing not fixed to the freehold, or instrument inanimate or beast animate' (H. B. 1845) could be a deodand, and William Bonefaunt's step (presumably fixed to the freehold) illustrates the deodand in all of its elusive ambiguity.

Its defining feature is a lack of definition. While the Coroner might play a key role in the analysis (Pervukhin 2005, 248), the decision to name an object deodand was at the discretion of the jury, and it was for the jury to assign a value to it.[8] It was an inherently contingent object – a chattel which through the jury's shaping of the narratives of death became linked to that death. The variability of the deodand's appearance in the law and the historical record means that few irrefutable assertions can be made about it, and its origins pre-date legislative attention. The earliest legislative mention is found in the reign of Edward I, in *De Officio Coronatoris* in 1275–1276, which includes no definition and clearly draws on pre-existing common law.[9] It did not appear again in a statute until 1833,[10] but was considered judicially and, probably most influentially, in the work of a handful of key jurists, including Fleta, Britton, Coke, Hale and Blackstone.

Unfortunately, in their attempts to set out the law – a task which, speaking about his wider project, Coke describes as 'a worke arduous, and full of such difficultie, as none can either feele or beleeve, but he onely which maketh tryall of it' (Coke 1809) – they only succeeded in creating more mystery and confusion over the meaning and purpose of the deodand.[11] In fact, as Pervukhin (2005, 239) shows, the creation of deodand law was driven by juries, and many of the rules around deodand were created as jurists and courts sought to make sense of the wide variation in jury decisions on deodand. Few inquest jury decisions were appealed for the courts to develop common law principles and, while jurists sought to impose clear principles on deodand law, there is little evidence to suggest that juries considered themselves bound by these principles.

This is not to suggest that Coroners and juries entirely ignored these rules. For example, courts emphasized the role of movement, and juries

---

[8] Although this valuation could be, and was, challenged; see, for example, Hunnisett (1961a, 33).

[9] *De Officio Coronatoris* states: 'Concerning horses, boats, carts (mills) etc., whereby any are slain, that properly are called deodands, they shall be valued and delivered into the Towns, as before is said.' Hunnisett (1961a, 5) contends that this was not a statute proper, but was rather an excerpt from Bracton, a 13th-century jurist, which came to be regarded as a statute.

[10] 1833 3&4 Wm IV c 99 (Fines Act).

[11] Including making errors of law, as noted in Hunnisett (1961a, 5) and H. B. (1845, 191).

often suggested that movement[12] was important, as with Elyas Ide, a seaman who fell from a mast and 'immediately' died. The jury 'attribute his death solely to his drunkenness and the rope, and further find that neither the ship nor anything belonging to it was moving or being moved except the rope, which they appraise at 10s' (Sharpe 1913, 177). However, as court decisions acknowledged, movement was only one factor, and other jury considerations in finding and valuing a deodand seem to have included mischief, negligence, retribution and proximity.[13] Juries manipulated items said to have caused death – and the values of those objects – and 'tailored their findings to each individual case'.[14] This characteristic of the deodand, and the way in which it was tailored to each individual death, is what constitutes it as a device capable of producing a form of contextual explanation (and therefore accountability) for an individual death.

It is otherwise difficult to understand the deodand of a ladder in the case of William le Cupere of Bedford. The jury concluded that on 18 August 1272 he had

> climbed up Cauldwell church … to do his work. He saw two pigeons in the belfry, climbed up inside it to look for them, and by misadventure fell through the middle of an opening (*clera*), breaking his right leg and the whole of his body. (Hunnisett 1961b, 38)

William died the following day, and the ladder he had climbed up to get into the belfry was appraised at 6d and declared deodand. Suggestively, the report also states that the Prior of Cauldwell was fined for taking it without warrant, and although no explicit link is made between the Prior's behaviour in taking the ladder and the declaration of deodand, it is clear that in some way the jury linked William's death to the Prior, perhaps as an informal health and safety punishment. From our perspective, the ladder might be seen as peripheral; having used it to enter the belfry, the inquisition suggests it played no part in his subsequent fall. Declaring the ladder to be deodand and therefore supposedly – according to one definition (Wellington 1905, 16) – the immediate cause of his death serves to highlight the deodand's flexibility.

---

[12] The test is generally stated to be *omnia quae movent ad mortem, deodanda sunt* (a deodand is that which moves to the death).

[13] See, among others, Sutton 1999, 14; Pervukhin 2005, 239. Burke (1929) similarly states that there is evidence that in some cases, negligence or carelessness might encourage a jury to find a deodand or increase the value of it.

[14] Pervukhin 2005, 245. See also the range of jury decisions and valuations in Gray (2011).

The deodand as financial relief

One aspect of the flexibility of the deodand is that, although theoretically forfeit to the sovereign, it was sometimes used as a mechanism to provide financial support to those bereaved by the death. In 1837, Robert Cocking, a stuntman in Vauxhall Gardens, died when his parachute failed to open. Following the inquest, the parachute was declared deodand and was given to the Treasury. A fund to support his widow applied for the parachute, and this was granted (Smith 1967).[15] Similarly, in 1825 in London, deodands of £50 on a coach and horses and £10 on a cask of ginger were granted to the widows of deceased men (Sharpe 1913, xxvi). The coach and horses had run over and killed a hairdresser, while the cask of ginger was being carried by a labourer when he fell down a hole and died.[16]

Generally primary sources do not tell us what happened to the object, and sources differ over whether as a matter of law, the owner of the deodand could choose to forfeit the object, which would then be sold, or pay the valuation by the jury, or if it was not open to them to choose. Where the object was forfeit itself, it is unclear what role the jury's valuation played, but it is clear that in some instances, as with Robert Cocking's parachute, the object itself was given up. In many sources, there is slippage between deodand as an object and deodand as a sum of money amounting to a valuation of an object, as with the debates in Parliament at the point of abolition, where the Attorney General referred to the new system as 'making the deodand recoverable by an action at civil law'.[17]

The Sheriff, or other local official, is often stated to be responsible for the deodand (as in the case of William Bonefaunt's step) and may have been able to collect the value from the local community (Wellington 1905, 17), and there are examples of a deodand being awarded but not subsequently collected from the owner (see, inter alia, the cases discussed in Sutton (1997)). As with the definition of the deodand, the sources suggest a great deal of variability in practice and also in valuation, with at least one suggestion that where the Lord of the Manor publicly declared that the deodand would be given to the deceased's family, this encouraged higher awards (Gray 2011, 27).

However, while there is significant evidence that it was used to support the bereaved, it is not easy to establish how often this occurred, as the ultimate

---

[15] Smith goes on to note that Robert Cocking's wife did not collect the parachute, which was eventually sold at auction, probably to the owners of Vauxhall Gardens.

[16] The cask is not described as crushing the deceased man, but rather as being carried by him when he fell down the hole. Once again, it is not easy to understand how the cask might be seen to be the immediate cause of the death (although this might be an issue with what was recorded), but there is no doubt that it was a proximate object of value.

[17] HC Deb 11 August 1846, vol 88, col 626.

destination of the deodand is not generally included in the Coroners' rolls, which are the main source of evidence. One support for it as a widespread practice might be found in the rule which states that no deodand will be declared in non-moving cases where the victim was under the age of 14. Pervukin argues that this rule appears to have been inadvertently invented by Staunford based on Coroners' rolls and jury decisions, but without firm judicial authority (Pervukin 2005, 253). She contends that it is likely that the rule arose because most children would be killed at home and it was unlikely that juries would want to punish grieving parents. Another possibly complementary explanation is that if the deodand was regularly granted to the bereaved, there would be little need for a deodand for the death of a child at home, because the parents would both own the deodand already and be the beneficiaries of a declaration of deodand by the jury. Such an approach might explain the deodand in the case of Elena Gubbe, who on 1 November 1324 fell into the Thames while attempting to collect water. The stair of the wharf from which she fell (and which was again presumably fixed to the freehold) was declared deodand and appraised at 4d, while the earthenware jugs she had filled with water from the river (which presumably were the property of her family) were not (Sharpe 1913, 100). Whatever the explanation in this individual case, there is substantial support in other cases for the deodand playing a role in providing financial relief for the bereaved (Burke 1929, 16; Havard 1960, 14; Smith 1967, 398; Thurston 1976, 1; McKeogh 1983, 198; Sutton 1999, 16; Gray 2011, 27).

The historical origins of this practice are contested. Links to the deodand have been drawn (and disputed) with Biblical law, Roman law and Greek law, as well as the Anglo-Saxon concept of the 'bane', whereby family members of those slain would receive payment from the slayer to avert vengeance (see, inter alia, Anonymous 1841, 15–17; Wellington 1905, 14–15; Finkelstein 1972, 85; Jurasinski 2014). MacCormack argues that a definite conclusion cannot be reached (MacCormack 1984, 339), while Sutton considers that: 'It is quite possible that the deodand was at first a form of compensation which gradually developed into pure forfeiture' (Sutton 1999, 12).

The traditional narrative in relation to deodands is that they peaked in use in the 13th and 14th centuries, and gradually disappeared during the 16th, 17th and 18th centuries, before re-appearing with the railway age, when some significant deodand awards were made (Wellington 1905, 17; Havard 1960, 14; Sutton 1997, 46). Some near-contemporary sources support this analysis (Anonymous 1841, 15). However, Sutton has identified 'extensive and valuable deodands' in Holderness in Yorkshire in the 18th century, as well as examples in Marlborough and Westminster (Sutton 1997, 48–50), and Pervukin suggests that the deodand might have continued to be levied, but had slipped out of official attention (Pervukin 2005, 248). The presence of the deodand in popular culture (for example, appearing in Andrew Marvell's poem 'The Nymph Complaining for the Death of her Fawn' c. 1650) also provide supportive evidence for awareness of, and therefore some use of, the deodand in the 17th century.

From financial relief to cause of action

Crucially, by the time the deodand came to be abolished, its abolition was mirrored by the introduction of a right for the dependent family to claim compensation, reinforcing the link between the bereaved family and the deodand. This technical legal line of transformation, from a discretionary decision by the inquest jury to a claim outside the inquest, is explored in three short sections, in which I outline the deodand's role in financial relief for the bereaved, before discussing the debates in Parliament and, finally, assessing the replacement – the family's right to bring a claim.

Discretionary relief

A crucial plank in the argument against the deodand as a compensatory tool was that it was based in the 'defective machinery of a Coroner's court', in the arbitrary exercise of discretion by the inquest jury.[18] From the perspective of the dependent bereaved and the need to replace lost income resulting from the death of a family member, the wide scope granted to the jury in relation to both the award of a deodand and the valuation of the item doubtless carried risk. There was little guarantee that if any relief was awarded, it would cover the loss, and there was a risk that the jury would award no deodand at all. Smith argues that juries may have declined to award significant deodands because of the stigma attached to such awards, and inquest juries might have objected to mistreating otherwise responsible citizens by taking away their property or fining them (Smith 1967, 395). In 1845, H. B., albeit in an article seeking to juxtapose the unreasonable use of deodands in the 1840s with previous decisions, describes it as being 'clear from the ancient authorities, that jurors always determined the amount of deodand to be imposed with great moderation, and with due regard to the rights of property and the moral innocence of the party incurring the penalty' (H. B. 1845, 190).

There was also the risk that large deodands could be struck down by the court, leaving families with nothing (Cawthon 1997, 141–144; Kidner 1999, 321). In 1842, a decision of Lord Denman nullifying an £800 deodand was

---

[18] According to the Attorney General, Sir John Jervis, first author of the still widely read textbook *Jervis on Coroners* (now in its 14th edition), see HC Deb 11 August 1846, vol 88, col 626.

'an example of the venom which Coroner's courts could excite among high court judges' (Cawthon 1989, 144), and there were a sequence of cases in the early 1840s in which the Queen's Bench deployed a variety of technical arguments to invalidate large deodands[19] (although not all appeals by owners of deodands were successful).[20]

It was not only the jury that exercised a discretion in relation to the deodand. Once declared, the deodand was forfeit to the Crown or to whomsoever the Crown had granted the right – a local landowner or a local institution. Thus, in order for a bereaved family to receive financial relief, a second hurdle sometimes needed to be crossed, as was the case with friends and relatives of the nine individuals who died in the Sonning railway crash on Christmas Eve 1841. Despite the reluctance of the Coroner, the jury levied a £1,000 deodand, attaching 'great blame' to the company for placing passenger coaches (filled with 3rd class passengers) close to the engine, so that the heavy goods which formed most of the train crushed their coaches when the train hit a landslide. Subsequently, *The Times* reported that 'friends' of the nine deceased would get £100 each. It seems that Mr Palmer, the local lord of the manor, received petitions from these friends based on the article in *The Times*, as he then wrote to the paper to state that it was questionable whether a deodand would belong to him, and in any case it was too early to say how the money would be distributed. Sutton notes from the accounts of Great Western that there was indeed no apparent subsequent payment to Mr Palmer, but the company did pay out money for hospital bills for those injured.[21]

A possible response to both the risk of having a deodand struck down and the family not receiving compensation was for a jury to threaten a deodand, and thereby to negotiate a solution with the deodand owner. In one example of this, in 1833, the jury apparently extracted financial support for the widow of John Skinner from the shipowner Mr Mellish by threatening a deodand (Cawthon 1989, 146–147).

The implication of these cases is that either through a direct grant or through indirect means by jury negotiation, the deodand could be deployed as a tool to give money to the family, but the bereaved could not oblige the Coroner, jury or state to provide them with financial relief. Smith, reviewing these developments, suggests that the deodand was moving towards a system of compensation, 'although at a painfully slow rate and in an incredibly haphazard fashion' (Smith 1967, 389).

---

[19] For example, *R. v Great Western Railway Company* 3 A&E, NS 333; *R. v William West* (1841) 1 QB 826.

[20] *The Queen v The Grand Junction Union Railway Company*, 113 Eng Rep 362 (1839).

[21] Sutton 1997, 46. See also Matheson (2014, Chapter 2); and Gray (2011, 31), who suggests the deodand was in fact £1,100.

Passage of the Bills

However, in the debate in the House of Lords on its abolition, Lord Campbell asserted that under the deodand, relatives could receive no compensation, whatever the degree of negligence.[22] Lord Campbell's critique focused on the incoherence of a law which compensated where injury was short of death, but not where death ensued, as well as the deodand's consequent failure to deter poor practice leading to deaths.[23]

In the other House, Thomas Wakley set out an alternative account of why the deodand 'ought not to remain in its present state'.[24] He cited an example of a fatal accident which was caused by a railway employee previously found to be guilty of very gross offences, but nevertheless retained by the company. The jury had imposed a deodand of £2,000. As Coroner, Wakley was concerned that 'if it was tried in a court of law, the inquisition was not very likely to stand'. He therefore consulted the Attorney General[25] and leading Counsel,[26] and was advised that the result would withstand the scrutiny of the Queen's Bench. Having satisfied himself:

> He said to himself 'Well, it is now clear that for their gross misconduct the company will have to pay 2,000*l*.' He was however sadly disappointed by the result. The case was taken by the defendants into the Court of Queen's Bench, where the inquisition was at once declared to be utterly worthless – it was cast aside and treated as almost worse than waste paper. He believed that no inquisition had ever been drawn with so much care and attention as that to which he was referring; and he thought it was quite clear, from the result, that the law ought not to continue in its present state.[27]

For Wakley, the problem with the deodand was the inconsistency of its application, which gave a reactive and conservative Queen's Bench the

---

22 HL Deb 24 April 1846, vol 85, col 967. Lord Campbell's speech echoes a similar statement by H. B. from 1845, and it may be that this was his source for the statement; see H. B. (1845, 193).

23 See, for example, HL Deb 24 April 1846, vol 85, cols 967–969; and HC Deb 21 August 1846, vol 88, col 926.

24 HC Deb 22 July 1846, vol 87, cols 1372–1373.

25 It is not clear whether he is referring here to the then Attorney General, Sir John Jervis (the first author of *Jervis on Coroners*), who had been in post for five days, or an earlier Attorney General.

26 Mr Serjeant Stephen, first author of *New Commentaries on the Laws of England*.

27 HC Deb 22 July 1846, vol 87, col 1373.

opportunity to defeat just punishments with legal technicalities.[28] As highlighted earlier, Wakley was eager to use the position of Coroner to promote public health and had found 'no benefit whatsoever to arise from the present law of deodands'[29] because it failed as an effective tool that he could use to force change. Instead of reinforcing a rational investigation dedicated to preventing future deaths, the deodand permitted the jury a wide degree of discretion at the end of the hearing, granting them the ability to declare a deodand against a gentleman's horse when his servant may have been to blame for the death, failing to punish a livery stable keeper who lent a drunken apprentice an unmanageable horse which then killed someone, or unjustly punishing a railway company which had properly examined a train before it left the station.

And this last concern of Wakley's tapped into a deeper concern: that the arbitrary and unpredictable deodand inhibited the increasingly valorized risk takers in charge of industry (Simon 2004). In contrast, the deodand, representing a tool available to the local community for the collectivized management of risk, clashed with dominant conceptions of risk as either a matter of individual responsibility, dealt with by contract law and thrift, or else something to be spread through rational, predictable and institutional mechanisms (O'Malley 2000 and 2002).

Support for the principle behind the conjoined Bills was overwhelming; they were approved by large majorities in both Houses of Parliament and were supported 'by the Lord Chancellor, the Lord Chief Justice, by all the law Lords, and by the Judges of England'.[30] The only unease expressed about abolition was raised by Mr S. Wortley MP, who argued that despite its problems, the deodand provided 'a cheap and ready compensation [for] the poor'[31] that avoided expensive and risky legal proceedings. Additionally, he argued that the Bill would not enable claims against a company, but only against a servant 'who was in most cases a man of straw, and could pay nothing'.[32] His concerns, which were immediately dismissed by the Attorney General, would prove prescient.

---

[28] In a later debate, noting differences between the Attorney General and Mr S. Wortley, he noted that, despite having received an entirely similar education, they had widely differing views on the deodand. Indeed, 'if either of these Gentlemen were elevated to the Bench, the law of Coroner would entirely depend on the opinion of which of them happened to be the judge'. HC Deb 11 August 1846, vol 88, col 626.

[29] According to Lord Campbell, HL Deb 22 July 1846, vol 87, col 968.

[30] HC Deb 7 May 1846, vol 86, col 173.

[31] HC Deb 11 August 1846, vol 88, col 625.

[32] HC Deb 11 August 1846, vol 88, col 625.

The abolition and institution of dependency claims

On 18 August 1846, Queen Victoria assented to the abolition of deodands.[33] Eight days later, Lord Campbell's Act came into effect,[34] the rule in *Baker v Bolton*[35] that death of another could not form the basis of a civil claim was bypassed, and claims for bereaved relatives were instituted.

The impact on the inquest was to limit the possibilities opened up by the deodand. As well as a tool for financial relief for the family, the flexibility of the deodand enabled financial relief for others. It could provide relief if the family was not constituted in a way formally recognized by law, or provide relief to others if there was no one who came within even the broadest definition of family.. Alternatively, monies could be put to community benefit – fixing bridges or providing financial relief to those with leprosy (Burke 1929, 18; Sutton 1999, 16) – or as a negotiation tool to effect health and safety improvements (Smith 1967, 397; Cawthon 1989, 147). Abolition of the deodand was a way of managing the unruly juries that sought to use the deodand in this way, whether with the support of a local Coroner, or without, as Thomas Wakley discussed with such chagrin in the House of Commons. At the same time, the creation of a right to sue for the bereaved dependants was part of a process of formalizing the family, and framing them as properly and primarily responsible for instituting responses to the death. The abolition of the deodand and the implementation of the Fatal Accidents Act were thus central to strategies to manage both community and kin.

Prior to abolition, the most famous way in which the deodand was used as a tool of resistance for the community related to the industrialization of Britain and the railways. As discussed earlier, abolition was closely linked to the protection of risk takers driving the burgeoning rail network. As Wellington dryly notes, 'the date of this statute (1846) may suggest the great inconvenience which the law, if it had remained in operation, would have caused … to railway and other enterprises in which loss of life is a frequent occurrence' (Wellington 1905, 18; contrast Kidner 1999, 323).

The railways expanded dramatically in the first half of the 19th century, as huge investments were made in their development. As Mr Williams MP noted in 1846, in just the last two preceding sessions of Parliament, Bills for railways requiring private funding of £210,000,000 (over £100 billion in the contemporary context) had been passed, which had 'caused great apprehension in the money market, that the monetary affairs of the

---

[33] 1846 9&10 Vict c 62.
[34] 1846 9&10 Vict c 93.
[35] *Baker v Bolton* (1808) 1 Camp 493, 170 ER 1033.

country would be deranged, and its commerce considerably retarded, by the application of so much capital to railway undertakings'.[36] Passing a Bill did not guarantee that this precise amount would be invested by private finance, but the growth of railways was undeniably staggering: 'a mindless juggernaut, grinding private rights into the ground in the blind quest for profit'.[37] As deaths at the hands of the juggernaut became a frequent occurrence, some inquest juries reacted to defend the private rights of those killed by the railways. The *Mechanic's Magazine* of 1842 cast the railways as 'The Modern Mechanical Moloc' and severely censured 'the railroads for the numerous accidents that had occurred, attributing them to a general lack of precaution and scarcity of safety measures'. As a result: 'Deodand after deodand has been imposed by honest and indignant juries – deodands in amount surpassing any previously known in our criminal history' (Burke 1929, 28). Case reports bear this activity out, and in a number of cases in the late 1830s and early 1840s, juries found trains and carriages to be deodands, and valued them at significant amounts.[38] The *Monthly Law Magazine* in 1841 stated that 'in 1840 we have seen [deodands] rapidly ascend to £500, £800, and at length, £2,000'.[39] Railway companies took such inquests very seriously, 'almost always sending legal counsel and at least one director' (Cawthon 1989, 145), and successfully challenged many deodands which were awarded.[40] Railway deaths provided the backdrop to the debates in Parliament,[41] and Cawthon highlights the 'behind the scenes' intervention of the 'railway interest': 'A combination of outraged lawyers, employers and judges [who] got in the ear of Parliament in the matter' (Cawthon 1989, 147).

Before this lobby succeeded in abolishing the deodand, Smith suggests that the law left juries with little choice but to declare trains and carriages as high-value deodand, as an ancient rule that the deodand moved to the death bound them to recognize them as such and it was 'hard to pretend they were low value' (Smith 1967, 395). This version of events ignores the

---

[36] See HC Deb 11 August 1846, vol 88, col 623.
[37] J Kellett, quoted in Wolmar 2005, 19.
[38] See Cawthon (1989) for a detailed discussion of this development, and see also a deodand of £1,400 awarded against the Stockton & Darlington railway, discussed in Fellows (1930).
[39] Anonymous 1841, 15–16. This may well have been the deodand which Thomas Wakley discussed in the House of Commons in 1846.
[40] See, for example, *R v William West* 1 A&E 826 (1841); *Leeds and Selby Railway, R v Midland Railway Company*, 8 QB 587 (1844); *R v Great Western Railway Company* 3 A&E, NS 333.
[41] See, for example, the 'mildly humorous exchange' (Smith 1967, 399) between Lords Campbell and Lyndhurst, in HL Deb 7 May 1846, vol 86, cols 174–175, and the pointed remark by Lord Campbell in which he stated that he trusted that the 'great many' House of Commons members who were also railway proprietors 'would forget that they were directors, and consider only that they were citizens and subjects' (see HL Deb 24 April 1846, vol 85, col 969).

place of active resistance in the deliberations of these juries, which could have decided on a low value,[42] or chosen, as in other deodand cases, to separate part of a moving object from the whole (for example, Hunnisett 1961a, 33). Instead, some Coroners and juries explicitly deployed the deodand as a tool to exact concessions, and while this may not have been the norm, it was a vital and potentially progressive development, curtailed by the abolition of the deodand (Cawthon 1989, 147; Gray 2011, 29–31).

Without the ambiguity available in the deodand, the inquest jury lost this tool, and also lost the possibility of expressing a formal retributive reaction to deaths deemed to be by misadventure. The inquest, the 'only court in which working class people could participate as jurors' (Sim and Ward 1994, 263), was shorn of a tool for the community to produce a contextual, local form of accountability.

Shifting out of the potentially populist Coroner's court meant that arguments over compensation lacked the energy which an inquest in close physical proximity to the death could generate. By contrast, after abolition, financial loss was principally a dispassionate question for objective determination by the law, and while the mechanism purportedly gave agency to bereaved families, it was in fact extremely limited from their perspective (Cawthon 1986, 201), with workers – legally deemed to have voluntarily taken on risk by signing an employment contract – being particularly poorly served (Kidner 1999, 331; Stein 2008).

Judges compensated bereaved families 'rarely and begrudgingly' (Cawthon 1989, 147)[43] and while there was an increase in claims, particularly for railway passengers (Kostal 1994; Oliphant 2013), legal, social and cultural barriers prevented many claims from getting as far as a courtroom (Bartrip and Burman 1983; Bartrip 1987, 7; Kidner 1999, 321; Stein 2008, 956–957). Section 2 of the Fatal Accidents Act required action by the estate of the deceased, which was impractical for those too poor to proceed to probate, and the courts restrictively interpreted the Act to require pecuniary loss, thus replacing the uncertainty of the deodand (Sutton 1997, 50; Pervukin 2005, 245) with the vagaries of establishing negligence and financial loss. According to the Mines Inspector in 1853: 'However gross may have been the neglect which caused the husband's death, all interests are arrayed against the survivors.'[44]

Thus, compensation, based on an increasingly structured assessment of loss, itself shaped by documentary evidence generated in a civil action to a specific

---

[42]   As other juries did, for example, in relation to the first recorded railway deodand, awarded in April 1833, for Jane Hazell, a girl killed by a train of three wagons of sand. A deodand of £2 was levied on one wagon and the sand in it; see Fellows (1930, 73).

[43]   Although railway companies complained that in their cases, juries awarding compensation were overly generous; see Kidner (1999, 333).

[44]   H. Mackworth, quoted in Bartrip 1987, 7. See also Smith 1967, 401–403.

standard of proof, replaced discretionary and flexible financial relief. At the same time, juries in civil claims were warned not to take the opportunity to punish railway companies with large awards against them (Kidner 1999, 328) and were instead to focus on the law. Dependants better able to establish family connections or pecuniary loss – those with formally sanctioned relations recognized by the law[45] and with licit, certain and evidenced financial affairs – were in a far stronger position than those with less formally recognized intimate relationships or financial affairs (Stein 2008, 957). The question of financial relief shifted from the inquest arena to the civil courts: from a local space, a hearing held in a pub shortly after death and attended by neighbours, into an 'extended, expensive process' in a formal courtroom (Cawthon 1997, 144). The dependent family became a key actor: plaintiff and later claimant moving from the periphery of the law into law's direct gaze, while in that courtroom, the jury, potentially capricious in the inquest, was shackled in the civil jurisdiction by legal technicalities, expertise and evidence.

In this process, despite being re-engineered as the vehicle of justice, legislators fretted over whether families, and in particular widows, could be trusted to behave responsibly. A widow, left to herself, as Viscount Sandon observed in the House of Commons, might marry another man and 'the money might all be expended the day after the verdict in a drunken frolic'.[46] Such families had to be controlled, which meant that widows, cast either as domestic angels to be protected or fallen women to be anxiously managed (Ward 2014), had to be restrained and the money secured for the children.[47]

Happily, from the perspective of Parliament, the risks for business were made more predictable,[48] as new technology drove the development of tort law (Oliphant 2013, 837–838), but financial relief for the bereaved may not have appeared any less arbitrary and was certainly less immediate. The family were given rights, but (almost precisely a century before the introduction of legal aid) only the richest families had the ability to enforce such rights, and the informal, negotiated and uncertain gave way to the impenetrable, constrained and putatively certain.

Contingency

There was nothing inevitable about the form that this development took. Some Victorian and subsequent commentators argue that, with its very basis

---

[45] Categories of potential claimants were set out in ss 2 and 5 of the Act, and relationships falling outside these formal categories could not form the basis of a claim.

[46] HC Deb 22 July 1846, vol 87, col 1369.

[47] See Lord Campbell, HL Deb 21 August 1846, vol 88, col 926; see also s 2 9&10 Vict c 93; and the discussion in Kidner (1999, 325).

[48] Although some companies railed at the awards given by juries; see Kidner (1999, 333).

in superstition (Burke 1929, 16), the deodand could not survive modernity (Finkelstein 1972, 207; Berman 1999, 53). The deodand as an evil object could not be reconciled with reason, 'which is the soul of law' (H. B. 1845, 191). However, this account of the irrational deodand underplays the contingent nature of the deodand and its abolition. MacCormack argues that it is not clear that juries were engaged in declaring an object to be evil (MacCormack 1984, 339) and, immediately prior to its abolition, sources demonstrate that the primary narratives around the deodand were of prevention of death and compensation of the bereaved. Adaptation of the deodand was not impossible. It could have been remodelled into compensation for the family within the inquest, as Smith has argued was happening (Smith 1967, 389). Additionally, adopting the justifications of Hale and others, modification of the deodand could have increasingly focused on the deodand in a narrative of prevention of death (Hale 1800). Exploring what might have been (Tomlins 2016), such a shift could have maintained and obscured the symbolism of the banishment of the object, allowing the ambiguity of the deodand to continue to reflect different concerns.

Having criticized the irrational deodand, one Victorian commentator proposed exactly such an adaptation in the *Monthly Law Magazine* of 1841:

> When we consider how often the death of a husband and a father plunges the wife and children in a state of extreme destitution, how frequently a whole family is thus by one blow deprived of the very means of existence, we must surely lament that it is not left to the discretion of the inquest to deduct a certain portion of the deodand for the relief of the sufferers. Thus the same means which have been adopted to instil a horror of inflicting death, might also tend to the support and nourishment of life. (Anonymous 1841, 24)

This proposal was not acted upon. Crucially, this was not because the deodand as an object which caused death was no longer sustainable. The deodand was never solely such an object, but was instead a flexible community tool which could meet various ends, forming a vital part of accountability for death. It was this very freedom and flexibility which could not be tolerated, as a jury could not be relied upon to be objective and rational.

Conclusion

The irrationality of the deodand is from the perspective of an external observer. From the perspective of the jury deciding in an individual case, the approach to a deodand is far less clearly irrational, and it is much easier to understand the jury's decision as making material a form of meaningful, local, contextual accountability. Viewed as a legal device, the practice of declaring deodand is a practice of jurisdiction, part of the representation of the jury's co-constituted authority in the inquest. In its decline, it is possible to see the emergence of the family in both the way in which family provided a basis to argue for abolition and the way in which family claims had to be provided for in the course of reform.

But critically, in the course of that provision, family was transformed, being formalized and severed from other forms of kinship. Examining other shifts in this same period of history, Donzelot describes the transformation of family into the re-organizing principle of society as 'as a positive form of solution to the problems posed by a liberal definition of the state rather than as a negative element of resistance to social change' (Donzelot 1979, 53). He analyses the way that in this period, family became the foundation of the liberal state's response to pauperism and indigence, with philanthropy focusing efforts on the family, encouraging family saving and thrift, and making the family 'agents for conveying the norms of the state into the private sphere' (Donzelot 1979, 58). In the course of these developments, Donzelot argues that the malleability and lack of definition of family, and its continual creation and re-creation in response to governing priorities, means it becomes the key tool by which social cohesion is maintained. Increased engagement with family, in this account, becomes a key method of establishing responsible behaviour. However, in the inquest itself, as I will turn to explore next, reforms and modernist reimaginings of the system were slow to see a central role for family, resulting in a diminishing role for forms of accountability other than a triadic, technocratic approach.

3

Accountability Reconceived

Introduction

In Chapter 2, I suggested that the participation of the community (including but not limited to the declaration of deodand) and the notification which called the community to take part were important characteristics of the historical inquest jurisdiction. These two elements – notification and enabling participation – can be understood as legal devices and are practices which have re-emerged in the context of the role of the family in the contemporary inquest. In this chapter, I argue that they are constitutive elements of the contemporary jurisdiction and can provide a basis for a conceptual understanding of an inquest law in which the bereaved are at the centre.

To explore this issue, this chapter examines accountability and authority in the shifts from the historical, to the modern, to the contemporary inquest. These are not definitive, clear-cut periods of time, but are instead ways to characterize the contested, contingent and changing nature of the inquest over time.

The chapter is divided into five parts. It opens by focusing on the modern inquest and the shifts which defined it as a modern system, before moving to explore the changes which characterize the contemporary jurisdiction. In this analysis, I return to examine the ways in which Morgan's (2006) discussion of technocratic and community forms of accountability assist in understanding the changes in the inquest. Focusing on the family, I turn to examine the contemporary jurisdiction in more detail, with particular analysis of notification, the expansion of the category of family and the participation of family – in particular, the basis for family being involved and able to ask questions during the inquest.

The modern inquest: important, limited and factual

The traditional account of authority in the modern inquest focuses on the legal authority and wide discretion of the Coroner. This approach emphasizes the legislation, precedent, guidance and best practice which underpins (and, to some extent, directs and constrains) the work of the Coroner, who acts to answer the four questions of who the person was, and how, where and when they died (see, for example, Thurston 1976; Dorries 2014; Matthews 2020). In the classic statement of the law, in 1994, the then Master of the Rolls Thomas Bingham declared that 'an inquest is a fact-finding inquiry conducted by a Coroner, with or without a jury, to establish answers to four important but limited factual questions'.[1] The Coroner is 'the public official responsible for the conduct of inquests, whether he is sitting with a jury or without' and it is his duty

> to ensure that the relevant facts are fully, fairly and fearlessly investigated.
> … He fails in his duty if his investigation is superficial, slipshod or perfunctory. But the responsibility is his. He must set the bounds of the inquiry. He must rule on the procedure to be followed. His decisions, like those of any other judicial officers, must be respected unless and until they are varied or overturned.[2]

The dual focus is on a narrow[3] but vital inquiry to establish facts and on the authority of the Coroner to determine that inquiry. The Coroner speaks the law (subject to the supervisory jurisdiction of the courts) arising from an investigation which is not superficial, slipshod or perfunctory, but which is otherwise theirs to determine. The central emphasis is therefore placed on the Coroner's authority to investigate and judge.

This framing grew out of a long process in which possibilities of accountability through the inquest narrowed, and authority held by the community in the inquest diminished. The abolition of the deodand (as discussed in Chapter 2) foreshadowed this trend, which also included a series of Victorian rationalizations founded on concerns over bribery and corruption (see, inter alia, Hunnisett 1961a, 169; Richardson 2001, 2150; Glasgow 2007, 95–96), as well as reforms as a result of the development of modern medicine. Efforts were made to standardize fees and powers of Coroners,[4] and the holding of inquests in public houses was banned (although this continued nonetheless for many years; see Burney (2000, 80)). The

---

[1]   *R v North Humberside Coroner ex p Jamieson* [1995] 1 QB 1, 23G.
[2]   *R v North Humberside Coroner ex p Jamieson* [1995] 1 QB 1, 26B–D.
[3]   I choose this term to emphasize the distinction with the widening jurisdiction which is a result of Article 2, despite comments in case law in which the High Court 'reject[s] the suggestion that the scope even in a Jamieson inquest is especially narrow'; see *R (Worthington) v HM Senior Coroner for Cumbria* [2018] EWHC 3386 (Admin), para 49.
[4]   See, inter alia, the Coroners Act 1860.

office of the Coroner was refounded in statute in 1887 and, a year later, 600 years of history were wiped out as elections for county Coroners were replaced with local authority appointment.[5] In 1926, the role of the jury was further reduced when the requirement to view the body was removed and inquests without a jury were initiated. Furthermore, the 1926 Coroners (Amendment) Act professionalized the role of the Coroner, reshaping the office so that five years of legal or medical experience were required, a development which can be read in the context of Day and Klein's description of a privatization of accountability, 'in so far as professionals and experts claim that only their peers can judge their conduct and performance' (Day and Klein 1987, 1).[6] The impact was a shift in which the community moved from agents to observers of an – in many ways practically inaccessible – investigation into death.

By this time the inquest's role in criminal investigations was already diminished as Coroners had fought (and ultimately lost) a long battle with the police and Justices of the Peace for primary responsibility for violent crime, and this role was further reduced in the 20th century (Toulmin Smith 1852; Havard 1960, 32; Dorries 2014, 6– 7). The 1926 Act obliged Coroners to adjourn an inquest when criminal charges were brought in another court, but the inquest still had the power to name an individual guilty of homicide and commit them for trial. This power was criticized by the Wright Report (1936, 22–31) and then again by the Broderick Report (1971), and was eventually abolished by the Criminal Law Act 1977 following the high-profile decision by an inquest jury to name the disappeared Lord Lucan as the guilty party for the murder of his children's nanny. In relation to civil liability, the role of inquests was also diminished, as criticism by the Wright Committee was followed by a specific restriction in the first Coroners Rules in 1953. The recommendation that 'Coroners' courts should be prohibited from dealing with questions of civil liability' (Wright Report 1936, 34) was translated into a rule that the verdict could not be framed in such a way as to appear to determine any question of civil liability.[7] The Coroners (Amendment) Rules 1980 further limited the role of the inquest, removing the power of juries to add 'riders' or recommendations to their verdict.

Throughout this period, there was also administrative reform linked to professionalization of the office, most notably the gradual enlargement of Coroner districts. The impact of this was a slow reduction in Coroners running a jurisdiction on a part-time basis and fewer Coroners concentrated

---

[5] In the Coroners Act 1887 and the Local Government Act 1888.

[6] See also Leslie (2016) for reflections on this in the contemporary Canadian context.

[7] Coroners Rules 1953, SI 1953/205, r 33.

in larger districts, from 309 districts in 1936 to 164 in 1982 (Scraton and Chadwick 1987, 45) and down to 128 in 2003 (Dorries 2004, 7). This effort to reduce areas has continued subsequently, with 97 in 2015 and 85 in 2020, with an aim to eventually reduce to 75 (Chief Coroner 2020, 11).

The impact was a stop-start, gradual reimagination of the jurisdiction. The inquest shifted from its historical form of a legal forum which brought together legal and medical expertise with local participation and knowledges[8] to a modern technical, professional jurisdiction which was more distant from the immediate population, the deceased and the family. The final particular form was not inevitable and elsewhere around the world, similar pressures resulted in very different forms of the Coroner and the inquest.[9] However, as Glasgow argues in an analysis of the role of medical expertise, the impact of the 1926 Act in England and Wales was that 'the campaign for a more expert medicalized inquest gained momentum whilst the campaign for medical Coroners declined' (Glasgow 2007, 228). As a result, much of the subsequent official concern focused on questions of consistency and the accuracy of decisions (see, for example, Green and Green 1992, 34), and reforms were aimed at producing improved technical outcomes.

By the 1980s, as Prior argues, it was a jurisdiction in which a public health/ medical focus on pathology compelled particular forms of knowledge about death, concentrating on the 'recording, measuring and (causal) explanation of human mortality' (Prior 1989, 12).[10] Prior's groundbreaking analysis of the 'social organisation of death' in Belfast in the 1980s argued that death only remained visible through 'an objective and scientific language which speaks of mortality, disease and causation, rather than one which speaks of attitudes, sentiment and awareness' (Prior 1989, 11). His work emphasizes this with a division between public and private accounts of death, with public narratives focused on medico-legal discourse (including the work of the Coroner) and private discourse, which include the perspective of the bereaved. Drawing on Weber, he argues that the public investigations he identifies 'tell us nothing about the meaning of the world or of the objects within it' (Prior 1989, 11).

Fincham et al suggest that Prior's approach 'seems to assume that the medicalisation of death is always oppressive because it denies human agency'

---

[8]   But one which, as I noted in Chapter 2, should not be romanticized as necessarily progressive – as Scraton and Chadwick (1987, 26) note the power of the Coroner in particular was closely tied to class and wealth.

[9]   For insights into some of these differences, see, for example, Timmermans (2006); Moore (2016); Scott Bray, Carpenter and Barnes (2018) (which also reflects on the Coroner and coloniality); and Matthews (2020, 579–605).

[10] See also Buchanan and Mason 1995; McGowan and Viens 2010; Hill and Cook 2011; Hawton et al 2014.

(Fincham et al 2011, 68). They note that some families in their study of inquest case files linked to suicide welcomed a diagnosis of mental illness. For my analysis, the value of this insight is the way in which their account demonstrates a combination of technocratic and community accountability, as family support appeared in the files, suggesting that family participated in the production of a conclusion which was meaningful for them. Twenty-five years earlier, Prior's research and account of a dominant medico-legal discourse was not able to establish this space for family, potentially suggesting a change in the place of the bereaved or a different cultural context between the two sites investigated. In either case, Prior's account of the inquest, and the emphasis on expert communication in his analysis, corresponds closely to Morgan's account of technocratic accountability, as does the modern emphasis on the Coroner as a disinterested, neutral and arm's-length adjudicator. With a focus on forms of accountability, it is an understanding of the Coroner and inquest which can be contrasted with what came before.

Dowdle (2006, 4–6) argues that an inability to identify 'the people' to whom accountability is held led to accountability being defined through institutional architecture: from the democratic to the bureaucratic-organizational and judicial-legal. Morgan (2006) suggests that in each of these, the model of an arm's-length decision maker has prevailed, and the focus should be on seeking the ways in which community participation can generate meaningful revelation, explanation and justification. The Victorian Coroner is an interesting illustration of these tensions, demonstrating a combination of the three modes of accountability – an elected local judicial official, embedded in and generating a nascent public health-oriented bureaucracy – but in a jurisdiction in which the role of the community remained key. In this context, as Burney argues:

> At [the inquest's] theoretical core lay the proposition that the public circulation of information concerning potentially disturbing deaths was a tool of social stability. In giving a formal context for the airing of the gossip, rumour, and suspicion generated by such deaths, the inquest diffused a tension that, if left to fester, might pose a threat to the reign of sense and reason. (Burney 1994, 34)[11]

It was these narratives, with a simultaneously contained and enabled community, and productive tension between discourses of public health and the liberal state, which constituted the basis of the development of the modern inquest (Burney 2000). The historical inquest is revealed as

---

[11] In relation to viewing the body in the Australian context, see Trabsky (2015).

a jurisdiction holding out the possibility of combining both technocratic and community forms of accountability, while the development of the modern inquest crowded out possibilities of participatory accountability linked to a tacit community. The inquest came instead to rely on an expert triadic approach to revealing, explaining and seeking justification for sudden death, in which the Coroner and their independence and expertise were central.

Prior's critique of this modern jurisdiction was not limited to deaths in controversial circumstances, but campaigning associated with such deaths raised 'serious questions over the adequacy of the role and function of the coroner' (Scraton and Chadwick 1987, 14).[12] At the start of the 21st century, a combination of this critique, combined with pressure from reform from official sources, began to effect change. These are shifts which can be characterized as a shift to the contemporary inquest jurisdiction.

The contemporary inquest: a widening focus

Official pressure for reform of the system grew as a result of the intertwined impact of human rights laws and scandals about systemic failures in the death investigation and reporting systems. Key to these moves was the incorporation of the right to life in Article 2 ECHR through the 1998 Human Rights Act. A central feature of Article 2 is the requirement for structures for the investigation of all deaths and for an enhanced, detailed investigation where the state was somehow implicated in that death. It also emphasizes the importance of family participation in the investigation. In relation to the role of family and in other respects,[13] it has had (and continues to have) a dramatic effect on the domestic law of the inquest, beginning with the key House of Lords decisions in *Amin*[14] and *Middleton*,[15] which will be discussed further later on.

It is often stated that 'there are two types of inquest'.[16] Common legal shorthand describes the first as *Jamieson* inquests, named after the 1994 decision of Bingham MR, in which the inquest is required to determine 'by what means' the deceased came by their death. These are cases in which the responsibility of the state under Article 2 ECHR to conduct an

---

[12] A criticism which was dismissed by some in power as 'anti-authority'; see Scraton and Chadwick (1987, 46–47).

[13] See, inter alia, Dorries (2014); Thomas et al (2014); Simor (2015); Baker (2016a); and Matthews (2020).

[14] *R (Amin) v Secretary of State for the Home Department* [2003] UKHL 51.

[15] *R (on the Application of Middleton) v West Somerset Coroner* [2004] UKHL 10.

[16] *R (Paul Worthington) v HM Coroner for Cumbria* [2018] EWHC 3386, para 10.

enhanced public investigation into that specific death is not engaged.[17] The second is the *Middleton* inquest, which was given a statutory foundation in the Coroners and Justice Act 2009, in which the state's duty to investigate under Article 2 is engaged as the state 'may bear responsibility'[18] and an inquest is required to explore the wider circumstances of the death.[19] This ostensibly clear division between cases which engage Article 2 and those which do not hides significant legal complexity, and the Court of Appeal has noted, for example, that: 'The Strasbourg jurisprudence on the question of engagement of the obligation of investigation is not always easy to understand and successive courts in this country have struggled to interpret it.'[20] Particular challenges for the courts have been identifying the ways in which the obligation relates to deprivation of liberty and forms of detention, as well as efforts to draw distinctions between healthcare and non-healthcare-related deaths, while a series of applications for judicial review of Coronial decisions have sought to clarify a number of questions, including the trigger for engaging Article 2, of conclusions to such inquests, requirements of what ought properly be left for a jury to consider and how that relates to a PFD Report.

The year 2003 was a critical one in relation to the development of the contemporary form of the inquest. In addition to the decision in *Amin*, two substantial official reports were published which imagined a fundamental restructuring of the inquest. The review headed up by Tom Luce (Luce 2003) had come about as a result of general concerns about the failings in the certification of deaths following a series of scandals. These included the actions of GP Dr Harold Shipman, which also provoked a parliamentary inquiry – the Shipman Inquiry – led by Janet Smith, which eventually produced five separate reports into the systemic failures which had allowed him to murder so many of his patients. Her third report (Smith 2003) included a particular focus on the inquest system.

In their conclusions, both of these reports rejected the wholesale scrapping of the inquest system, with Janet Smith drawing on history to declare that 'I think that the tradition of the Coroner's inquest is so well rooted in this

---

[17] This is a slight simplification for ease of reading, as Article 2 will always be engaged at the highest level in such cases in the sense that it obliges a state to have a legal system which will investigate death. See, for example, the discussion in *R (Humberstone) v Legal Services Commission* [2010] EWCA Civ 1479, which notes that: 'The system provided in England and Wales, which includes the availability of civil proceedings and which will in practice include a coroner's inquest, will always satisfy that obligation' (para 67).

[18] *R (Maguire) v HM Senior Coroner for Blackpool and Fylde* [2020] QB 409, para 11.

[19] See s 5(2) in contrast with ss 5(1) and (3).

[20] *R (Humberstone) v Legal Services Commission* [2010] EWCA Civ 1479, para 52.

country that most members of the public would regret its loss, even though they are critical of the way it is operated at present' (Smith [2003], para 19.11). Both also emphasized the ways in which the system was not responding to the needs of families, and the Shipman inquiry in particular framed the family as key participants in the oversight of procedures for investigating death. It argued that had family members been involved in certification procedures, it would have been a real deterrent to Dr Shipman and would have increased the chances of his crimes being detected.[21] The Luce Review was more cautious, emphasizing the involvement of family where appropriate and the need for informed participation, in line with other public services,[22] but notably proposing, in its consultation document, that family should be at the centre of the inquiry.

Neither set of recommendations was implemented in full, and the government's response to the reports in 2004 makes little reference to the role of the bereaved (see, for example, the foreword to Home Office (2004)). Instead, they framed the possibilities for reform, organizing and informing the policy debate[23] which resulted in the eventual (and not inevitable) passage of the Coroners and Justice Act 2009 and its introduction in 2013, together with significant associated secondary legislation.[24] These shifts – the development of human rights jurisprudence and the legislative reformulation in 2009/2013 – can be seen as the jurisdiction re-engaging with the possibility of community accountability, but now focused on the family.

The rise of the family

There are two specific legal techniques involving the family which are crucial in creating jurisdiction: notification of kin and the enabling of their participation. These 'technologies of jurisdiction' (Dorsett and McVeigh 2012, 54–80) have clear parallels with those legal practices which constructed the place of the community in the pre-modern inquest; the ways in which the instruction to attend initiated the inquest jurisdiction and community participation was key to shaping the process and outcomes. The analogy with the place of the historical community is instructive, enabling analysis of authority in the inquest other than from the top down, and the possibility of picking apart what it might mean to describe the family as having authority in the inquest.

---

[21] Smith (2003), summary, para 51, and see the discussion at para 19.39.
[22] Luce 2003 Chapter 8, p 143, paras 7–8.
[23] And see also Constitutional Affairs Committee, 8th Report of Session 2005–2006.
[24] See, inter alia, Glasgow 2004; Luce 2010; Thornton 2014.

Calling the family to law: notification

Under the pre-2013 procedural rules (the 1953[25] and 1984[26] Rules, which will be discussed further later on), relatives were not automatically notified that the Coroner was involved in investigating the circumstances of death, with, for example, no specific requirement to notify before a post-mortem was carried out (if they notified the Coroner that they wished to attend or be represented at the autopsy, they were to be informed that it would be going ahead). Writing before the 2009/2013 changes, Thomas et al (2008, 127) state that despite there being no statutory duty to notify, there were 'an increasing array of reasons why this should be done', citing 2002 Home Office policy, Article 8 ECHR and case law which 'has noted it is good practice to seek the views of the family prior to the post-mortem'.[27] However, despite this emerging obligation, longstanding problems with communication – a common cause of complaints raised by family members – continued, including discrepancies in information provided and methods of notification.[28]

In 2013, in a significant change, specific statutory provision was made. The Coroner was now required to 'attempt to identify the deceased's next of kin or personal representative and inform that person, if identified, of the Coroner's decision to begin an investigation'.[29] Following this, further notification requirements arise.[30] Notification, primarily linked to disposal and management of the deceased, was detached from a sole focus on the body and was linked instead to the initiation of the inquest jurisdiction. Importantly, where previously it was something which arose upon request, it shifted to a proactive duty.

---

[25] Coroners Rules 1953, SI 1953/205.

[26] Coroners Rules 1984, SI 1984/552.

[27] See Thomas et al (2008, 127), citing the case of *Kasperowicz v HM Coroner for Plymouth* [2005] EWCA Civ 44, para 15.

[28] See, inter alia, Beckett 1999; Davis et al 2002, 27; Prisons and Probation Ombudsman 2013, paras 4.1 and 4.1.7.

[29] Coroners (Investigations) Regulations 2013, SI 2013/1629, reg 6; see further discussion of the practice of notification in Chapter 4.

[30] Where an investigation requires a post-mortem, the Coroner must inform the next of kin or personal representative of the decision to hold a post-mortem under reg 13 of the 2013 Regulations. See Angiolini (2017, 206) for a critique of the operation of this in practice. Further notification requirements arise where material is preserved or retained (reg 14), or a decision to discontinue is taken following the post-mortem, and reasons for that decision have to be given (reg 17). The body must be released as soon as reasonably practical and, if more than 28 days has passed, the Coroner must notify the next of kin or personal representative of the reason for the delay (reg 20). Additional notification requirements in relation to the process of the investigation and inquest are set out in the following section on participation.

As with the requirement to call the community together to inspect the body, the requirement of notification is a technology of jurisdiction. Jurisdiction in this sense must be understood as something which is continually being remade and re-established through practice rather than a more static product of direction from above. In this account of jurisdiction, notification of the next of kin is a legal device which is directed at the establishment of the inquest as a place of law in an individual case, and the involvement of the next of kin is a critical part of that creation. It is unlawful not to notify them; it is notification which calls them to the inquest and initiates the lawful role they are expected to play. Unlike the historical community, the law does not compel the acceptance of this place, but enables their engagement. As I will explore in later chapters, the impact of their absence, from a system which represents them as central and frames them as having a need to know (on which see McIntosh 2016; Dyregrov and Kristensen 2020; Ngo 2020), is therefore more problematic and raises more existential questions about the inquest than the absence of a historical community who could be directly disciplined if they did not respond to law's demands.

In relation to the body, this early notification of the family represents a shift in the representation of the family from residual recipients of the remains of their member to active informed agents in the management of the body and the initial stages of the construction of an explanation for death.[31] It also reflects the fundamental shift in the representation of the role of the Coroner — the Coroner is not just a custodian of the remains of an individual for a specific time and for a specific purpose, but together with their responsibility for the physical body, must also take custody of the relationship of the next of kin and the body. This goes beyond granting a family member rights if they initiate contact with the inquest by permitting them to attend the post-mortem or carry out their own post-mortem.[32] Instead, it is a proactive role structured by legislation in which the defining characteristic is engagement, and thereby an acknowledgement of the family's special relationship with both the body[33] and the inquest. In these ways, notification becomes the first step in drawing tacit knowledge into

---

[31] This move can be considered in relation to debates about dignity in the context of political and legal debates over ownership and control of bodies and body parts arising out of numerous high-profile instances of the retention of body parts; I will return to consider this in Chapter 5.

[32] *R v Greater London Coroner ex p Ridley* [1986] 1 All ER 37.

[33] See Human Tissue Act 1961, s 2 and Human Tissue Act 2004, s 1 — once the body is released, the permission of relatives is needed before a further post-mortem is allowed. See also *Bristol Coroner ex p Kerr* [1974] 2 All ER 719 and the discussion in Thomas et al (2008, 134).

the jurisdiction and instituting the possibility of the inquest as a place of meaningful participatory revelation.

Enabling participation I: expanding family

Once notified, the family take their place as privileged participants. The 2009/2013 changes give all interested persons, including designated family members, the right to disclosure on request and further associated rights, as will be discussed further in subsequent chapters. However, the rhetoric of family at the heart, combined with human rights jurisprudence, represents family as more than simply possessing the right to be involved. There are two ways in which this representation can be explored and analysed, which I will examine in turn: firstly, through the gradual extension of categories of those family members entitled to ask questions and, secondly, through the subtle but vital reimagination of the family's right to ask questions.

The first appearance of the bereaved family in legislation relating to inquests is in the 1887 Act, which includes only one mention of the relatives of the deceased. Section 18(6) provided that a Coroner holding an inquest can authorize a body for burial prior to the verdict and, if he does so, he should deliver the burial order to 'the relative or other person to whom the same is required by the Registration Acts to be delivered'.[34] Otherwise statute law was silent as to their involvement, albeit in the context of very few procedural rules about the way in which inquests should be managed. The Coroners (Amendment) Act 1926 included provision to make rules for the running of inquests, but a decade later, the failure to put such rules in place was decried by the Wright Committee, which described Coroners labouring under the 'disadvantage of having no general rules of procedure' (Wright 1936, 51). The Wright report did note that in practice it was common for family to be permitted to be represented, but that this was at the discretion of the Coroner (Wright 1936, 55).

When Rules were eventually made in 1953, these allowed relatives who notified the Coroner to be represented at the post-mortem.[35] In addition, the 1953 Rules provided that an otherwise undefined 'properly interested

---

[34] Interestingly, for deceased members of both Church of England and non-Church of England, orders to bury could be delivered to relatives or persons responsible for the funeral, but for non-Church of England funerals only, an order to bury could also be delivered to a friend: compare s 17 of the Burials Act 1874 and s 11 of the Burials Act 1880.

[35] Coroners Rules 1953, r 4. Such representation had to be by a legally qualified medical practitioner, and the Coroner was required to notify them of the post-mortem. The rules did not include any right for relatives to request a second post-mortem, but it was subsequently held that the Coroner's power to hold a post-mortem is not exclusive, and they cannot refuse a reasonable request for a second post-mortem from an interested

person' should be entitled to be informed of the hour, date and place of the inquest hearing, and to put 'relevant' and 'proper' questions to witnesses at that hearing.[36] Effectively declaratory of the pre-existing non-official guidance on Coronial practice (Melsheimer 1888, 35), the proactive family was permitted procedural entry, but their involvement was limited and circumscribed.

This increasing statutory regulation can be seen as a response to dissatisfaction with inconsistencies and individual injustices across the inquest jurisdiction, constraining the discretion of individual Coroners and imposing a minimum level of best practice, and these concerns continued, such that in 1980, new Rules were published that amended the 1953 Rules.[37] Rule 5 of the 1980 Rules provided the first statutory definition of who had a right to examine witnesses at the inquest, inserting a list into the 1953 Rules of people with an automatic right, opening with 'a parent, child, spouse and any personal representative of the deceased'[38] and also including a beneficiary under a life insurance policy.[39] The Coroner retained a general discretion to include any other properly interested person, but after 1 June 1980, for the first time, some family members had an automatic right to participate in the inquest hearing, although automatic and discretionary participants alike often continued to be described as properly interested persons. The content of Rule 5 was repeated in the 1984 Rules, which were chiefly consolidating,[40] while in 2005 the category of automatic entrants was expanded to include civil partners and partners, defined as persons of the same or opposite sex who lived together in an enduring family relationship.[41] Finally, in the Coroners and Justice Act 2009, this right shifted from secondary into primary

---

person (this is discussed further later on). See *R v Greater London Coroner ex p Ridley* [1986] 1 All ER 37.

[36] Coroners Rules 1953, r 16.

[37] Coroners (Amendment) Rules 1980, SI 1980/557.

[38] Coroners Rules 1953, r 16(2)(a), as amended by r 5 of the 1980 Rules.

[39] Coroners Rules 1953, r 16(2)(b), as amended by r 5 of the 1980 Rules.

[40] They also provided that properly interested persons were entitled to see documentary evidence during and after the hearing (but not in advance), and that they should be notified if criminal charges were preferred in relation to the death; see Coroners Rules 1984, rr 33, 37 and 57. The rights in relation to notification of the post-mortem remained identical in the 1984 Rules, and in both Rules, relatives could request a different pathologist if the proposed pathologist worked in the hospital in which the deceased died. The 1984 Rules supplemented these rights with notification rights where material from the body was preserved, or where special examinations for toxicological or other purposes were to be undertaken. This right to be notified included the requirement that the relatives be told what material was being preserved or tested, the period for preservation, and options for disposal after expiry of period of preservation (rr 9 and 12).

[41] See Coroners (Amendment) Rules 2005, SI 2005/420.

legislation and the categories of family members were further expanded. Those entitled to be automatically involved under s 47 of the 2009 Act now include brothers, sisters, grandparents, grandchildren, children of a brother or sister, stepfathers and stepmother, and half-brothers or half-sisters. At the same time, the definition of 'partner' was amended so that instead of an enduring family relationship, a partner was someone in an 'enduring relationship'.

It is this expanded category of family which is represented as being at the heart of the contemporary inquest jurisdiction, and which is an essential participant in the creation of a legal space represented as responsible for combining community and technocratic forms of accountability.

The historical trajectory is a shift from a role outside statute or case law, based in practice, over which the Coroner has absolute discretion to allow participation, to an automatic right to participate founded in primary legislation.[42] The impression is one of a slow and incremental development of rights, which hides the contestation and contingency in their institution, but also hides the radical nature of the shift in the contemporary jurisdiction. Drawing on Riles (2006), attention to the legal reasoning in relation to the right to ask questions in cases engaging Article 2 ECHR illustrates the depth of this radical rupture. Furthermore, the shift illustrates a fundamentally different way of understanding the conceptual foundation of the jurisdiction, breaking, or at least severely disrupting, law's pretensions to continuity (Tomlins 2016, 5).

Enabling participation II: asking questions

The historical explanation of why questions by kin are permitted is described in the 1888 edition of *Jervis on Coroners*, the leading authority on inquest law and practice,[43] in which it is stated that:

---

[42] In addition to this automatic right to participate, a raft of notification rights are attached to the family's role as participants. New notification rights are set out in the 2013 Rules where an inquest is to be resumed (for example, after a criminal trial) (r 10) or is to be transferred to another Coroner (r 18). As well as longstanding requirements to notify of the date and the right to examine witnesses, the new rights also include a right to advance disclosure, and to consider views regarding witness screening and videolink. Notably, the Coroner is not required to notify family where a report is made to prevent future deaths; instead, reports and responses to reports should be sent to 'every interested person who in the Coroner's opinion should receive it' (rr 28 and 29).

[43] Melsheimer 1888. An indication of the esteem in which the analysis by the authors of *Jervis on Coroners* is held is shown in the fact that the battered, bindingless copy of this 5th edition of *Jervis* held by the British Library is stamped 'Home Office, Under Secretary of State's Room'. For discussion of the authoritative role of manuals like *Jervis*, albeit in the Australian context, see Trabsky (2016).

> It is the duty of the Coroner to examine the witnesses himself, but he has a discretion, in cases where he thinks that it will be of any assistance, to allow questions to be put by, or on behalf of, persons interested. And after each witness has been examined, the Coroner should inquire whether the jury wish any further questions to be put. (Melsheimer 1888, 35)

As discussed earlier, this involvement of the jury was an integral part of the process, while the place of the family was at the discretion of the Coroner. The purpose of permitting questions by them was where the questions will assist – the family is framed as a useful assistant, potentially capable of helping the inquest achieve its goals, but their participation is not an essential constitutive part of that process.

While the discretion of the Coroner to choose to permit the involvement of (some) family members was removed through the 1953 and 1984 procedural changes, the same logic for their role in asking questions remained central. This is clear in the leading case on the exercise of discretion by a Coroner when deciding who ought to be allowed to participate: the case of *Driscoll*.[44] In this case the High Court reviewed the refusal of a Coroner to permit the participation of two sisters in the inquest into their brother's death. Under the CJA 2009, they would automatically be granted the right to take part, but in 1994 their application fell to be considered under the test of a 'person who, in the opinion of the Coroner, is a properly interested person'. The High Court held that there could be circumstances in which a Coroner could conclude that even a close relative (outside the automatic categories) was not properly interested.[45] In the key section of the judgment, Kennedy J held:

> What must be shown is that the person has a genuine desire to participate more than by the mere giving of relevant evidence in the determination of how, when and where the deceased came by his death. He or she may well have a view he wants to put to the witnesses, but there is no harm in that. Properly controlled it should assist the inquisitorial function.[46]

The role of individuals, even where their relationship is very close to the deceased, is focused on assisting in the inquisitorial function. The scope of

---

[44] *R v HM Coroner for the Southern District of Greater London ex p Driscoll* (1993) (1995) 159 JP 45.

[45] A conclusion which now seems difficult to sustain, following *Platts v HM Coroner for South Yorkshire* [2008] EWHC 2502; see the discussion in Chapter 7.

[46] *R v HM Coroner for the Southern District of Greater London ex p Driscoll* (1995) 159 JP 45, 56B–G.

inquiry is determined by the Coroner, and the law represents the role of the family as assistant to the Coroner. That involvement may be of value, but they pose a risk to proceedings if they are not properly controlled and directed to the purpose of the inquiry. Their view of the case does not cause harm as long as it assists with the investigation, and they must be corralled so that irrelevant or illegitimate questions are organized out of the process. This is part of a narrative in inquest law in which the family 'not infrequently strain to pursue their quarry well beyond the bounds set by the Coroner'.[47] The Coroner sets the boundaries in the quest to seek answers to the questions required by statute and, within those boundaries, the family's participation is permitted because it might make for a more effective investigation.

In contrast, Article 2 ECHR has fundamentally changed this, refashioning the right to ask questions in the contemporary inquest jurisdiction, starting with cases which clearly engage the right to life, but with wider implications. For Article 2 cases in particular, instead of an opening concern with constraint of kin, the family's right to ask questions is fundamental to the jurisdiction – a key part of their necessary effective participation – and is not grounded in their ability to assist the Coroner.

This development can be first seen in Strasbourg jurisprudence relating to Article 2 ECHR, including the classic formulation in *Jordan v UK*,[48] which included the requirement that

> there must be a sufficient element of public scrutiny of the investigation or its results to secure accountability in practice as well as in theory. The degree of public scrutiny required may well vary from case to case. In all cases, however, the next-of-kin of the victim must be involved in the procedure to the extent necessary to safeguard his or her legitimate interests.[49]

In the domestic context, it was the deployment of a key piece of judicial historicization by Lord Bingham in the case of *Amin*[50] which pulled pre-Human Rights Act inquests into line with this ECHR jurisprudence. In the application by Imtiaz Amin, uncle of Zahid Mubarak, a young man killed by his racist cellmate, Lord Bingham stated that it was 'very unfortunate that there was no inquest, since a properly conducted inquest can discharge the state's investigative obligation [under Article 2 ECHR], as established

---

[47] *R v North Humberside Coroner ex p Jamieson* [1995] QB 1 (CA).

[48] *Jordan v United Kingdom* (2001) 37 EHRR 2.

[49] *Jordan v United Kingdom* (2001) 37 EHRR 2, para 109.

[50] *R (on the Application of Amin) v Secretary of State for the Home Department* [2003] UKHL 51, [2003] 4 All ER 1264.

by *McCann v. UK*.[51] In his discussion in relation to the duty of the state to investigate deaths in custody, Lord Bingham found that

> effect has been given to that duty for centuries by requiring such deaths to be publicly investigated before an independent judicial tribunal with an opportunity for relatives of the deceased to participate. The purposes of such an investigation are clear: to ensure so far as possible that the full facts are brought to light; that culpable and discreditable conduct is exposed and brought to public notice; that suspicion of deliberate wrongdoing (if unjustified) is allayed; that dangerous practices and procedures are rectified; and that those who have lost their relative may at least have the satisfaction of knowing that lessons learned from his death may save the lives of others.[52]

Alongside other key cases, principally *Middleton*, Lord Bingham's decision in *Amin* established a sometimes uneasy relationship between the requirements of Article 2 ECHR and the inquest system, and his characterization of the inquest as providing space for family participation was a key legal manoeuvre permitting the joining of the two jurisdictions. As discussed earlier, family may have sometimes been given a chance to take part in the past, but this opportunity was by no means centuries-old or an essential part of the process. Bingham's narrative move, inventing a traditional place for the family in inquest law, is thus akin to the invented traditions of Hobsbawm (1983) as a practice of a symbolic nature which establishes a continuity with the past. It is a response to 'novel situations which take the form of references to old situations' (Hobsbawm 1981, 2), with a clear parallel in the form of the importance of the participation of the community in the historical inquest.

In the same case, Lord Bingham went on to consider what family participation might look like. Dismissing investigations by the Prison Service and the Commission for Racial Equality as insufficient, he noted that

> the family were not able to play any effective part in [the] investigation[s] and would not have been able to do so even if they had taken advantage of the limited opportunity they were offered.[53]

The biggest single break with the past and the clearest link to the previously central role of the participating community is in the crucial emphasis on the

---

51 *Amin*, para 33.
52 *Amin*, para 31.
53 *Amin*, para 37.

effectiveness of family participation. The point is developed in *Humberstone*,[54] a Court of Appeal case which provides further guidance on the meaning of effectively participating in a hearing. It focused on public funding for representation at an inquest, and the guidance in place about when funding should be available. The decision of the court noted that

> the [Article 2] duty on the state is fulfilled by the Coroner's effective investigation. But, for the investigation to be effective, the family must be able to play an effective part. So, the [question] is whether [representation] is necessary to enable the family to play an effective part. In other words, the decision must focus on the effective participation of the family and not on the needs of the Coroner.[55]

This underlines the conceptual shift in the contemporary inquest. Family participation is not enabled to assist the Coroner, but is instead based on the need for family to be involved to safeguard their interests, as the Court went on to note:

> The duty to provide representation is derived from the fifth criterion which must be satisfied in an enhanced investigation as described in *Jordan v United Kingdom* [2003] 37 EHRR 52 . The requirement is that the next of kin must be involved in the procedure to the extent necessary to safeguard their legitimate interests. This requirement was adopted by Lord Bingham of Cornhill in *R (Amin) v Secretary of State for Home Department* [2004] 1 AC 653 at para 20. From that requirement flows the duty to provide representation where it is likely to be necessary to enable the next of kin to play an effective part in the proceedings.[56]

Therefore, in order to have an effective Article 2-compliant investigation, the state must ensure family can play an effective part. This goes beyond attending proceedings and raising any particular concerns with the Coroner, who can then put questions on their behalf, as:

> It is said that the ability to attend and understand the proceedings together with an opportunity to raise any particular matter of concern with the Coroner will be sufficient ... [this] seems to overlook the right of a close family member ... to question witnesses. Of course

---

[54] *R (Humberstone) v Legal Services Commission* [2010] EWCA Civ 1479.

[55] *R (Humberstone) v Legal Services Commission* [2010] EWCA Civ 1479, para 75.

[56] *Humberstone*, para 77.

some family members will be able to exercise that right competently, although I think it will often be difficult for them to do so. But to suggest that in general it will be enough for them to be able to tell the Coroner of their concerns seems to me to contemplate that they can properly be deprived of their right to question witnesses.[57]

It is thus the combination of Article 2 and the rules governing inquests which oblige the state to provide public funding for legal representatives. Underpinning this is a conceptual shift. The place of family is reimagined; their role is not solely about assisting the Coroner, but is also not founded solely on the need to have their concerns raised. Setting out all their concerns in advance, and listening to the Coroner explore them with witnesses and through documentary evidence is not enough. It is also not founded on their ability to understand proceedings. Instead, they must be enabled to participate, to play a role in shaping the process and producing an outcome. As noted in a later case, their purpose in taking part is not relevant and need not be only focused on assisting the Coroner reach a conclusion or on seeking to demonstrate that the state is culpable in some way, as:

> The family might simply wish to do no more than discover the truth. They might wish to obtain comfort that suspicions that they harbour or which are circulating in the press or on social media that the state was complicit are unfounded. They might crave for lessons to be learned to prevent what happened to their loved one happening to the loved ones of other families.[58]

The outcome is that from, at best, a helpful adjunct to the Coroner, their endeavours subordinated to the inquisitorial function, in a contemporary *Middleton* inquest, an effective investigation by a Coroner can only take place if the family are effectively involved and able to safeguard their own interests, and the effective involvement of that family is one of the purposes of the inquest (McIntosh 2012).

Furthermore, this conceptual shift in the role of the family is not limited to Article 2 inquests. To explain this requires some further exploration of the debate over the substantive difference between the two types of inquest. While it is clear that the question of whether it is a *Middleton* or a *Jamieson* inquest has a significant impact on the potential conclusions the inquest can reach, it is much less clear what other differences there are, and debate has focused in particular on the question of whether an Article 2 inquest

---

[57] *Humberstone*, para 79.
[58] *R (Letts) v Lord Chancellor* [2015] EWHC 402 (Admin), para 64.

necessarily has a broader scope; in other words, whether it must undertake a broader investigation than in a *Jamieson* inquest. For example, as Lord Chief Justice Lord Burnett of Maldon noted on behalf of a unanimous Court of Appeal in the case of *Maguire*:

> 77. … An analysis of the speeches in the House of Lords in *R (Hurst) v. London North District Coroner* [2007] 2 AC 189 and the judgments in [*R (Smith) v. Oxfordshire Assistant Deputy Coroner (Equality and Human Rights Commission intervening* [2011] 1 AC 1] does not deliver a clear answer to the question whether as a matter of law there is any difference in scope between article 2 and traditional inquests (see for example Lord Mance at para. 207 and 208 in *Smith*). (*R (Maguire) v HM Senior Coroner for Blackpool and Fylde and Others* [2020] EWCA Civ 738)

Matthews (2020, 140–142) disagrees, arguing that there must be a difference in the scope of the inquiry by virtue of the requirements to produce a limited conclusion in *Jamieson* cases, and an obligation to reach a conclusion on the wider circumstances of the death where Article 2 is engaged. The question was not at issue in *Maguire*, but the Court of Appeal did hint at some sympathy for this view, noting the 'peculiarity' of the way in which Article 2 has impacted on inquests, with a focus on 'the product and not the content of the investigation'[59] where it is engaged, as opposed to 'what must happen in a medical case. Beyond an obligation to provide a cause of death, no further investigation is required of the state's own motion by article 2'.[60]

The context was a decision about whether the failings in medical treatment provided to Jackie Maguire required the inquest to reach a conclusion which explored the wider circumstances of her death. Jackie Maguire had cognitive disabilities, lived in a residential care home and was subject to a Deprivation of Liberty Safeguards (DoLS) authorization. She died in hospital, but concerns were raised by her family about failures by healthcare professionals while she was in the care home in the days leading up to her death, and the Coroner initially agreed to hold a wider investigation, including an examination of those failings. However, at the conclusion of the inquest, the Coroner held that the evidence did not indicate that the positive obligation to protect life under Article 2 arose, and therefore the procedural obligation to reach wider conclusions about the circumstances of the death did not arise. Directed to do so by the Coroner, the jury returned a conclusion of natural causes and provided a short narrative description of the events which led up to Jackie Maguire's death. The family, concerned that the jury had not been given an

---

[59] *Maguire*, para 77.
[60] *Maguire*, para 78.

opportunity to comment on any of the failings which had preceded death, challenged the conclusion of the inquest by way of judicial review.

In the Court of Appeal, all sides agreed that the investigation and the hearing had met the requirements of a broader investigation, so the key question for the Court to decide was whether the conclusion of the inquest should have answered 'how' Jackie Maguire had died or ought to have considered 'how and in what circumstances' her death had occurred. The Court concluded that her 'undeniable vulnerability'[61] and the existence of a DOLS authorization was not determinative of whether an Article 2 inquest was needed, that the facts and circumstances were key, and her death ought to be treated in the same way as other deaths in which concerns about medical negligence were raised. In these cases, the Strasbourg Court has endeavoured to distinguish between medical negligence, systemic deficiency and the denial of emergency healthcare (Kapelańska-Pręgowska 2019), in which, in essence, ordinary negligence[62] will not engage Article 2. Following this approach, the Court of Appeal upheld the decision of the Coroner that Article 2 was not engaged in Jackie Maguire's case.

As was noted earlier, in the course of this discussion, the Court considered the question of scope, stating that all of the legal attention paid to the question of the conclusion of an inquest and whether it complied with Article 2 is because – recalling Lord Bingham's judicial historicization – the inquest otherwise provides a mechanism to meet the criteria in Article 2. It stated that:

> There is no issue that the other indicia of an article 2 compliant investigation identified by the Strasbourg Court in *Jordan v. United Kingdom* (2001) 37 EHRR 2 will be satisfied by a properly conducted inquest.

The vital point is that, as identified by *Middleton*, the only problem with the inquest, from the perspective of Article 2, was that the limits on conclusions might not produce an outcome which enabled the process to identify state responsibility for the death. The conclusion in *Maguire*, albeit clearly obiter, is that in every other respect, the properly conducted inquest meets the requirements in *Jordan*. This means that the rights to be involved, including the specific right to ask questions – based on domestic inquest law rather than arising out of Article 2 requirements[63] – satisfies the requirement in

---

[61] *Maguire*, para 70.

[62] See the discussion in *R (on the Application of Parkinson) v HM Senior Coroner for Kent* [2018] EWHC 1501 (Admin).

[63] Notably, not all Article 2 cases (that is, non-inquests) require the ability to ask questions; see, for example, *R (on the Application of Mousa) v Secretary of State for Defence* [2013] EWHC 2941 (Admin), para 38.

Jordan that the next of kin be involved 'to safeguard his or her legitimate interests', whether or not the inquest is a *Middleton* or a *Jamieson* inquest. In other words, the conceptual basis for involvement of kin is the same, whatever the scope or conclusions of the inquest – they are involved in order to safeguard their interests, not to assist the Coroner.[64]

In practice this makes sense, because of the potential difficulty of identifying whether Article 2 or not is engaged, given the complexity of the legal requirements and the way in which evidence may emerge in the course of the investigation and the hearing. As was noted earlier, in *Maguire* the Court of Appeal suggested that whether the Article 2 procedural obligation is engaged or not is 'unlikely' to affect the scope of an inquest and evidence called, which chimes with an earlier decision in which the it had noted 'in practice little difference … as far as inquisitorial scope is concerned'.[65] Matthews suggests a threefold approach, in which Coroners err on the side of a wider investigation, casting 'the net wider rather than narrower' (Matthews 2020, 141, para 6-23), unless and until it is clear that Article 2 is not engaged. This means that being attentive to what emerges in the investigation, including the pre-hearing process, is even more vital, as is the role of the family, particularly where they are seeking to push for a broader investigation. However, this is not to suggest that the family are no longer constrained and corralled, and their involvement remains subject to the limitations placed on them by the Coroner,[66] as well as by virtue of public funding if they are fortunate enough to have it,[67] and constraints imposed by their own lawyers and by other family members. These are all concerns to which will I return in later chapters.

Conclusion

The place of the family in the contemporary inquest can be seen in the conceptual basis of the right to ask questions, as well as the broadening of who can establish themselves within the category of family and the shift to proactive notification of kin. These are all practices of jurisdiction, all part of an emerging understanding of the law of the inquest in which kinship is represented as playing a key role. Unlike the approach of Tait and Carpenter (2014), for whom therapeutic approaches to family are a new and distinct

---

[64] I return in Chapter 8 to consider the potential impact of this conclusion in relation to public funding for the bereaved in inquests.

[65] *R (Sreedharan) v Coroner for the County of Greater Manchester* [2013] EWCA Civ 181, para 18 vii.

[66] For example, irrelevant questions remain capable of exclusion by r 19(2) of the Coroners (Inquests) Rules 2013.

[67] See, for example, *R (Joseph) v Director of Legal Aid Casework* [2015] EWHC 2749, para 49.

theme within the inquest, this places family as the heir of community. However, unlike the historical community, the family's authority is not encapsulated in the authority of a verdict or materialized in the form of a deodand. Where the law of the historical inquest was inaugurated by the gathering of the community, the institution of the contemporary hearing is a more complex, piecemeal and crafted process. It is a process in which the family must be called, cannot be excluded[68] and must be engaged.[69] The family is therefore perhaps more critical to the representation of the law of the contemporary inquest than the community was in the historical inquest. Where the historical inquest saw the community gathered metaphorically, if not actually, around the body of the deceased, the contemporary inquest can be understood as gathering around the family,[70] their involvement represented as critical in achieving a process and outcome which contains the possibility of going beyond the mere technical identification of cause of death. The provisions requiring their involvement establish participation as a key feature of the contemporary jurisdiction, while the way in which law represents this as involvement for their own ends rather than to assist the Coroner frames the process as an endeavour to provide for a meaningful accounting that is not solely oriented to the requirements of a technocratic conclusion.

This is not uncontested, and there is more than a remnant of the modern, solely technocratic approach which can be identified in understandings of the current system, which I will explore in context in the next four chapters. This alternative account emphasizes the authority of a neutral, expert Coroner to decide, and limits family to the exercise of formal legal rights. It is, anecdotally, probably an account which is dominant in the view of those in practice. However, as I have sought to show in this chapter, there are important ways in which this understanding is flawed.

Discussing the ways in which law 'maintains a monopoly over its own speech', from Jonathan Swift to Maurice Blanchot's trial for his involvement in the revolt against French rule in Algeria, Daniel Matthews notes that:

---

[68] Unlike the public, who can be excluded; see Coroners (Inquests) Rules 2013, r 11(4) and (5) and see also *R (Secretary of State for the Home Department) v Assistant Deputy Coroner for Inner West London* [2010] EWHC 3098 (Admin) and the way in which the European Court distinguishes between the role of next of kin and the wider public in *Jordan v United Kingdom* (App No 24746/94) [2003] 37 EHRR 2, para 109, approved by Lord Bingham at para 43 of his decision in *Amin*.

[69] It is this constitutive role where my account perhaps differs from those engaged in exploring a therapeutic jurisprudential approach to the inquest.

[70] Perhaps a legal fiction, but if so, drawing on Pottage (2014, 156), perhaps a fiction operating not at the level of metaphor, but as an 'effective legal construction'.

The law maintains itself through the denial of the other's speech, *who* speaks and *how* they speak in relation to the law – the magistrate warns Blanchot, 'there are things you do not say here' – are crucial to the crafting of law's authority. Such procedural technicalities aimed at disavowing the voice of the other expose a jurisdictional logic at work. (Matthews 2014, 5, emphasis in original)

Attending to these questions in the inquest means attention is focused on who speaks and how they speak, revealing the ways in which the jurisdiction is constructed. Crucially for the contemporary inquest jurisdiction, both questions are underpinned by a question of why kin speak. My attention in this chapter has been on the changing nature of *who* and the foundational question of *why*. The question of *how*, and the ways in which this relates to the complex manner in which the voice of the family may be disavowed or amplified is something I will return to in subsequent chapters, starting with the notification of next of kin.

4

First Contact and the Next of Kin

Introduction

First contact with family is a vital part of analysing understandings of both family and the contemporary inquest. In particular, it is essential in exploring the role that family are understood to play in establishing the system as a process of community accountability, in which tacit, meaningful connection to the deceased can enable the possibility of a meaningful explanation for death. It is also a critical moment for beginning to analyse the ways in which kinship can be constructed in the process of the inquest in the interplay between indeterminate law, official understanding and family practices.

The chapter is divided into five parts. It opens by examining the legal category of 'next of kin' and the importance of focusing on practices and processes, before moving to provide details on the vignettes I used to explore the way in which the decision makers understood the role of family. Following this, I elaborate on the ways in which the first contact with next of kin establishes kinship, use insights from scholarship on decision making to help to understand this process, and close with an explanation of my use of 'framing' as a way of understanding how decisions about family in the inquest system are made. Two frames are identified: one which corresponds with the modern understanding of accountability in the inquest as technocratic, and one which can be seen to emerge from a contemporary approach to the inquest, in which family participation is linked to the production of community accountability.

Making decisions, indeterminacy, and practices of family and kin

The opening obligation to the family is set out in Rule 6 of the Coroners (Investigations) Regulations 2013 SI 1629/2013:

A Coroner who is under a duty to investigate a death under section 1, must attempt to identify the deceased's next of kin or personal representative and inform that person, if identified, of the Coroner's decision to begin an investigation.

'Next of kin' is not used in the Coroners and Justice Act 2009 and first appeared in the 2013 Regulations. As *Jervis on Coroners* notes: 'The phrase "next of kin" has no current technical meaning in English law and it is surprising that it is not defined for the purposes of the Coroner legislation' (Matthews 2020, 198). The documents accompanying the legislation do not assist in defining the phrase, as the only relevant reference to the provision in the Explanatory Memorandum for the 2013 Regulations is an undefined reference to putting 'the needs of bereaved people at the heart of the Coroner system'. There is also no direct case law on the point, but the courts have considered the meaning of 'next of kin' for the purposes of entitlement to funding at an inquest in *Joseph*,[1] where the High Court held that:

30. ... the meaning of the phrase cannot be confined to a dictionary definition of 'the single nearest living relative'. Nor, in my judgment, can it be appropriate simply to import a definition which might be appropriate in other areas of the law, such as intestacy. I readily accept ... that the phrase 'next of kin' must be capable of extending in an appropriate case to more than one close relative of the deceased: hence the various passages in the case law mentioned to me in which the phrases 'close relatives', 'close family', and 'next of kin' appear to me to have been used largely synonymously.

31. Thus in my view, depending on the circumstances of a particular case, 'next of kin' may mean the single nearest living relative, but it is also capable of meaning one or more persons who (a) were closely related to the deceased; (b) qualify as properly interested parties for the purposes of the inquest: and (c) were sufficiently close to the deceased around the time of his death to be treated for these purposes as his next of kin. Identifying the person or persons who fall within this category will necessarily be a fact-specific decision in each case.

The emphasis is on considering both formal categories and also the facts and contexts in which family is practised – identifying who was sufficiently close at the time of death. Family, for these purposes, cannot be reduced to static categories, but is something which results from everyday regular

---

[1] *R (Joseph) v Director of Legal Aid Casework* [2015] EWHC 2749 (Admin).

activities (Morgan 2011, 6). In such an analysis, formal categories are not irrelevant, but they contain fluidity and ambiguity ('closely related' and 'sufficiently close'), and highlight the ways in which law and the practice of family are intertwined (Morgan 2011, 28), as well as the ways in which 'notions of "family" are rarely static but are constantly subjected to processes of negotiation and re-definition' (Morgan 1999, 18, drawing on Weeks, 1999). This focus on a combination of formality with practices and closeness is also evidenced in the approach advocated in *Jervis on Coroners*, which notes that

> the phrase next of kin is used to denote a person or persons who should be informed of various stages or events in the investigation. It is always an alternative to the deceased's personal representative. Closeness to the deceased, ability to receive and act on information and smallness of number are more important for these purposes than, say, the rules of inheritance or the principle of representation, which work better for the (passive) purpose of obtaining a share in the deceased's estate. And marriage or civil partnership is closer even than blood. (Matthews 2020, 198)

This formulation, even more than the approach of the court, emphasizes the family as something active, with closeness combined with the ability to receive and act on information understood as far more important than passive, formal categories based on inheritance. Conceptions of the family as something which is done, rather than something which is, can be seen here both in the way that everyday mundane practices of family link to closeness, and also in the way in which the system relies on those practices to identify family. In the most direct possible sense, these are practices which 'are not simply practices that are done by family members in relation to other family members but they are also constitutive of that "family membership" at the same time' (Morgan 2011, 32). However, continuing to examine *Jervis on Coroners* reveals that these practices will only take putative next of kin so far, and formal conceptions of family intervene. Intriguingly, and revealingly, this is not a formal conception of family which has a clear legal foundation.

Jervis on Coroners goes on to set out a list of who, drawing in part on an assertion of what is in the 'lay mind' (Matthews 2020, 198), ought to be treated as next of kin, submitting that it means 'the first available adult or adults with capacity in the following classes of person' (Matthews 2020, 198): spouses/civil partners, children, grandchildren, parents, grandparents, siblings, uncles and aunts, nieces and nephews, and cousins. In the assertion of this hierarchy, Matthews argues that an emphasis on marriage over blood is based on the list of those entitled to be interested persons in the inquest in s 47 of the Coroners and Justice Act.[2] However, despite being listed after a spouse/civil partner and ahead of blood relatives in s 47(2)(a), a non-married partner of the deceased is a glaring absence in the list of next of kin in *Jervis on Coroners*.[3] The absence of partners highlights that the approach recommended by Matthews is not one which is founded in the legislation, but is rather one which is based in extra-legal ideas of what constitutes family.

Paying attention to the ways in which state agents make references to family norms is something Bourdieu suggests is essential in analysis of the ways in which family is constructed (Bourdieu 1977, 1996). In his account, activities of the state continually create and re-create the family, in a cycle in which subjective categorization by official actors constructs the objective social truth of family, which then acts to create the subjective category of family in the understanding of the decision maker (Bourdieu 1996). In the inquest context, as both the *Joseph* case and *Jervis on Coroners* demonstrate, this cycle includes the interplay of both official categories (whether founded in law or based in a conception of family outside law) and an engagement with practical kin (Bourdieu 1977; Atkinson 2014). Critically, family is not fixed in these formulations; instead, it is tacit and negotiated, and practice may be privileged over formality. This was perhaps most clearly revealed in one interaction I had with an officer

Ed: I'm interested in next of kin – where does it come from? If you have someone who has a brother and a sister, how do you decide which one is next of kin?

Officer: We have got a list.

Ed: You've got a list?

Officer: On my wall, the priority of who would be first.

Ed: Could I have a photocopy of that by any chance?

Officer: Yeah, will have to think where, I've put it on my wall somewhere.

After the interview, the officer gave me a copy of the list from somewhere on the wall. It had come from a training course the officer had been on and I reproduce it in what follows (see Figure 4.1).

It is not drawn from the order of interested persons in the statute or based on the criteria and list in *Jervis on Coroners*, and I found the lack of reference for its baldly asserted hierarchy fascinating. It generates its own authority; a

---

[2]   On which see further discussion in Chapter 3, and see also Chapter 6 in relation to the ways in which it is considered in practice.

[3]   For linked discussion, see Conway (2016, 63) for criticism of the use of intestacy rules in relation to rights to make decisions in relation to a body.

Figure 4.1: Next of kin flowchart

Spouse

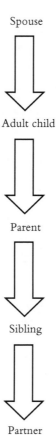

Adult child

Parent

Sibling

Partner

source-free statement of law to which no lawyer would automatically accede, but which represents law, structuring the approach of those administering the law. Its location is also important; putting it up on the wall further reinforced it as authoritative statement, a tool for quick reference which summarizes the norms to be applied in case of dispute. But it had also disappeared on the wall somewhere and, instead of being a rigid hierarchy, had become a flexible guide:

> 'But you would tend to phone whichever one on the list. You would just pick and sort of get an idea, you know, obviously 'I've got your details and your sister's details, which one of you is it best to contact?' And usually they say it's best to speak to me or actually can you contact my sister that would be better and they usually sort it between themselves. Again if they both wanted to be contacted then we would

contact both of them but majority of time they would, usually they are all together anyway and talking to one of them so just go through me, so yeah, it is usually not a problem.' (Officer)

As 'they usually sort it out between themselves', this is a first engagement which indicates the potential flexibility of approach and a concern with pragmatism and practicality, with the additional possibility that next of kin is not a single point of contact, but is a shared responsibility and a route into a group which is 'all together anyway'. I explored the same issue in interviews with Coroners, and asked one Coroner specifically how they decided who family was:

'Well, that is a very good question. Technically of course, we have got s.47 of the CJA 2009, which spells out the identifiable, what we might describe colloquially as, next of kin. But my normal sources of information are either going to be the hospital if it is a hospital death to identify primary members of the family, or if the police are involved then police to identify members of the family. It will be impossible to contact each and every family member, we normally would go to, obviously the spouse if there is a surviving spouse, mother and father, a brother or sister if they were taking an interest, but there can be family and I have dealt with them before where there are loosely competing interests between for example the brothers and sisters. I had a case where a sibling was in complete logger heads with another sibling, and applied for an injunction to stop me releasing the body to his sister. They were at each other's throats, so we try and be as inclusive as possible, can I say hand on heart that we succeed every time? No I can't, we try and do our absolute best to make sure that we know.' (Coroner)

As these answers demonstrate, the question of who is next of kin is perceived to be a technical legal question capable of being conclusively identified (as Atkinson (1978, 90) found with the meaning of suicide), but is treated in practice as a question which is open to negotiation and determination by the people within the category of family.

The emphasis from this very first engagement is on informing multiple members or the entire family, not simply notifying a single next of kin. This frames next of kin as responsible for engaging with the wider family, and they play a critical role in defining that wider family: who is legitimately involved, who should play a limited role and who should properly be excluded.

In these accounts, family represent a link to the deceased, but they are not responsible in law for representing the deceased. Next of kin are there in their own right, not on behalf of the deceased,[4] and there is little provision made in law or practice for the deceased's wishes to play a part. As Matthews (2020, 198) notes, there is no provision enabling individuals to nominate another individual to be their next of kin for the purposes of an inquest. The only way in which an individual could lawfully nominate another to act on their behalf would be by appointing them as executor in their will,[5] but a personal representative and next of kin are not the same. Furthermore, while Rule 6 states Coroners must attempt to notify next of kin or personal representatives, there were no references in any of my interviews to contacting personal representatives. The clear implication is that the wishes of the deceased are not central to the decision[6] and that the next of kin is perceived to have priority over any personal representatives.[7] Finally, as subsequent examples show, there was a clear preference for making decisions about who was next of kin informally wherever possible, and only resorting to formal declarations where it was deemed to be necessary.

These insights illustrate the limitations of a positivist approach which ignores the interpretative work that goes on in these processes (Tait and Carpenter 2014). A positivistic analysis of decision-making presupposes that a final decision maker is provided with factors and has a range of possible decisions, while a systemic approach seeks to explore how earlier decisions can shape, require or avoid a final 'legal' decision. These earlier decisions range from a formal explicit decision to implicit informal and unevidenced or hidden decisions, and might mean that effective power to decide might thus be consciously or unconsciously exercised by individuals not granted the formal power to decide (Lukes 1974).

An account of the engagement of the family which only engages with the explicit final 'legal' decision of the Coroner (if there is one) is incapable of providing an account which engages with the subtlety and nuance of the interactions that combine to create a place for the family in the inquest. The way in which family is involved can include decisions made as a result of

---

[4]   *R (Joseph) v Director of Legal Aid Casework* [2015] EWHC 2749, para 54.

[5]   Compare, in this regard, the different treatment of family and non-family personal representatives before the European Court of Human Rights; contrast *Scherer v Switzerland* (Application No 17116/90) and *Thevenon v France* (Application No 2476/02) with *Malhous, v Czech Republic Dec* (Application No 33071/96).

[6]   A reflection which can be compared to reflections on testimonial autonomy – see Douglas (2014); Hacker (2014); Leslie (2014); and Monk (2011), (2014) – although, as noted in Chapter 3, beneficiaries of a life insurance policy are automatically interested persons if they wish to be involved in the inquest, but the relationship between interested person status and next of kin is not clear.

[7]   Further reinforced by references in interviews to the fact that even if estranged/out of contact, family members had an important role to play if they became involved in the inquest.

explicit engagement with the law, but not necessarily, and in any event they are also often made in a context in which the explicit rules are not definitive and are open to negotiation (Gilboy 1991). Any analysis also cannot ignore the central role of the officer in this process, with – for example – one Coroner characterizing their officers as having the responsibility to notify and explain: 'As far as a lot of the contact is concerned it is through the officers, and of course putting the family central is partly reflected in the range of duties of notification by officers and explanations and we do our best to support the officers in meeting that.'

The officer is framed here as expert in engaging with the family, while in contrast, another Coroner emphasized their role:

'I may have contact with the bereaved family very shortly after the death ... I normally don't allow my staff to do these difficult conversations because sometimes I have to do them because I am the horse's mouth, so quite often I will have to speak to families shortly after [the death].'

It is because of this variability and flexibility that I adopt an approach which highlights practices and the 'lived-in and taken-for-granted world' that is 'constantly being created and reproduced through the day-to-day activities' of those within it (Morgan 1999, 21), in contrast to a focus on difficult cases, breakdown or dysfunction (Morgan 2011, 6). The practices in which I am interested are those that link to decisions which determine or shape the place of the family in the inquest. To understand these decisions, the crucial question is not what items of information (or factors) are part of making a decision, but rather how the decision maker understands and organizes the information they are presented with (the 'frame'). Hawkins (2002, 52) argues that the frame, as a structure of 'knowledge, experience, values and meanings', is always contingent and will 'instruct a decision-maker how to understand a case, a problem or a person'. Developing this, and drawing on Kennedy (2008), my account is one in which frames can be seen to be deployed strategically. These frames are intimately linked to the decision maker's understanding of different forms of accountability within the inquest.

To explore the understandings of decision makers, I devised a series of vignettes, which I will discuss next.

Vignettes

Spalding and Phillips note that vignettes have been productively used in social science research since the late 1970s (Spalding and Phillips 2007, 954), and Finch uses vignettes to examine kinship relationships, noting that interviewing using vignettes invites statements about normative beliefs in a contextualized set of social circumstances (Finch 1987, 105). Finch also argues that, rather than depicting extreme situations, the vignette should focus on the mundane, although it can be advantageous to include some unusual features (Finch 1987). They also acted as miniature case studies, allowed the participants to explore holistic issues (Yin 1994, 12) and encouraged participants to describe their own experiences (Barker and Renold 1999). I was clear that the vignettes were my creations, drawing on case law as well as my experience from practice, and so contained something of me (Spalding and Phillips 2007, 958). Therefore, rather than relying on an approach which emphasizes the desirability of the controlled experiment and the isolated objective feature (Epstein and Martin 2014, 4–7), I explored the responses of the interviewees and my role in constructing those vignettes, drawing from critical reflections on the dynamic instability of law and society (Pavlich 2011). In my analysis of the answers, rather than testing the responses against each other and against doctrinal law to establish truths, I used the vignettes and my interviews to develop and deepen contextually grounded theoretical insights (Yin 1994, 13).

One interesting feature to emerge was that while my research design envisaged that the vignettes would provide more detailed substantive reflections on definitional questions about who constituted family and that the opening questions would enable the interview to engage in wider systemic questions, in fact many of the most interesting systemic insights came through consideration of the vignettes. This was perhaps because of a common law-style preference for working from cases to principles. Alternatively, it may be because the vignettes provided circumstances which potentially challenged some of the broader assertions in the earlier stages of the interviews. They were not designed to be particularly hard cases, but rather to be facts and circumstances which provoked discussion, yet they did enable me at times to return to previous answers and to unpick them further in the light of the vignettes. Whatever the explanation, there is some irony in the fact that it was the examples of individual cases which provoked some of the most interesting systemic responses.

Vignette 1: The non-adopted daughter and the missing wife

A tree alongside a public footpath falls onto a pedestrian, a 65-year-old male, killing him. The police attend his address and inform the occupant, who identifies herself as his daughter. After initial contact with her, she tells your office that she does not think she was ever formally adopted by him, but lived with him as his daughter from the age of five (for the last 35 years). She says she thinks he was married once, and she thinks he would not have got divorced because he was a staunch Catholic.

In follow-up questions, I teased out further explanation – for instance, whether officers would permit the daughter to be involved, whether they would seek details of the wife and how they would go about seeking those details. With this, as with the other vignettes, I asked Coroners how they would expect their officers to act, how they would decide what to do, and how they would respond if their officers came and discussed this scenario with them.

Vignette 2: The girlfriend

A soldier in a barracks in your district is found shot dead. Internal Army investigations suggest the gunshot was self-inflicted. His girlfriend contacts your office. She had been going out with him for ten months at the time.

Follow-up questions included testing how additional information would affect the decision, as well as suggestions that it would change things if, for example, she is pregnant with his child, they lived together and he was an orphan with no other relatives. I was surprised to discover that for many participants, the fact that it was a soldier with a boyfriend/girlfriend relationship suggested it was either possible or even likely that the deceased was also married, a factor I had not envisaged in the vignette design.

Vignette 3: The mother, biological father and the new partner

The school bus which should have picked up a five-year-old girl was cancelled at the last minute, but no one informed her parents, and she walked home from school. On the way, she was run over and killed. The police have informed her mother and her partner. The mother informs you that the father is not on her birth certificate and she had an old (now expired) non-molestation order against him after he was violent towards her. He has had no contact with the child, who was born after she left him. She says her new partner has effectively been the father and she wants him to be treated as such in the inquest.

With this vignette, I sought to raise further questions about the extent to which Coroners and their officers would expect to search for further possible next of kin once they had identified an obvious next of kin, as well as questions about the way in which decisions were made about who else might participate.

Vignette 4: The long-lost sister

A man dies in police custody. He was homeless and police were unable to find any next of kin. After the post-mortem, his sister contacts your office. She says she has had no contact with her brother for 30 years after a family dispute, but wants to be involved.

My attention in this scenario focused on two areas: what evidence, if any, might be needed to support the sister's claim; and whether the length of time she had been out of contact with her brother would make any difference in the way she was approached.

The lack of information in the vignettes was deliberate; as Finch (1987) notes, ambiguity forces interviewees to invent factors which would help them decide, and in so doing, I hoped they would reveal ways in which they would understand and frame the situation. I selected the ways in which the deaths had occurred from real cases to ensure they would be believable for the participants. In relation to the relationships, these were invented by me as possible scenarios which might arise and which could require an exercise of discretion on the part of the Coroner (that is, not falling into the automatic categories of family in the legislation) or might raise questions about the differences between close emotional ties and formal kinship links.

Keenan (2009; see also Canetto 1993) shows how race, class and gender can be reinforced by systems which self-describe as neutral, and in an analysis of the ways in which the inquest process can be revelatory of patriarchy, she notes the importance when researching of recognizing your own standpoint. My identification as a male with professional qualifications and some experience in representing families in inquests (as a solicitor rather than as an advocate) impacted in particular in relation to the construction of my vignettes. Although I had reflected on aspects of gender in my work, I did not reflect on the gender make-up of the vignettes until after my interviews. I created the vignettes by drawing on reported cases and my own experience, and on further reflection was struck by the gender bias within them, with three of the four deceased being male, and five of the seven family members identified as female, and I realized that my experience in practice was commonly in situations where the deceased was male and I was instructed by a female family member.

This gendering in the system is borne out to some extent in the literature, with, for example, a higher rate of inquests among men (accounting for 65 per cent of inquest conclusions in 2020; see Coroners Statistics 2020), with a large amount of scholarship on the higher prevalence of self-inflicted deaths among men (see, for example, Murphy 1998; Scourfield et al 2012), while

Maple et al (2014) argue there is over-reporting of women's voices in suicide literature (Maple et al 2014). In this context it is relevant that Barker and Renold (1999) emphasize the importance of plausibility of vignettes and, like Spalding and Phillips (2007, 959), I experienced validation of my vignettes in some of my interviews, with interviewees stating they had had a case like this or asking if these were examples taken from their jurisdiction. However, one officer described the circumstances in Vignette 3 as implausible. As discussed in Chapter 6, this officer stated that this set of circumstances would not happen – the new partner would not be treated as the father because the mother was available to be next of kin. Here, the very implausibility of the scenario was itself revealing, as this response revealed the way in which the officer would play a part in tacitly ensuring that these circumstances would not arise.

These vignettes produced insights which run through my chapters on the contemporary system, and as shorthand I refer to the individuals in these scenarios as the non-adopted daughter and the missing wife (Vignette 1), the girlfriend (Vignette 2), the mother, biological father and the new partner (Vignette 3), and the long-lost sister (Vignette 4).

Constructing kinship

Vignette 1 provided particularly revealing answers in relation to the construction of next of kin, with some interviewees asserting that the missing wife was still legally next of kin. However, all interviewees answered that the non-adopted daughter would be likely to be involved in a significant way, even, through negotiation, taking precedence over the wife:

'I think the daughter would be entitled to disclosure and probably would be entitled to the body but the wife has precedence and I would expect reasonable steps to be taken to try and chase down the wife. What happens on the ground really is that there is then a conversation between the wife and the daughter, they say I have never seen him, I am quite happy for you to take the body. That is what really happens on the ground in this sort of situation, they speak to each other and people are very civilized, usually.' (Coroner)

This illustrates a common theme across all interviews that the tacit connection with the non-adopted daughter would form the basis of her acceptance as next of kin despite the lack of a formal relationship. The answers re-emphasized the potentially critical place of the first contact in acceptance and precedence of kin:

'Well, the daughter at the moment is the only person who you have got, so she automatically becomes an interested person at the outset, by virtue of her being brought up as a daughter, other people may well emerge, and we will clearly be looking for them, and they may also be interested persons.' (Coroner)

The non-adopted daughter is thus automatically rendered an interested person and next of kin, and the officers and Coroner will be 'clearly' actively seeking others. Her role may not formal, but

'You would treat her as his daughter wouldn't you, she is his daughter, she might not be adopted by him, but she is still to all intents and purposes his daughter, you would treat her as his next of kin.' (Officer)

The length of time is important:

'She's saying she's lived with him for 35 years, she's not aware of anyone else, we would have to accept that she's not lying to us.' (Officer)

And in relation to their investigation:

Ed: Would you ask [the daughter] for details of the wife if she was able to give them?

Officer: If she was able to give them, I would just like to know, I mean, legally speaking his wife is still the next of kin, and I mean, I guess there would be some sort of duty down the line somewhere for her to be informed that he had died, and we would ask the police to do that on our behalf, but if the daughter didn't know that we might make some inquiry with the police to see if they can find this individual, but I think we would tend to stick more with the daughter to be totally frank.

In these responses, it is clear that what is at stake is not the identification and application of technical legal principles, but rather an amalgam of those principles with other considerations, and an insistence on considering the context in which the relationship arose. Crucially, central emphasis was placed on the longstanding family practice of treating their relationship as father–daughter, mirroring a formal kinship tie.[8]

---

[8] See *R v Coroner of the Queen's Household ex p Al Fayed* (2001) 58 BMLR 205, [2000] Inquest L.R. 50; and *Platts v HM Coroner for South Yorkshire* [2008] EWHC 2502. However, it should be noted that these are cases relating to the test for interested person status, not next of kin.

A core theme of many interviewees' responses emphasized the role of family in gathering and providing information to the inquest, and the special place of the family is constructed in the way in which the family are given responsibility for individualizing the deceased; fashioning context and history, providing feedback on the process and setting out concerns. This represents the family as having a responsibility for re-introducing contingency in the investigation, and possibly providing a counterweight to systemic processes which rely on typical approaches to routine situations.

Decision making in the inquest

Routinization and typification

In his work on decision making, Hawkins argues for the need to pay attention to the role of typification, or the way in which routine decisions are made the same way (Hawkins 2002, 35–38). Typification enables individual decision makers to act more swiftly, ordering their work and separating out the routine from the complex. This categorization of routine decisions, relying on experience, can provide a defence against criticism and justify a particular course of action. In this context, it is important that my interviewees all reflected on the importance of experience, with both Coroners and officers placing importance on the place of experience in being able to do the job properly, as one officer explained:

Officer: From first point of contact you can usually get an idea of what kind of family you are dealing with, you can get quite a good idea. The more and more you do it the more and more you get it.
Ed: OK, so that is experience?
Officer: Yeah, absolutely yeah.

The crucial aspect of experience here is that experience is valuable for being able to 'deal' with the family, including gathering information from them, engaging them in the investigation and potentially managing a family perceived as disruptive.

Processes of typification can also mask aspects of a situation, as decisions are made that assume particular features of a case, drawing on information from referrals (Emerson 1991), and this is closely linked to sequential decision making (which will be discussed later). An example of this in the Coronial context can be found in the ethnographic study of the inquest system by Atkinson in the 1970s, and his observation that deaths on the road were not generally investigated as possible suicides (Atkinson 1978, 118). However, it is also important to explore how their own awareness of the impact of routinization can affect decision makers. In the inquest context, this awareness is reflected in two key discourses: an emphasis on the need to get and give information to the family to individualize the deceased; and a repeated emphasis on responsiveness to the particular facts of the case. A doctor might say who the next of kin is, but could then say the following:

'You might want to speak to the daughter rather than the wife. Especially with very elderly people, a lot of the time it is not necessarily appropriate to speak to the wife, it may be better doing it with the children but it is all dependent on the situation, ascertain the actual next of kin and start at that point [and] go from there.' (Officer)

Similarly:

'Sometimes if you get a next of kin, like if I have an elderly gentleman, really confused, doesn't really understand what you are saying so we then would say, is there someone else there or have you got a relative that we might be able to contact? Then you would go through that person as well, obviously keep that person aware of what we are doing but just so that we are 100% sure that that next of kin knows exactly what the process is because you sort of get the idea that he may not be sure of what is happening so yeah, we would then take it to find someone else to give the information to as well.' (Officer)

This important role of the family is amplified by another consequence of typification: the way in which it can produce administrative precedent, whereby organizational and administrative rules can take on the same force as legal rules (Hawkins 2002, 36). As the priority list provided to me illustrates, even administrative rules of unclear provenance can take on the force of legal rules:

'I suppose one of the main difficulties is, if someone has been with someone … 20 odd years, not married and there are children, things like that. Sometimes, depending on how the relationship went down with the family, that can be a bit of bother. Obviously there are certain things – common law marriage and cohabiting and other things like that – but it is difficult if you have got someone who has been with someone for say ten years and they might have never married and they have got a daughter, and she's like 'no I'm next of kin' but you are not married and it can be hard because obviously she's lived with that person day in day out, but they just didn't choose to get married. Sometimes can be hard.' (Officer)

This is an account in which hardline rules create particular difficulties and apparent injustices,[9] but in other instances, even as they appear to be binding rules, the actors may not act as if they are bound by them, and instead seek to solve problems as they arise (Hawkins 2002, 40). This was illustrated in an exchange I had with an officer in relation to the biological father in Vignette 3. I asked if the officer would take steps to seek the father, and the officer stated no, but if he turned up:

Officer: We'd have to, you know, weigh up the pros and cons, because, but you know, we would cross that bridge when we come to it.

Ed: So weighing up the pros and cons, what sort of things would you be wanting to find out or wanting to know in that?

Officer: What, if he came to us? He would have to come to us, we would not go to him, because basically we are saying there that, she doesn't want him told, well I mean that is a matter for her, nothing to do with us, but he is going to find out that his daughter has died, unless he is in Antarctica or somewhere like that, it is going to be in the press isn't it, and he is going to read it, and he may well then make approaches to us, for information, and that is when we would then have to consider his ex-partner. When I talk about weighing up the pros and cons, you just can't sit here and go well, I'd look at that and I'd look at this, because every case has its different merits and different difficulties, so you have to look at it in isolation at the time, I think in the long run you would talk to them, you would certainly start off by talking to the chap, and then you would be taking things on from there but for me to say now what I would do, I couldn't do that, unless you said to me, well, you know, this is what he is like, what are you going to do now?

This lengthy answer illustrates the emphasis on flexibility and responsiveness to the facts as presented to the inquest, but also demonstrates the way in which the actors can be framed as essentially reactive, responding to the presentation of events and information, and (critically here) to the way in which the absent father presents himself. It also highlights the flexibility in the system and the ways in which the system engages with family

---

[9]   And here, I would suggest, an unlawful interpretation of next of kin – see the discussion in Chapter 3.

relationships; there is no provision in the law for the biological father to be treated differently from the mother or for her needs to be taken into account when considering his role, but the officer administering the system has the power to shape family involvement, depending on the way in which their understanding of the context is organized.

Sequential decision making

It was emphasized by many interviewees that the ultimate decision in relation to next of kin status was not a decision for the inquest system and that if family members disagreed about whether they were next of kin, they would need to go to court to get a decision.[10] It was also emphasized that decisions taken within the inquest system would often rely on decisions taken by actors before the inquest system was engaged, and the role of the decision makers in the inquest was consequently circumscribed. For example, in relation to the missing wife in Vignette 1, officers suggested they could make some investigations themselves (with some noting that they could check marriage registers or use a company to investigate), and Coroners stated they would expect inquiries to be made, but most of my interviewees emphasized the following point:

> 'There is a limit, officers are not expected to go to unreal lengths to trace family and everyone else, so if she says to you there is a husband, it is not for the officers to go round searching all the counties' telephone directories or whatever.' (Coroner)

At this point, an officer came in, and the Coroner took the opportunity to ask what steps they would take. The officer stated that they would ask the police, who would check the police intelligence database:

> 'So the police do it, and if that comes up negative, we are not going to go running. We say to the daughter well, we haven't managed to find him, and it may be for witness statements something will come up, or very often when someone has died people come out of the woodwork.' (Coroner)

---

[10] While there is no case law directly on this point, this assumption does not appear to be correct. In the event of a dispute, the courts have jurisdiction to determine who is entitled to determine how to dispose of a body (see Conway 2003), but the question of who is next of kin for the purposes of the inquest is not necessarily the same (although it is closely linked, as the discussion in Chapter 5 illustrates). The decision is therefore the Coroner's, subject to the jurisdiction of the High Court in the event of a perverse or irrational decision.

As this (and similar references to 'coming out of the woodwork' in other interviews) illustrates, family can emerge as part of the inquest process, and it was clear that the interviewees were used to responding to ongoing situations where individuals sought to be involved as the investigation developed. This quote also illustrates a common theme of the role of trust and expertise in systems of decision making. As the fortunately timed interruption by the officer shows, my Coroner interviewees expected their officers to have expertise and to act on initiative, with perhaps some assistance or guidance:

Ed: You would just say to your officers I think you should try and find them and your officers would?

Coroner: Well that is their department, I mean we might brainstorm it together – can either of us think of any other avenue we can explore.

Importantly, the Coroner and their officers operate in a system in which the police and other agencies have some responsibilities for the efficient conduct of the investigation:

'As far as we are concerned, it is down to the police to track down next of kin, they do obviously present themselves when, you know, they'll realize something, they'll hear through the grapevine locally that something has happened, then they'll telephone us, and things sort of unravel a bit or become clearer but initially we have the one point of contact and find out as much as we can as we go on.' (Officer)

Furthermore, as with 'big' – that is, newsworthy – cases in regulatory authorities (Hawkins 2002, 35), 'big' inquests have more serial elements, with greater scope for the decisions to be shaped by decisions taken in external investigations by, for example, the police or investigatory/regulatory bodies like the Independent Police Complaints Commission (INQUEST 2013, see also the discussion in Angiolini (2017, 205, 209–10)) as with the long-lost sister in Vignette 4:

'In a case like this, she would probably come to us via the police. People don't necessarily think to contact the officer first, if someone has died in police custody, they would ring the police first and then they would speak to the investigating officer who would get the details and often we would then get a call saying this woman has rung up she is the sister and give us the telephone number and we will contact them. We don't sort of take everybody on trust, but it generally pans out that they could make an inquiry and people who aren't legitimate wouldn't go through the police.' (Officer)

The longstanding relationship between the police and the inquest system has been the subject of a great deal of academic discussion and criticism (Cowburn 1929; Thurston 1962; Scraton 2002), but they are only one in a range of actors who can make important decisions which affect the inquest, as another officer emphasized:

> 'A death in the community, in hospital, or an expected death we may have GP or hospital doctors contact us and we may be able to get the next of kin details from them as well, and a lot of [the] time they might advise us who the best person is to talk to and who they would prefer to be our point of contact.' (Officer)[11]

Furthermore, it is not only state agents. My interviewees also emphasized reliance on the family, as excerpts from four separate interviews illustrate:

Officer: Unfortunately we have to trust what the police provide us as next of kin or doctors or GPs, and just speaking with the people that you have got details for and trusting what they are saying to you.

Coroner: It is slightly a question for the officers what level of proof, I would take people on trust.

Officer A: The problem is with identification of next of kin obviously we can only do so much establishing who that is because we are not private detectives. (Officer B) And we trust people don't we, if they say, we are next of kin then we don't argue.

Coroner: Well, we can ask who she is, but you ask who they are, you ask their contact details name and address, but there is good faith in this, you know.

All of these answers illustrate the way in which the process is shaped by a range of other decisions made by individuals inside (and outside) of the category of family, by external actors, including the police or the hospital, as well as by the officer.[12] In relation to a decision about interested person

---

11 On the relationship between doctors and the inquest system, see, inter alia, Gilleard (2008); Tuffin et al (2009); Barnes, Kirkegaard and Carpenter (2014).

12 For example, in relation to the impact of decisions by the family on other decisions, see discussion of suicide verdicts in Tait and Carpenter (2014, 9–11). In relation to the important role of otherwise hidden 'non-legal' actors, see Castellano 2009.

status, for example, a combination of prior decisions might force a Coroner to decide in a particular way, or alternatively might mean the decision is made before a Coroner ever needs to make a formal ruling. An approach to analysis of the law recognizing the contemporary role of family cannot ignore the multiple ways in which these actors act in reliance or in response to those earlier decisions, and the ways in which expertise and conceptions of jurisdiction are employed to respond in particular moments in that process. This conception also draws attention to the ongoing nature of such decisions in a lengthy process – that decisions can be revisited, affirmed, subtly reshaped or radically revised, but cannot be seen as separate from the processes which have created the circumstances that require (or obviate the need for) a decision.

These answers also re-emphasize the ways in which the actors perceive themselves to be responding to facts and to the family, and reacting to their presentation of themselves and their concerns, as the following discussion between two officers about initial contact with the long-lost sister in Vignette 4 demonstrates:

Officer A:	We tend to take people on face value.
Officer B:	Yeah, we don't say, well, look, can you come in with your birth certificate, no we tend to take people on face value, I mean, I think, once you start talking to people, you would pick up if there was something wrong.
Officer A:	If it was something dodgy, yeah.
Officer B:	If somebody was to ring me up and say well I am Jimmy Smith's sister, I perhaps wouldn't tell her everything on the first telephone conversation, I might talk to her and try and establish just a few little facts, before I was to really relay everything to her.

As this answer also illustrates, these are not solely abstract considerations; they are bound up with material evidential concerns like attending the office with a birth certificate and assessing the credentials of a putative family member based on their telephone manner. Exploring the place of writing in particular is crucial in an account of how a jurisdiction is created and shaped, and who is engaged in that jurisdiction.

Evidence and legal writing

Vignette 4 provoked interesting reflections on evidence, in particular in relation to what the long-lost sister might need to produce in order to be recognized as next of kin. One Coroner proved very willing to accept non-formal family relationships in earlier discussions of a case in which an informal adoption had occurred, but was also clear that evidence was needed to support a claim to be next of kin:

Coroner:	She can presumably establish that she is the sister?
Ed:	Well that was going to be a question, would you take any steps to seek to establish that?
Coroner:	Yes, I would want her to establish the relationship.
Ed:	What would you be expecting from her to establish that?
Coroner:	I would want a birth certificate that shows she has the same parents or same parent singular at least, as him. And if she was saying well, you know we weren't formal but we were brought up together, she'd have to establish something otherwise she's just Joe Public who has popped out of the woodwork and said 'oh, I'll play a hand in this'.
Ed:	So she would need to provide some evidence to persuade you that they were brother and sister?
Coroner:	Yeah, whether real or de facto.

The emphasis on evidencing the informal family reveals this Coroner's engagement with balancing the requirements of formality and tacit connection. The technical, detailed face of law is both deployed (in the request for evidence) and subverted (in the emphasis on non-formal but substantive connections) with the aim of engaging law with a contingent kinship construction. Key to this is the 'routine sharing and the sharing of routine [which] consolidates care and integration' (Atkinson 2014, 226).

In relation to precisely what evidence might be needed, another Coroner suggested that a letter from the sister would usually suffice, while a different Coroner stated that they would want evidence, and when asked what evidence:

'I suppose what we tend to do, thinking about it now, is they ask them to write in, because we get phone calls, so we always ask them to write in, and probably we would take it very much at face value.' (Coroner)

The emphasis here is on a written record, not as a way of transmitting information, but as a means of establishing truth in itself. At one level, this is the material of law at its most abstract, with little attention to form as compared to some other documents, such as consent forms (Jacob 2012, 58). The content and form of the letter are largely unprescribed and are relatively unimportant, as with the illegible *tofes haskama* or consent form Jacob found used in an Israeli transplant centre (Jacob 2012, 59–61). However, unlike the *tofes haskama*, the existence of the letter is crucial, introducing a 'reflective pause' (Jacob 2012, 54), and limiting flexibility and liquidity (Hogle 2003,

87). As with the evidence from the missing sister, the letter introducing the family represents ongoing endeavours to satisfy the demands of both community and technocratic forms of accountability – where relationships are taken at face value in an endeavour to bring in the tacit connection, but are also subject to a minimum of law-type oversight, capable of being objectively justified and evidenced. Part of an ongoing process, and so capable of reversal or re-affirmation, it is a moment at which the family is reified and perhaps otherwise tacit relationships are made concrete. It is the moment at which family are identified as something separate, and it occurs through the operation of legal writing, because a telephone call is not enough.

It can therefore be seen as a vital moment in the process of family being engaged in the jurisdiction. As Dorsett and McVeigh argue, legal writing inaugurates the power of law; from a claim form to a parking ticket (Dorsett and McVeigh 2012, 60). Here, the letter from the family is part of a process of family being called to law – a process which, as well as the letter from the family, could include telephone calls and letters and official forms being sent from the Coroner to the family. These material processes carry the authority of law, and it was revealing that I was told anecdotally that some actors in the inquest system felt the statutory forms (enclosed within both the Coroners [Investigations] Regulations 2013 and the Coroner [Inquest] Rules 2013) lacked official authority because of their layout. In this context, I was told of some Coroner's offices who acted to 'improve' them by inserting a crest at the top of the form.

Decisions do not stand alone

Another criticism of an approach based on positivistic decision making is the emphasis on making each individual decision independent of other organizational concerns. In my interviews, it was clear that that converse was true and that in the inquest context, a great deal of attention is paid to the implications of the current handling of a case for a particular way of handling other cases, and the relationship between an individual case and the wider context. One example of this was a Coroner's reflections on relations with a wider community:

> 'In this area we have a large Muslim and Jewish population and quite often there will be representatives of the Muslim or Jewish faith who want to make representations to me about, for example, not having a post-mortem or releasing the body sooner, and I will regularly meet them.' (Coroner)

These comments, along with a range of other comments by Coroners about their caseloads and comparisons with the activities of Coroners in other districts, including decisions to hold post-mortems, made it clear that decisions are regularly made which take into account the impact of a decision in one case on other cases. This wider context, together with the implications of typification and serial decision making, mean that an analysis of decisions in the inquest system which looks at individual cases without considering the broader systemic issues would be necessarily flawed, and it is for this reason that I turn to framing as a way of understanding how decisions are made.

Framing and the Coroner's first contact with the family

I use framing as an analytical tool to explore the ways in which my interviewees made sense of the situations we discussed in our interviews. The frames deployed by my interviewees reveal how questions are understood, how issues are organized into or out of a particular decision, and how factors are classified and interpreted. They were sometimes used strategically by my interviewees and sometimes engaged with apparently less deliberately, and the emphasis in them on striving to combine forms of accountability or, alternatively, a concern to constrain kin and emphasize solely technocratic accountability links my empirical work to the themes developed in my historical and jurisprudential analyses.

Returning to Bourdieu's account of the reproductive cycle of family, framing can be understood as a method of subjective categorization, which follows from, and reproduces, the objective social category of family. Importantly, however, this is not a perfect cycle, reproducing precisely the same conception of family in both the mind of the decision maker and the world their decisions create. Instead, my interviewees emphasized some agency on the part of family to determine their own edges and an emphasis on practices and, in particular, on caring practices (Held 2005), as shown by the contrast between the automatic involvement of informal relationships (the non-adopted daughter and the 'de facto' sister) and those with formally constituted relationships, but circumstances which suggested a lack of caring ties (the missing wife who may not be sought and the biological father, who was only reluctantly permitted engagement by most interviewees). Examination of the deployment of framing provides a tool for a critical exploration of those decisions and the way in which the same factors, framed differently, can reveal differences in approaches. To explore how framing operates in relation to factors, and how I reached my two core frames, I draw on answers to my initial substantive question in interviews with Coroners, which was: "How and when do you first have contact with the bereaved?"

The answers I received illustrated the ways in which the same factors could arise, but be given opposite interpretations. In these interpretations, two themes were clear: on the one hand, a focus on triadic forms of accountability and the need to avoid or mitigate risks to the effective operation of that approach, often linked to constraining the family; and on the other hand, a concern to effectively engage the bereaved, to enable their contribution and to make the investigation meaningful beyond the legal technicalities.

For example, in answering my opening question, one Coroner adopted a frame of focusing on the need for combining forms of accountability, perceiving the role of the family as central to the meaning to be given to judicial independence. For this Coroner, independence was a factor to be demonstrated to the family through direct early contact. I asked whether this would be via telephone or in person:

> 'I will do both if necessary, what I can't do is I can't compromise my judicial independence, because the Coroner's job is somewhat unusual in that you are not an arbiter between two parties, you are an inquirer, and sometimes it is necessary to have hands-on contact with the family either on the phone or in person. A lot of it is simply explanation, and sometimes the families like to see the person that they are actually going to possibly have the inquest dealt with. ... For example in the inquest I have just completed, I had to speak to the deceased's father very quickly because the post-mortem [raised questions over the quality of the emergency care received], which then introduced the topic of second post-mortems, and I had to explain the pros and cons of all this.'

The essential components of an approach to the inquest which engages community accountability are here – meaningful explanation is allied to an inquiry in which the family plays an effective part. They are also combined with formal concerns to avoid threats to perceptions of judicial independence which might arise from failing to get 'hands-on' contact with the family at an early stage. In so doing, this Coroner demonstrates a concern with evidencing the independence of an inquiry to the family similar to that advocated by a Select Committee in relation to statutory public inquiries.[13]

In contrast, for another Coroner, while judicial independence was also a factor in the decision, the issue was framed by reference to concerns about the risk of appearing to be biased, and the technocratic need to maintain neutrality and the triadic form:

> 'Usually, the first contact with the bereaved that I have personally will be in the courtroom. And that is because of the appearance of bias. Because the bereaved is only one of any number of interested persons

---

[13] See the recommendation by the Select Committee on the Inquiries Act 2005 that chairs of inquiries should meet victims and families as early as possible in the inquiry process (Select Committee on the Inquiries Act 2014, 73–74).

before the inquiry, it is inappropriate for me to have any close contact or communication with them before the inquest.'

Other interviewees emphasized the general nature of the rule:

'General legal principle is, you don't have contact with interested persons directly, you do it through the officer, in that way you can never be accused of bias.' (Coroner)

'As far as Coroners are concerned, we don't come into contact with the bereaved until the inquest.' (Coroner)

These three answers did not start with concerns the family might raise or with attention to making the process meaningful for the family, but instead focused on insulation, a framing in which judicial independence meant they were obliged to keep their distance from the family. The question was understood as a matter of general principle, in which an adherence to a general legal principle promised to control the risk of a perception of bias. Alternatively, it was framed as a discretion open to the Coroner, but interpreted through a desire to avoid the risk of bias by appearing to be too close to the family.

My interviews suggested that many (but not all) of the decision makers perceived an ideal inquest as one which would seek to combine forms of accountability, but their accounts of this could swiftly shift to an approach which emphasized an inquiry in which accountability for death is achieved through expertise, distance and neutrality, as I will explore in my next three chapters. It could also change the other way, and interviewees for whom first contact was framed through concerns with neutrality and expertise could emphasize ways in which they understood their role to be focused on combining accountabilities in relation to subsequent questions.

However, one common theme (as is regularly identified in inquest scholarship) was tensions between protecting the understanding of the inquest as a fact-finding jurisdiction which does not include blame for death, and perceived illegitimate efforts by family to seek to understand who and what might have been at fault for the death. This is something which could emerge from the point of notification. As quoted previously, experience meant that first contact would give an officer an idea of "what kind of family you are dealing with" I asked this officer more about what they meant by the 'kind of family' and they explained it was linked to blame. I asked if they would act differently if they thought a family was seeking to place blame on someone else in an inquest:

'Yes probably to be perfectly honest. There are certain people who would 'quote' you [*made quote marks in the air*], well you told me this and it might not even be in the right context, but yes, we are aware that people can take things you say and twist them a little bit to get, to get, what I am I trying to say, to get an advantage over you but yes, some families you would be aware of what you were telling them, obviously you would tell them what they were entitled to but you wouldn't expand on things that you don't need to.' (Officer)

In this account, from the first instance, the perceived risk posed by a family challenging the officer leads to an engagement of the family focused on providing the minimum required. At the same time, it highlights a potential paradox: that those families who are not perceived to be trying to get an advantage are able to access an expanded engagement. It is this potential tightrope which bereaved families are required to walk in a system in which, as the case of *Brown*[14] demonstrates, officers can lawfully privately brief the Coroner about a grieving father who is 'difficult' because he 'would not accept what he was being told'.[15]

Conclusion

The first engagements between the bereaved family and those investigating a death are crucial. Concerns by family members often begin with questions about discrepancies in the information they are given in their first few contacts with officials, or with concerns about the way in which they were told of the death (Beckett 1999, 273; Davis et al 2002, 27; Luce 2003, 142–152; Prisons and Probation Ombudsman 2013, paras 4.1 and 4.1.7). This first contact is therefore key for the people involved in an inquest and sets the tone for future encounters, but remains under-examined in scholarship. I have focused on this first engagement in this chapter for two reasons: the impact on the jurisdiction of the inquest; and to reveal and illustrate my conceptual approach.

In relation to jurisdiction, as was argued in Chapter 3, the law of the contemporary inquest represents the family as active and involved for their own legitimate ends, while the modern technocratic approach represented them as assistant to the Coroner. These different representations of the role of family feed into different understandings, or frames, linked to accountability, one which draws from the modern inquest and focuses on a technocratic form of accountability, and one which understands the inquest as responsible for combining the technocratic together with community forms of accountability. These frames organize the ways in which the role

---

[14] *Brown v Norfolk Coroner and Another* [2014] EWHC 187 (Admin).
[15] *Brown*, para 19.

of family is understood, even when the law itself is not specifically followed, in a process of systemic decision making. The tone setting undertaken in this notification and first contact plays a role in shaping the conduct of the investigation, and the jurisdiction of the inquest, in a process in which both practices can be seen to make and remake family and the inquest.

In the contemporary inquest, notification represents the place of family as responsible for introducing contingency and context and resisting typification. In the next chapter, examining the body in the inquest, I will develop this further, with a particular focus on the question of dignity.

5

Dignity, the Family and the Body

Introduction

> The body implies mortality, vulnerability, agency: the skin and the flesh
> expose us to the gaze of others, but also to touch, and to violence,
> and bodies put us at risk of becoming the agency and instrument of
> all these as well. Although we struggle for rights over our own bodies,
> the very bodies for which we struggle are not quite ever only our own.
> The body has invariably public dimensions. (Butler 2006, 26)

Those public dimensions and struggles over rights do not end when life
ends. After a sudden death, the body is both the remains of the person
who was and vital evidence for the investigation into how they died.
What should be done with and to the body is an early and potentially
very contentious issue in an inquest, and the way in which the body is
treated can be the cause of significant distress for bereaved kin. Specific
decisions will often need to be made about the need for a post-mortem
and what form this should take, whether further tests are required which
involve removing samples from the body, and who the body should be
released to when investigations are completed. Such decisions may not be
straightforward in many cases and can be a particular source of contestation
where the perceived requirements of the investigation clash with religious
or cultural responses to the body.

This chapter focuses on decisions around the body and, in particular, on
the ways in which the inquest system understands the relationship of the
family and the body of the deceased. Central in that are competing framings
of dignity, and the coverage here begins by exploring two competing ways
to understand dignity in this context. This discussion initially examines
the exhumation of bodies, but then turns to apply these two approaches
to dignity to the inquest in order to suggest that approaches to dignity can
be either framed through a concern with formality, office and civility or

through a concern with morality and conscience. This latter understanding emphasises paying attention to care, humanity and kinship, with attention to dignity.[1] These different understandings of dignity link closely to different framings of accountability in the inquest, and examining the place of the body in particular highlights conceptions of race, religion and culture in relation to perceptions of the role of family in the inquest.

This chapter is divided into four main parts. In the first, I set out the two competing accounts of dignity and develop them by drawing on two cases relating to exhumation. Turning to the inquest, I examine the ways in which the law represents the bereaved family as responsible for the dignity of the body while it is under the control of the Coroner. Critically, while dignity is at stake in these decisions, its form can shift, and the two frames of conscience versus civility can be seen in those adaptable understandings of the place of kin. The final two parts explore these framings in relation to post-mortems and the way in which kinship is constructed in the release of the body when investigations are concluded.

Jurisdictions of conscience and jurisdictions of civility

Dorsett and McVeigh's analysis (2012) contrasts two approaches to dignity. They differentiate between a 'thin' account of dignity, concerned with questions of office (Condren 2006), civility and public status, and a 'thick' account which focuses on the complexity of the individual person, and on questions of morality and their humanity (Dorsett and McVeigh 2012, 81–97). In the examples they explore, they first examine approaches to assisted dying which start from considerations of the concerns of the state as to who can act and how they can act, and establish links to public status and honour. These approaches deliberately leave aside ethical questions of what it means to die well as concerns beyond law. They contrast these jurisdictions of civility with a jurisdiction of conscience, in which the law explicitly engages with 'the rights and dignity' (McGuinness and Thomson 2020, 843) of the deceased and the bereaved, with moral philosophy and a conception of dignity based on consideration of truth and autonomy, including addressing the meaning of a good death. They argue that 'attending to the jurisdictional variety of the regulation of the end of life also complicates the ways in which we might understand authority and the authorisation of

---

[1] For selected reflections on dignity in this context, see, for example, Partington (2004); Razack (2011). Importantly, despite its centrality to the issues, dignity is rarely an express consideration in the law in this area, and there is a great deal of discussion of dignity in other scholarship. For some discussion of the problems and potential of legal conceptions of dignity, see, inter alia, Hale (2009); Carr (2012); Dupré (2012).

law. To view such regulation simply as an act of sovereign will or reason is to impose more uniformity than is present in legal practice' (Dorsett and McVeigh 2012, 95).

Dignity: the body and the next of kin

This distinction is set in a context in which matters of conscience which originally arose in canon law have now been superseded by the common law's focus on honour, manners and ideas of office. In one example of the relationship between the two jurisdictions, they argue that the historical rule that there is no property in a body amounted to the common law declining jurisdiction for the body in favour of the law of the Church, and the demise of ecclesiastical law left the dead body without a clear place in law (Dorsett and McVeigh 2012, 44, 69–71; see also Troyer 2008). They note that one area in which ecclesiastical law continues to hold authority is in relation to burial, exhumation and reburial in consecrated ground (Dorsett and McVeigh 2012, 77). In contrast, burial, exhumation and reburial in non-consecrated ground is determined by the civil courts. Once buried, it is a criminal offence to exhume a body without a licence (from the Secretary of State in relation to unconsecrated ground and from the consistory court for consecrated ground).[2] This jurisdictional division enables an instructive comparison of approaches to dignity, which is highlighted in two leading cases relating to the bodies of Steven Whittle and Father Josef Jarzebowski.

In the case of *In Re Blagdon Cemetery*[3] in the ecclesiastical jurisdiction, the question was whether the court should permit the exhumation and reburial of Steven Whittle. The court set out general principles, emphasizing the 'aura of permanence'[4] associated with burial, and drew on a paper on the theology of burial by the Bishop of Stafford which contrasted 'commending, entrusting, resting in peace [against] "portable remains", which suggests the opposite: reclaiming, possession, and restlessness; a holding onto the "symbol" of human life rather than a giving back to God'.[5] As a result, the court approved the reluctance of the consistory court to grant faculties for exhumation and reburial, but still allowed the application, permitting Steven's exhumation and reburial. The decision of the court explored Steven's views, his parents' views and their needs, and the wider dictates of religious teaching. It was central to the decision that Steven had died suddenly when he was young, having expressed no opinion about where he would like to

---

2   See Burials Act 1857, s 25; see also the discussion of the law in Conway (2016, 181–211).
3   *In re Blagdon Cemetery* [2002] Fam 299.
4   *In re Blagdon Cemetery*, para 304D.
5   *In re Blagdon Cemetery*, para 305C.

be buried and was buried in Somerset in a community to which he had no links. His parents, employed in the pub trade, had moved regularly and lacked a permanent home at that time, but had made it clear they wanted to move him when they had such a home, eventually buying a triple plot in Suffolk when they retired. The court also discussed the increasing ill health of Steven's parents (making it difficult for them to travel to his grave) and the support of his other closest relatives for the move. The fact that there was community support was not important; the court held that the amount of local support, whether clerical or lay, would normally be irrelevant.

By contrast, there was considerable community opposition to the disinterment and reburial of Father Josef Jarzebowski.[6] Father Jarzebowski was a priest who, according to the judgment, achieved almost saint-like status among the Polish Roman Catholic community in the UK and is under consideration for beatification.[7] He was a member of the order of the Marian Fathers, and was instrumental in developing a school and church at Fawley Court in Henley in the 1950s. Upon his death in 1964, he was buried there on his own express wishes. In 2008, the Marian Fathers sold Fawley Court and decided to move his remains to an unconsecrated site in a local authority graveyard, requiring them to make an application to the Secretary of State.[8] The grounds for their decision were that moving his remains would mean he was buried with other Marian Fathers and it would be easier for those who wished to visit his grave to do so. Around 2,000 people wrote a letter of opposition, including Father Jarzebowski's first cousin once removed, Elzbeita Rudewicz (who, aged seven when he died, had never met him, but who had visited his grave on a number of occasions). Nevertheless, the Secretary of State approved the order to disinter and rebury his remains, as the views of the next of kin were regarded as of particular importance and, in his case, the Marian Fathers were the relevant next of kin. Father Jarzebowski's views on his place of burial were not relevant as the 1930 Constitution of the Marian Fathers states that the decision in relation to place of burial is for the head of the order. In addition, if his remains were moved, they would be reunited with the brothers with whom he worked, and it would be easier for members of the public to visit his grave. The Court noted as follows:

13. The Secretary of State did not ignore the countervailing factors, which he identified as (i) the priest's wish to be buried at Fawley

---

[6] R (Rudewicz) v. Secretary of State for Justice [2012] EWCA Civ 499; see the discussion in Hill (2013).
[7] See para 35 of the judgment and see 'Priest's grave moved at night' (2012).
[8] Under s 25 of the Burial Act 1857.

Court, (ii) the stress which would be caused to many members of the Polish community by the priest's disinterment, (iii) the possible feeling of 'disrespect' that his decision might be seen as signalling to the Polish 'heritage', and (iv) the objections of the priest's nearest living relative. Nonetheless the Secretary of State decided to grant the application.

Elzbeita Rudewicz sought judicial review of the decision on the public law grounds of mistake in law, irrationality and disproportionality. While the court did not expressly undertake a review of the merits of the decision, the judgment contains significant details, and the combined approach of the Secretary of State and the civil courts can be contrasted with the approach of the consistory courts. The decision found that the theology of burial and permanence is irrelevant in the context of reburial in unconsecrated ground (even where the original burial may have been in consecrated ground).[9] The court held that the principles applied in the consistory courts were peculiar to that jurisdiction (in particular, the theological emphasis on permanence) and could not be extended to provide interpretation for burials in non-consecrated ground simply because they were the same as the religion of the person buried. With this move, the court shifted the frame away from questions of conscience to focus on questions of civility and the public sphere (Kennedy 1997; Conaghan 2014). Father Jarzebowski, in his office as priest, was under the direction of his order, who as his next of kin had the clear right to decide where he should be buried. His express wish to be buried at Fawley Court was overridden, with attention instead directed to his accessibility to the public. The dignity of his burial was thus left primarily to be determined by the Marian Fathers,[10] and while concerns about disrespect to his wishes and the indignity of impermanence were noted in the proceedings, they were outside the jurisdiction of the secular orientation of the Secretary of State and the courts. In passing, the decision notes that the church at Fawley Court was built at the expense of an émigré Polish prince, Prince Radziwill. The prince was buried in the church, which was sold along with the rest of the site, and in relation to his remains the Secretary of

---

9   It was not clear whether Fawley Court was consecrated, although the court treated the site as if it was unconsecrated; see para 34 of the judgment. For a discussion of cemeteries as secular spaces, see Rugg (2000).

10 The judgment explicitly states that the constitution permits choice of burial site, but is silent on whether the constitution expressly deals with questions of exhumation and reburial. In the absence of an express reference to such a power, it must be presumed the constitution does not include such a provision.

State had refused an application to disinter and rebury following objections by his son.[11]

In Steven Whittle's case, the court had engaged with questions of the humanity of those before it, exploring the autonomy (or lack thereof) of both Steven and his parents, who had been forced into transience by their trade. Central to the decision are questions of conscience and the competing demands of a form of dignity focused on the individual, the theology and dignity of a Christian permanent rest, and the humanity and dignity of the desire for family unity.

In contrast, the decisions in relation to both Father Jarzebowski and Prince Radziwill emphasize the centrality of the decision of the next of kin in the treatment of the body. This is a 'thin' form of dignity, in which the determining factors are questions of status and in which those with the office of next of kin are primarily responsible for determining what amounts to a good death and a good resting place, whether this is final or not.[12] Where a jurisdiction of conscience picks apart the relationship of family and the deceased and examines their separate but interconnected humanity, here the status of kinship is conflated with the dignity of the body. Attention is directed to establishing status and, once established in the office of next of kin, the law both grants and draws authority from that status. Questions of the autonomy and conscience of the deceased fall outside law's jurisdiction, while questions of the dignity of family and next of kin become questions relating to the ways in which they have upheld, denied or despoiled their office rather than focusing on questions of their humanity in the context of their bereavement.[13] In passing, it is notable that this is a definition of next of kin which is far more clearly delineated than is the case in the inquest context.

Dorsett and McVeigh suggest that modes of jurisdiction are overlaid in modern law so that it can be hard to pick apart distinct jurisdictional engagements with conscience or civility (Dorsett and McVeigh 2012, 91), and the case of Father Jarzebowski also highlights this complexity. In the judgments of the court and the Secretary of State, a deeper consideration of humanity was engaged in the context of seeking to unite Father Jarzebowski with other Marian brothers. However, even here, his personhood was tied up with his office, as moving him would mean that access to his grave would be unimpeded and 'would have the advantage of being combined, for those who wished, with visiting the graves of his former brothers'.[14]

---

[11] In line with stated policy, see *R (HM Coroner for East London) v Secretary of State for Justice and Susan Sutovic* [2009] EWHC 1974, a case in which the family's opposition to exhumation was key.

[12] On which see Jassal (2015) on mobility as resistance to 'necropower'.

[13] Which might be framed as procedural, rather than substantive, dignity; see Carr (2012).

[14] [2012] EWCA Civ 499, para 12.

In their different approaches, these cases highlight contrasting ways to understand the family and their relationship with the body, and I turn next to explore these framings in the inquest.

The family and the body: from passive recipient to active supervisor

The shift from the historical to the modern form of the inquest included a disappearance of the body, shifting it out of public view. In the 19th century, the gathering of the community around the body had been transformed into a fundamental legal requirement that the jury view the body of the deceased. As Burney describes, in late Victorian Britain this requirement came under increasing attack on public health grounds.[15] Through these attacks, the body moved from essential evidential object to an insanitary and inefficient item which enabled juries to form judgments based on the inapposite external visage of the cadaver rather than the expert opinion of the pathologist. In addition: 'Local councils, concerned among other things with the cost and the specular "excesses" of inquests, looked to the abolition of the view as a way of scaling down the ritual' (Burney 1994, 41). In response, some Coroners resisted abolition, focusing on the central place of the dead body in the authentication of their office, but this opposition foundered by the 1920s, and the requirement to view the body was abolished in the Coroners (Amendment) Act 1926.[16] In the contemporary inquest, in practice, the body under the control of the Coroner is never viewed by the jury (Matthews 2014, 257) and not always by the family (Dix 1998). For example, as one Coroner told me in relation to deaths on the railways: 'The family are usually discouraged from viewing, and, they can, it is usually OK.' Photographs of the body are treated with great caution and Coroners are encouraged to share them first with relatives in a sensitive manner if it is necessary for them to be used (Dorries 2014, 157–158). The body is now a matter for the Coroner

---

[15] In relation to Victorian engagements with mourning, death and a nascent public health agenda, see, inter alia, Jupp (1999); White (2002), (2003); Rugg (2013b), Amadei (2014); Lemke (2014); Trabsky (2015). Public health was a critical plank in the argument of the early cremation movement; Sir Henry Thompson, founder of the Cremation Society argued that 'sentiment should choose for its beloved dead "a physical condition that is neither repulsive nor injurious to others"' (Jupp 1999, 25). Jupp links this to an Ariesian (Aries 1981, 614) concern with the invisibilization of death, in which a focus on public health was to the detriment of bereaved families, 'whose needs have too often been overlooked' (Jupp 1999, 25), and notes the development of rights of the next of kin in relation to the choice whether to cremate (Jupp 1999, 24).

[16] Although they could still see the body if a majority of the jury wanted, a right which was abolished in 1980; see Matthews (2014, 257).

and the family, who engage with the dignified management[17] and disposal of the body away from the public space of the inquest.

In the historical inquest, the role for the family in relation to the body was limited to receiving the body once the Coroner released it, and in the contemporary system, family remain primarily responsible for the body in practice. The responsibility for the body comes with a direction to maintain its dignity, to inter the body 'until it is properly buried',[18] and the formal legal right to possession falls on the personal representatives of the deceased rather than on the family or next of kin (Conway 2003). Where executors or administrators decline their duty, others can be granted responsibility (Matthews 2020, 226), with the local authority as the ultimate backstop,[19] but where a personal representative claims the body, their primary claim cannot be supplanted (Conway 2003; see also Bremenstul 2013). In the contemporary system, delays in obtaining a grant of probate means that in practice, administrators are unlikely to be involved, and in most cases, arrangements will be made by executors or members of the family (Matthews 2020, 227). However, the emphasis of my interviewees was on identifying family and one or more next of kin, not on identifying those with a formal legal right as executor (Hernandez 1998) – an emphasis which is understandable in the context of the majority of people who die intestate.[20] The implication of this is that the dignified disposal of the body falls within the family's autonomy to act[21] once the body is released to them by the Coroner.[22]

---

[17] There is a great deal of scholarship which explores the role pathologists play in relation to establishing particular forms of truth. See, for example, the discussion in Timmermans (2006) and Jones (2018). In relation to medical professionals more broadly, see Gilleard (2008); Tuffin (2009); Barnes, Kirkeegard and Carpenter 2014.

[18] *Dobson v North Tyneside Health Authority and Another* [1997] 1 WLR 596, 600E; see also the discussion in Haddleton (2006). While the majority of bodies in England and Wales are now cremated emphasis remains on proper and decent disposal; see, inter alia, Conway (2003, 426).

[19] Public Health (Control of Diseases) Act 1984, s 46(1).

[20] Research varies, with one poll in 2014 suggesting that 35 per cent of UK citizens had a will (Dying Matters 2014), while another survey in 2014 suggested that 48 per cent of the UK population had a will (Will Aid 2014).

[21] There is a wealth of scholarship on issues linked to autonomy and property in the body in the context of law in relation to human tissue; see, inter alia, Hernandez (1998); McEvoy and Conway (2004); Vines (2007); Gallagher (2010). I draw on this work, but it is important that where some of this scholarship focuses on one-off decisions about disposal/ownership of body parts, my attention is on decisions specifically located in the ongoing inquest process. My attention is also on the broader question of dignity, of which autonomy is only a part; see Woods (2014, 336).

[22] However, this is an extra-legal responsibility, as once a body has been passed on, unless another individual with a responsibility to bury complains, there is no enforceable

Prior to release of the body, the historical position was that the Coroner had a very broad discretion over the management of the body while it remained under the Coroner's control. Through a series of judicial decisions[23] and legislative changes,[24] the family developed enhanced rights in respect of the treatment of the body prior to the 2009/2013 reformulation of the inquest, and the family now have a raft of rights in respect of the body,[25] together with a significant narrowing of the discretion open to the Coroner. For example, where the Coroner previously had the discretion to release the body early, the 2013 Regulations have shifted this into a requirement to hand over the body as soon as is reasonably practicable[26] and, if it is not released within 28 days, to explain the reason for the delay to the next of kin or personal representative. Notification and participation rights for the next of kin similarly arise in relation to the keeping and disposing of material preserved or retained from the body,[27] and the family's voice has become increasingly important in relation to decisions about the post-mortem.[28] However, it remains at the discretion of a Coroner, who may (not must) request a post-mortem where they are investigating a death or consider it necessary to decide if the death falls within their responsibility to investigate.[29]

This responsibility to notify, explain and engage with the family is a duty to account to the family for the way in which the inquest system has treated the body. It is the family to whom transparency is particularly owed (Thornton 2012a), and they are the only people who are able to hold the Coroner to account if those requirements are not maintained.

---

obligation to actually dispose of the body through cremation or burial; see Matthews (2020, 228); and see also Metters (2003); Leiboff (2005). In contrast see contrary opinion (with no contemporary case law) in Archbold, as discussed in McBain (2014). However, it is a criminal offence to prevent the lawful burial of a corpse – see *R v Hunter* [1974] QB 95; *R v Skidmore* [2008] All ER 146.

[23] See, for example, *R v Bristol Coroner ex p Kerr* [1974] 2 All ER 719.

[24] Including the right to be informed of and represented at the post-mortem examination and to reject a pathologist if they work at the same hospital, as introduced in the 1953 Rules; see rr 3 and 4.

[25] For example, see, para 7.2 of the Explanatory Memorandum to the Coroners (Investigations) Regulations 2013: 'The Coroners (Investigations) Regulations 2013 … update relevant provisions in the Coroners Rules 1984, putting particular emphasis on Coroners notifying bereaved relatives and other interested persons of developments with the investigation.'

[26] Coroners (Investigations) Regulations 2013, r 20.

[27] Contrast, for example, *Dobson v North Tyneside Health Authority and Another* [1997] 1 WLR 596, where samples were kept and then disposed of, and there was no involvement of family members as they had not applied for probate, so were not entitled to body parts.

[28] *R (Goldstein) v HM Coroner for Inner London North* [2014] EWHC 3889; see also Cowan 2014.

[29] CJA 2009, s 14(1).

If the Coroner has not notified them and thereby has failed to meet the standards in the legislation, it is only the next of kin who would know and would be able to raise a complaint.[30] Similarly, in the event, for example, that a Coroner had refused to release a body to an eligible individual or had breached the requirements in relation to the retention of post-mortem material, the family would be likely to be the only people who would have a sufficient interest for the purposes of a judicial review. While both avenues of enforcement are highly circumscribed, the imposition of duties on the Coroner, allied with these potential avenues for recourse, places the family as responsible for primary oversight of the way in which the inquest system treats the body. It is important that the context in which these rules have been developed lies in high-profile scandals[31] in which families have suffered the distress of discovering after many years that body parts of deceased relatives had been retained. The private dignity of the deceased and family was subjugated in favour of a purported wider public interest. In the contemporary inquest, however, any understanding of family as a private interest in opposition to a public interest in the body is complicated by the ways in which family participates on behalf of a wider community interest. In this account, family is a conduit to the community and represents a public interest in transparency and the proper treatment of the body, juxtaposed with the indignity represented by a body under the control of an opaque, paternalistic and inaccessible medical bureaucracy (contrast Mason and Laurie 2001).

This account of the law re-envisages the relationship as one founded on dignity, under which the family, acting for themselves, the deceased and the wider public, uphold and enforce the dignity of the deceased while the body is under the Coroner's jurisdiction.[32] The focus is on the family's humanity and bereavement, on an ethical framing based on the recognition of relationality and care (Held 2005, 9–28) and the family's role in what Partington (2004) has described as 'salvaging the sacred'.[33] The attention of

---

[30] See Guide to Coroner's Services, paras 11.4 and 11.5: https://www.gov.uk/governm ent/uploads/system/uploads/attachment_data/file/363879/guide-to- and also see CJA 2009 Sch.3, para 13. However, it is important to note that these possibilities are limited, and the procedures closely prescribed; see the Judicial Discipline (Prescribed Procedures) Regulations 2013; Constitutional Reform Act 2005, s 115; and note, as Matthews states, that examples of what constitutes misbehaviour are 'rare' (Matthews 2014, 48).

[31] See, for example, the foreword to the Home Office Position Paper (2004, 2), which explicitly refers to the Bristol Royal Infirmary and Alder Hey public inquiries. See Kennedy 2001; Royal Liverpool Children's Inquiry 2001.

[32] And the body here is not limited to the entire body, but extends to a broader concept of remains, as is discussed further in Prior (1989).

[33] Partington (2004, 16) describes her trip to 'rescue and protect' her sister's remains while they were under the control of the Coroner, placing memorial items with her bones as

the inquest, as a jurisdiction shaped by the technologies of notification and enabling participation, is on meaningfulness and understanding, and on the dignity of family as conscience. I asked one interviewee why the family got involved in an inquest:

'Well, there are several answers to that question at different levels, firstly because it is a legal requirement, because we have got to notify them, under the new Coroners Investigations rules. They have rights to express for example, about what happens to tissue and organs taken at post-mortem, so we need to ascertain their wishes with regard to that. Some families will take a keen interest and it is so variable, some families will want everything, some families won't want anything, some families don't want to participate at all, I think it is important that they do participate because it is their loved one and it is so they can have an understanding of what happened to them.' (Coroner)

The legislation phrases this as an opportunity for the family, but from a systemic perspective, it is important that they do engage, not only to exercise their rights, but also to achieve understanding. Thus, notification and opportunity are translated into encouragement, enablement and a need to understand, and where decisions are taken about the body, questions of memorialization and ethics (Woods 2014), and the ongoing relationship between the family and the body (Drayton 2013; Leichtentritt et al 2014) are taken into account.

The attention is on dignity as conscience, and the attention to nuance, context and meaning bring it into a framing focused on engaging with community forms of accountability. However, my interviews also demonstrated ways in which this framing could shift to focus on dignity as public status, through concerns with risk and a desire to protect and hide. As one Coroner put it:

'We have a dominant culture that is simply in denial, we do not generally discuss death of ourselves or our loved ones. As a country we have the lowest incidence of ever seeing a dead body, whereas in Ireland for example, it is on display and everyone sees it, so people are deeply shocked when they come to a Coroner, they don't know what has happened.'

'a chance to act in a situation that was still out of our hands' while the trial of her sister's murderer was ongoing and the remains could not be released.

For some of my interviewees, this concern with a shocked family provoked a desire to put up a defence to protect the family from being upset (Dix 1998), and to protect the family from threats from outside. In this framing, family becomes the protector of the private space around the body. This status was evident in some reflections on the role of the girlfriend in Vignette 2 and the role of family as gatekeepers. One Coroner who was not sure of recognizing the girlfriend as an interested person in the inquest stated that she would be encouraged to be in contact with the family, and in another interview, two officers discussed this together with explicit reference to the body:

Officer A: She is not his next of kin if that is what you are thinking about, we would treat her probably, as we would a next of kin.
Officer B: Well it depends what the family want you see.
Officer A: Yeah.
Officer B: If she is insisting on seeing him, we would have to ask his parents assuming they are still alive.

There is no basis in law for a requirement of consent by the next of kin where another individual wishes to view a body; it is for the Coroner to decide. However, as this quote makes clear, the practice is negotiated, with the family's wishes being key, even to the extent of potentially excluding other formulations of kin from contact with the body. The family is framed here as guardians of decency and dignity, determining the acceptability or otherwise of other kin, and the possibility of their entry into the privacy of death. Critically, this formulation, even as it is engaged with the private space around the body, is a focus on public status – those in the office of family are responsible for determining dignity, and the question for the girlfriend in Vignette 2 is whether she is able to negotiate with those in the status of family, not whether her bereavement needs to be recognized and acknowledged. It is only on her insistence that these concerns arise, and it is in this possibility of challenge that the framing slips from a concern with conscience to an engagement with risk. This is a thin form of dignity, focused on shielding the system from critique and providing protection for those confirmed in the office of family, and is thus an attention to the inquest as a public space separated off from the private space of family, with consequent attention to official duties and rights of family in those spaces.

The impact of this formulation is that in the public space for which the Coroner has responsibility for ordering, the family can also act in a way which is perceived as them failing to uphold their public office. The clearest example of this formulation was in reflections of some of my interviewees on post-mortems and cultural difference.

Dignity and the post-mortem examination

Drawing on Scott Bray's dissonance between 'representing the dead body in (medico) legal discourse and remembering, or memorialising, the dead in culture' (Bray 2006, 42), Carpenter, Tait and Quadrelli have explored the effect of 'a push towards therapeutic jurisprudence' (Carpenter et al 2013, 2) on autopsy (see Carpenter et al 2011, 2013, 2014, 2015a). Their research, along with other work (see inter alia Clarke and McCreanor 2006; Selket, Glover and Palmer 2015), highlights the tension between the treatment of a body as an object containing truth to be scrutinized and the role of the body in grieving practices, but also highlights a potential distinction between the Coronial system, with staff who 'are able to empathise with the position of families' (Carpenter et al 2014, 174) and medical and police staff, who valorize scientific method.[34] Their research in relation to post-mortems in Australia suggests that where religious objections are communicated to the Coroner, less invasive techniques of investigation tend to be prioritized (Carpenter et al 2011, 334). However, the communication of that religious difference, particularly profession of an Islamic faith, can engender distrust in a medico-policing environment in which Islam is invoked as 'culturally backwards as well as unyielding and dogmatic in its allegiance to faith' (Carpenter et al 2015a, 122) and which then feeds suspicion into the Coronial system 'as evidentiary truth' (Carpenter et al 2015a, 121).

The construction of the Muslim community as a 'suspect community' is also a feature of contemporary British society with a 'corrosive effect on the relations between Muslim communities and the police' (Pantazis and Pemberton 2009, 662; see also Greer 2010; Pantazis and Pemberton 2011). Two Coroners reflected on their engagement with members of the Islamic community, with the first in particular reflecting on the ways in which the uncooperative suspicious Muslim family could be framed as a risk to both an individual case and beyond:

'We have a fairly cooperative community. Perhaps there isn't the suspicion about us, we are not seen as the police. Some of the religious faith are more suspicious aren't they, than others, you do have Muslim deaths but you don't have as many as [somewhere else] where you tend to find with those kind of deaths, they are trying to push for religious reasons to arrange for the funeral to take

---

[34] Even in the light of evidence of poor practice; see NCEPOD Report (2006); Jones (2014). However, for some reflections on the value of post-mortems and scientific method, see Ambade et al (2011); Chattopadhyay (2014).

place, or they don't want a post-mortem and all that sort of thing, and when you have got that conflict between the laws of the land and their religious beliefs, it does bring about suspicion, and they do think that you are being difficult etc etc, and I think that then permeates out.' (Coroner)

'We are increasing, we find particularly the Muslim community don't want post-mortem examinations done, more than the Jewish, but some sections of that community will make complex complaints where they expect everything to be done the day before yesterday, but expect you to do that in a vacuum of no evidence, or making unsubstantiated allegations. I have to have evidence, and that is a problem.' (Coroner)

The accounts are of families posing a challenge to the system, unfairly seeing the Coroner as difficult, resisting the necessary management of the body, pushing and complaining. The response to this is an emphasis on the ways in which these families fail to uphold their office; charged with the status of next of kin, they are refusing to engage with their obligations by prioritizing private religious concerns over the 'laws of the land' and failing to grasp the place of the substantiation of evidence. This echoes Kasstan's suggestion (in relation to the Jewish Haredi community) that '[t]he state arguably views the hard to reach minority as failing in its moral responsibility to engage with biomedical and public health interventions, which presents a risk to the body of the nation' (Kasstan 2017; 108). Suspicion is framed in these accounts as unavoidable and cyclical, permeating out and presenting a risk to the link between the Coroner and the wider community. It also permeates downwards into the process, obscuring the caring links which give dignity and autonomy to the body.[35]

In contrast, a focus on dignity as conscience emphasizes a space for engagement with the family where the starting point was open to their contextual engagement. Another Coroner's reflections on this demonstrated this endeavour:

'We do our best but sometimes we have got to have PMs, and normally the families if they are explained, I mean it is, a lot of nonsense talked about this, Jewish and Muslim faiths have recognition and acceptance

---

[35] I draw here on reflections around the expression of autonomy through relational links; see, inter alia, the collected papers in Mackenzie and Stoljar (2000); Christman (2004); Mackenzie (2008).

of this, what has to be has to be, if it can be avoided or limited so be it, that is what we do.'

Critically here there is no opening initial concern with suspicion, and the potential for conflict does not mean that the decision is initially framed as a question of conflict with the bereaved. Any concerns they may have are not initially framed as irrational (McGuinness and Brazier 2008). The approach engages them in discussion, opening up space for reflections on questions of conscience and the dignity of both the family and the deceased. In this role, the family are not intransigent exercisers of oppositional rights, but are an essential effective part of a process engaged in combining the dual goals of meaningful revelation and satisfaction of technocratic responsibilities. The process is framed as participatory, and instead of a tension with the law or the conflict between the approach of family and the available evidence, the emphasis is on the possibility of avoiding or limiting if it can be done. This Coroner discussed the possibilities of non-invasive approaches to post-mortem investigation, highlighting that they were not appropriate in all cases, but with enthusiasm for their potential in providing a means of combining forms of accountability.[36] This approach is therefore capable of shaping an outcome which recognizes the legitimacy of difference and conscience, religious or otherwise, instead of a starting point of rights, office, responsibilities and status.

In a discussion about post-mortems which did not explicitly touch on religious or cultural differences, another Coroner also highlighted dialogue, stating that there were circumstances where people would request that there should be no post-mortem, or

> 'maybe there is some element of uncertainty about the death, but the doctor is reasonably confident and then the issue with the family is going to be well, if you are content to accept some degree of uncertainty, I can sign this one up, if you want better information we can go to autopsy, and they will have some choice in the matter, in the end the decision is mine of course, but we will listen to their views.'

The scenario is reversed, but the emphasis on flexibility and responsiveness is the same, recognizing that in some cases, some families are willing to undergo invasive post-mortem procedures to establish the medical cause of

---

[36] For a less enthusiastic review of these possibilities in the light of the *Goldstein* case, see Cowan (2014). For some reflections on the possibilities of non-invasive approaches, see, inter alia, PMFDI 2012; Brogdon 2013; Ruder and Ampanozi 2013; Ruder and Rutty 2013.

death (Rankin et al 2002; Sullivan and Monagle 2011), while for others an autopsy causes additional distress (Biddle 2003; Robb and Sullivan 2004; Drayton 2011; Barnes, Kirkegaard and Carpenter 2014). Critically, these framings of dignity are not fixed, and some Coroners and officers told me stories which illustrated the ways in which frames could shift.

Shifting dignities

In one interview, I read out Vignette 4 and asked two officers how they would respond to the appearance of the long-lost sister:

Officer A:	Fine.
Officer B:	OK.
Officer A:	Are you going to pay for the funeral then?
Officer B:	That's what we say, are you taking on the funeral?
Officer A:	And they say, no, we haven't seen him for 30 years, but – and then the local council or his executors have to do all the arrangements.
Officer B:	But even if the environmental health people deal with the funeral, if she says she wants to be involved, that is fine, it doesn't matter. We get people really upset because they cannot afford, they haven't seen Dad for years, he was difficult, he drank, they can't afford to pay for the funeral, but they are really upset, to us it doesn't matter, if they want to know what is going on and they are entitled to know what is going on, we don't judge, we just involve them as much as we can.

Here, the initial question of the dignified disposal of the deceased is for the family to resolve, but crucially in this account, the dignity of the family in the process is severable from the dignity of the deceased because of considerations of conscience.[37] The family, having justified their abandonment of office to the officers, are not judged, and are engaged with despite their failure. The upset family's demeanour and explanation – they were not in contact, he was difficult, they are poor – is understandable, forgivable and important. Evidencing their (frustrated) care and humanity, and invoking a conception of dignity as conscience, they provide for a shifting of the frame from a frame focused on office and duty to one which understands the role of family as central to efforts to combine forms of accountability. The impact

---

[37] Particularly in the light of growing funeral poverty (on which see Harris (2014); Woodthorpe et al (2013)) and the work of Quaker Social Action's Down to Earth campaign.

is that meaningful decisions about their involvement focus on endeavours to effectively engage them 'as much as we can'.

The account these officers provide reconfirms the crucial impact of the way in which family are perceived to approach the system. One Coroner contrasted families who "act with dignity" to "people who make a fuss and sit down and scream and wail", while an officer contrasted "graceful" and "ghastly" families. Another Coroner told a story about a scenario perceived to be laden with risk, in which illegality, immigration and "strangeness" were central concerns. However, the mother's calm display demonstrated dignity as public status and honour and thereby fulfilled aspects of office, in particular, providing justification for conduct which the Coroner had otherwise found inexplicable:

Coroner: We do have such strange requests. We had one where a skull and the legs of a body was retrieved from the sea after months, and the lady concerned had been born, I can't remember the country, somewhere in Africa. Her mother wanted to view the remains, she said she'll identify the body, I said we've got DNA, we are satisfied, no – she will do her own DNA test. And she insisted, and we were very concerned, I mean we had two concerns, one was she using this as a reason to get into the country, to utilize that route as a means of getting access, but two, was she someone strange? I spoke to my officer later and she said, she was absolutely quite cold and calm, and she smelt the bones and she said she was satisfied that that was her daughter, and I think, I don't know whether perhaps it was the look that the officer gave or something, but she said 'in our country people vanish and what we find are the remains after leopards and lions and jackals and hyenas have been at them, it is not always possible to make visual identification, we smell them, they smell of our family'. Now I can't explain how precise that is, whether it is to be relied upon at all, whether it is a load of rubbish, I don't know, but that lady went away satisfied, that it was her daughter whose remains had been found and retrieved from the sea.

Ed: Did you have an inquest in that?

Coroner: I had to have an inquest yeah.

Ed: Did she have questions, was she involved?

Coroner: No, she didn't come. She came over, viewed the limited remains we had, and went back to Africa, and took no

further part, in fact we never managed to make contact
with her again.

Ed: What happened to the remains?

Coroner: They were dealt with by the local authority I believe. The
local authority buried them or cremated them. The officer
was the only person at the funeral.

The composed and politely insistent mother had engaged with office on
her own terms, acting on her right to see the remains, but resisting its
requirements in respect of the investigation. Her dignified actions engaged
the dignity of the remains of her daughter, creating a narrative shift from
remains to personhood, with the conclusion that the officer attended the
funeral. Cultural difference is here framed as difference, but not illegitimacy;
while initially presented as strangeness and false intention, the mother's
approach transforms the frame into a focus on humanity and her meaningful
contingent revelation. It is therefore another account of a way in which a
frame concerned with risk can move to a frame of conscience and combining
forms of accountability through perceptions of the dignity of the family.

In contrast, another account engaged with a narrative shift of dignity
from a conception of dignity as conscience to a concern with risk and
conflicting offices:

Coroner: We had a body found on the rocks, and the evidence
suggested he had been dead for some time. He was lying
comfortably on his back, and had a hat he had taken off
and put under his head. The cause of death was impossible
to determine but the pathologist view was that it had
probably been hypothermia, died of exposure. He was
a refugee from Iran or Iraq or somewhere, and he had a
cousin in this country who was the sole point of contact.
He was a medical doctor, and he wrote to me and said you
have got to carry out extra tests because he couldn't accept
that the cause of death couldn't be ascertained. I said there
aren't any other tests to carry out, [the] pathologist's done
everything they can, no more information we can get, 'he
would not have laid down and died like that, that doesn't
happen', 'it does happen, I have had other cases where
people have died of exposure'. It was a bit disturbing for
a doctor who couldn't see this at all, and I think, at the
bottom of it, he believed that because his cousin had been
a refugee, he had been overlooked, mistreated, kicked
about, police had a hand in it, all sorts of insinuations,

	not outright allegations but insinuations, that were just not supportable.
Ed:	Did he attend the inquest?
Coroner:	No, I don't think they were particularly close, but because he was the only family member here, apparently the burden fell on him, because that is their culture apparently, I think of course, he got stuck with the costs of the funeral and the whole expense over here. I found it disturbing that a doctor could be absolutely adamant that there must be more tests; you are a doctor, tell me what tests, 'he would not have done this, he would not have laid down and died' – people do, they don't intend it to happen, it is not a conscious decision, I mean, 'he should've been found' – why? He was out of sight, there was no one, I've been to walk and he couldn't be seen from above because the cliff overhung where he was.

In this account, the body is portrayed as dignified, hidden and comfortable. The actions of the family challenge this dignity, raising questions of foul play, racism and mistreatment, which the Coroner resists as misplaced, emphasizing the cousin's medical expertise. At the same time, the cousin is perceived to be reluctant to act, but is obliged to do so because of the dignity and honour of his family. The Coroner is sympathetic to a cousin who was not close to the deceased, who has been apparently compelled into an unwanted status and obliged to speak for the deceased. However, the Coroner is critical of that cousin's failure to properly uphold the status of doctor, to mediate between the inquest and the wider family, and to approve the dignity of the corpse, and is ultimately left disturbed by a case which threatened the dignity of their professional office.

Dignity and disposal

Often in my interviews, these shifts in framing focused on the crystallization of disputes over who was entitled to receive the body and arrange the funeral. The starting position for all of my interviewees was very similar – that it was a question for family to decide. However, such answers revealed a complex interplay of considerations, with attention to both office holders and legal rights to possession, and considerations of conscience and the relationships within which the deceased lived and died. In relation to the non-adopted daughter in Vignette 1, as one Coroner quoted in Chapter 4 stated, they would be keen to pass the body of her informal father on to her, but there might need to be negotiation with the absent wife if she presented herself or was found. Similarly, an officer would 'happily go along' with the non-adopted daughter if she wanted to organize a funeral. Thus, answers emphasized the autonomy of family to determine the dignity of the deceased, with an emphasis on caring links, but also raised the possibility of the system intervening to protect the interests of the dead as provided by law:

> Yeah, I mean we try and get the family to tell us, do it that way round rather than us saying right the body is going to you, or whoever, and we do have circumstances where there is a dispute, and before, when I first started here it always used to seem to be whoever got to the funeral directors first to get the body, but we tend to insist that it is the legal next of kin, that is what we try to do, and then the onus is on them to say why that shouldn't be the case. (Coroner)

The emphasis on legal next of kin could be framed as a concern with office, but the Coroner understands their role as protecting the body from arbitrariness and focusing on the substance of the relationships. The next of kin is a rebuttable presumed recipient, but the potential malleability of the concept of next of kin leaves additional scope in this approach to engage with questions of morality, of the lived experience and of the conscience of the bereaved and the deceased. In these accounts, attention is directed to what people are willing to do, not in terms of their manners and status, but in demonstration of their humanity as expressed through relationships of care. Some interviewees described circumstances when broader conceptions of kin would be engaged if they were willing to 'take on the funeral'.

However, unlike decisions where the body remains under the Coroner's jurisdiction, the ultimate decision in relation to the release of the body is not for the inquest system (Conway 2003). This means that wherever a dispute crystallizes, the frame shifts swiftly to focus on formality and legal rights, in which the decision makers emphasize their lack of technical responsibility for the decision:

> One of the commonest disputes is, who do you release the body to? And I get that at least every month here, and the answer is reasonably simple, I need to be satisfied that it is to somebody who has that right to receive it and usually there is more than one person, it is not for me to judge between them, it is for the family to sort out, and so unfortunately sometimes the body is sitting here while they sort it out. I am not intervening, it is not within my power or jurisdiction to do that, so that causes problems. ... It is for you to sort, this isn't my job. Of course that then doesn't please the local authority because of the costs of storage, there comes a point where I might have to make a decision, sometimes I release it and then another next of kin pops out of the woodwork

and we never knew they existed and they are up in arms and need an explanation, I am going to have to explain that we only have to notify the people that we know about and we are very sorry, there was not a preference for one person or another, we just did our duty. (Coroner)

All of my Coroner interviewees emphasized their ultimate lack of capacity in relation to this decision. For this Coroner, it is a common issue (it was not for others) and is not for them to decide, but importantly sometimes a decision has to be made. When this happens, the too late indignant family can present as a challenge to the legitimacy of the system, to which the Coroner responds with an apologetic reliance on legal technicality and practicality. The focus in these situations is on status and on the right to claim the body, but also on avoiding litigation where possible, and many interviewees indicated that despite a lack of jurisdiction, actors in the inquest would seek to avoid the cost and indignity of litigation between family members:

'Try and see if you can come to some sensible agreement amongst yourselves because I am not empowered to decide for you, all I can do is give an indication of the pecking order and that I would be likely to agree to release it to the spouse or the parent or whatever.' (Coroner)

It might not even get as far as the Coroner, as officers play a part in judging when a dispute has crystallized between family members which needs to be communicated to the Coroner. The perspective of the officer is therefore particularly important, and all of my officer interviewees emphatically emphasized the autonomy and responsibility of family to decide. One example illustrates this where I had asked about a potential dispute between siblings:

Officer: I would send them away, and tell them to bang their heads together and sort it out. ... That does happen and you have got to say to people look you have got to be grown up about this, be adults, sort yourselves out ... you get that with opposing sides of families that the poor chap is resting up there in the hospital for weeks until they sort themselves out.

Ed: And your place would be to say to them, you have to sort this out.

Officer: Well I would yeah, we all would the same. I think we'd speak quite curtly to them as well and say well, look, grow up, well I would, certainly I would.

The indignity of the deceased alone and isolated in hospital is contrasted with his family members behaving like children, eschewing their public facing responsibility to behave with dignity; they need to grow up, as their behaviour is affecting the dignity of their poor father. The possibility that there might be a legitimate disagreement about how to respond to the body is dismissed, along with questions of conscience and ethics, because the risk of disrespect to the deceased is framed through their failure to fulfil their office. Similarly, one officer told a story of a body which had been in the "freezer at the hospital" for "years" because his mother believes he had been murdered:

> 'He has had several investigations into how it was all dealt with and it is quite clear that he has taken his own life but Mum just refuses to believe it and refuses to do anything with his body.' (Officer)

Refusing to let the body disappear, the mother is confronting the endeavour to manage her through an official emphasis on her responsibilities. Her stance draws power from a law which cannot compel her to 'do anything' and challenges a discourse of duty to provide for a particular form of dignity; critically, rather than not doing anything with the body, the something she is doing – the act of resistance in which she is engaged – is perceived to be undermining her dignity, the dignity of the deceased and the dignity of the inquest process.

Conclusion

Once a body is released by the Coroner, the law envisages a hierarchy of responsibility for disposal, but in practice, as my interviews revealed, this is a negotiated process, with family at the centre of those negotiations. Prior to release, while the body remains within the inquest jurisdiction, the role of the family has significantly changed in the contemporary inquest – a change which amounts to a reimagined role for family as responsible for the scrutiny of the management of the body.

The potential paradox for the inquest as a site committed to caring for the dead (Matthews 2014, ix) is that indignity has been found to lurk in the strategies adopted to respond to the appearance of the dead, from the inaccurate and insanitary jury view to the indignities which lie in a medicalized disappearance, the disconnection from memorialization and the invasion of autonomy represented by the autopsy, and the deep indignities and distress caused by the ad hoc appropriation of remains in Alder Hey (Royal Liverpool Children's Inquiry 2001) and Bristol (Kennedy 2001). The representation of the place of family in the contemporary inquest system is an endeavour to bridge this paradox, to explicitly situate dignity in the inquest as the recognition of the centrality of bereavement. It looks to account for a form of dignity in the ties between people (Butler 2006), a dignity which does not start from liberal individualism, but which starts from an acknowledgement of 'persons as relational and interdependent, morally and epistemologically' (Held 2005, 13). The challenge to this account occurs when the frame emphasizes constraint of kin and the requirements of a formal accounting, overwhelming the nuance and context of this dignity; when the tacit relationships of kin are transformed into the status, duties, rights and responsibilities of office, whether as next of kin or – as will be explored in the next chapter – as an interested person.

6

Family in the Driving Seat

Introduction

This chapter explores decisions taken (or not taken) in the pre-hearing investigation phase of an inquest. It focuses on the ability of kin to participate in that investigation and, in particular, on two apparently mundane procedural questions which are vital in understanding the contemporary pre-hearing context: the interlinked questions of who is entitled to be an interested person; and what documents they are entitled to receive in the process known as disclosure.

Interested persons are those people entitled to be involved in the investigation, with rights which include the right to be notified about developments in the proceedings, the right to make submissions about the process (including the scope of the inquest – in other words, what issues it will cover), the right to receive disclosure of documents and the right to ask questions of witnesses in any hearings.

The chapter is divided into two substantive parts. In relation to decisions about interested persons, I explore firstly the need for someone to represent a connection to the deceased and the emphasis on implicit decisions about their involvement. I then move on to examine the ways in which, when forced to make a decision, those decisions can be framed as focusing on concerns with kinship and connection (and therefore are focused on seeking to combine forms of accountability), or with formal family ties, but will also involve considerations of purpose and assertions about a natural hierarchy of family.

In the second part, I focus on disclosure and the entitlement to receive documentary evidence as part of the investigation. In particular, I focus on the ways in which decisions about disclosure can again be analysed as based on an understanding of combining accountabilities or a concern to privilege technocratic forms of accountability.

This chapter further emphasizes the importance of not focusing solely on the hearing and its outcome, but also examining systemic decision making in the time before the hearing, and the impact of family participation in those investigations. For example, in one account related to me, an officer described how they had acted on their own initiative without consulting the Coroner in relation to a natural causes death which involved a previous period in detention, seeking additional reports in response to concerns and questions raised by the family. A focus on systemic decision making also demonstrates the ways in which involvement of the family is a series of decisions about how they are involved. While statute law focuses on status and associated rights, practices in the system can ignore or defer questions of threshold, preferring to deal in contingency, equivocation and informality. The impact is that traditional legal understandings of status do not necessarily play out in the ways in which law would expect them to, and attention to legal rights and duties does not capture the reflexive and reactive relationship of the family and the system.

Interested persons
The need for connection

Other than the next of kin, the only appearance of family members in inquest legislation is through the lens of the 'interested person': either as an automatic interested person or, for those who fall outside those categories, permitted entry at the discretion of the Coroner. As was discussed in Chapter 3, the category of those given automatic entry has gradually expanded as the rules have changed, and the notification and participation rights attached to all those deemed to be interested persons have been set out in more detail. Legislation does not differentiate between the rights of interested persons, whether next of kin, family or non-family:[1]

'The law requires that those who are interested persons have an opportunity of disclosure, have an opportunity to make submissions on the scope of the inquest, have an opportunity to participate. So they are very much, all of them, in the driving seat, it is not to say

---

[1] Interested persons are set out in s 47(2)(a)–(m) CJA 2009 and include specific classes of family member, beneficiaries of a life insurance policy, anyone who might have caused or contributed to the death, and a range of other possible interested persons, with a final catch-all category of other individuals with a sufficient interest. Potential family members included in s 47 are a spouse, civil partner, partner, parent, child, brother, sister, grandparent, grandchild, child of a brother or sister, stepfather, stepmother, half-brother or half-sister, and, separately, a personal representative of the deceased or a beneficiary of a life insurance policy: CJA 2009, s 47(2)(a), (b) and (d).

that the decision is theirs, the decision is still the Coroner's, but it is to say that there is an accountability – I think is probably right – to interested persons ... I have to consider all interested persons equally, it would be quite wrong of me to consider the family because of their bereavement were primus inter pares, they are not. Of course they need to be handled sympathetically.' (Coroner)

They may not have any additional formal rights, but the role of the family in practice is very different from that of other interested persons. Many interviewees described active families expanding the evidence needed (see Easton 2020), while another reflected as follows:

'I see the family as driving the investigation, because with a hospital death, to you it may look natural, when you go to take the statement from the family, the family say well, they weren't given any water, they weren't given any food, there was never any nurses around, all the care aspects, the neglect aspects come out at that point, and of course then you have to go down a different route for the investigation, so we are reliant on the family to almost point the investigation down the right channels.' (Coroner)

Family involvement impacts on what is investigated and how it is investigated, and, as all my interviewees stated, they are more likely to be involved than was previously the case. The impact is that, in many ways, the biggest challenge for the system is when there is no kin. Without the presence of someone connected to the deceased, as the Coroner quoted in Chapter 7 states, an inquest is a "bit sad" and it is unclear who is to be satisfied. Two other Coroners reflected on conducting an inquest hearing without the bereaved in attendance:

Coroner 1:   It feels somewhat daft sitting there, either nobody in court or one tedious reporter.

Coroner 2:   There are quite often occasions when I am sat in court with just me and the officer, and I am reading evidence even if the press aren't there.

Ed: How does that feel?

Coroner 2:   A bit odd, but you get used to it. It is recorded as well, and it wasn't always recorded, but now under the 2009 Act it is required, and a copy of the recording is available to interested persons, so the basic requirement for the inquiry and the inquest takes place even though there are no bereaved as such, no family and no one present.

> Of course it is not expanded any more than that unless
> I obviously have concerns.

While a 'tedious' reporter may not combat the 'daftness' of an inquest without family, the oddness of the empty room may be partly countered by the role of technology, extending the public space into the future. In either case, it is a diminished hearing, with no one to hear the outcome, following an investigation narrowed by the absence of the participating bereaved. Where the proper place of family to oversee the process is vacated, the Coroner is left trying to fill the gap, not simply in the public hearing, but also in the investigatory space which precedes and shapes the final hearing. As another Coroner said, if there is no family:

> 'Then we have to almost step into their shoes and look deeper. You may have some medical notes there and the doctor has given you a statement to say that they died from bronchopneumonia, due to immobility, following a fall, and if there is no family, then we may spend more time on the notes, just checking that we are happy with them, that everything was as it should be.' (Coroner)

This scrutiny by family is not the forensic examination of the expert, but the contextual scrutiny which comes from a caring relationship with the deceased. The protection which family is represented as offering is here extended into death (Figueiredo et al 2015), and the Coroner cannot fully take their place, but will be forced to do so if necessary. However, it is a better investigation if the Coroner does not have to rely on medical notes or almost step into their shoes and, when it gets to the inquest, where the audience is not the tiresome media or an imagined future listener. Family's engagement represents social connection, generating and buttressing a narrative of relationship resistant to themes of isolation and abandonment (Searle 1995; Klinenberg 2001; Kellehear 2009). If there is no family, the system is forced to turn elsewhere for kin. One Coroner told me they would not recognize the girlfriend in Vignette 2, and in response I asked if this would be different if there was no other family:

> 'If he didn't have any other family it might be, but – in a case like this, goodness gracious you would want someone there. This is the sort of case that can run for years, it will be subject to loads of inquiries, and I would like to have somebody represented, to represent the interests, so I would be looking for, someone, even if it was a cousin or an uncle or something like that, we would want a next of kin for this, and if there is absolutely no one else then I would consider it, but you do have to have some contact.' (Coroner)

Another Coroner said where there was "absolutely no family" and a longstanding friend of 30 years wanted to participate, they would normally exercise their discretion. There does have to be some connection, "a closeness" or "a genuine interest; they are not just nosy parkers or interfering busybodies", as other Coroners put it, but the system will search for someone to represent kinship and connection.[2]

Not making decisions

There is no requirement that decisions about interested person status are publicly announced and my interviewees all emphasized the ways in which their general approach is rarely explicit and determinative. Instead, decisions are taken without formal rulings unless "there was any argument about it, there isn't usually". In most instances, as two Coroner interviewees told me, it is "usually blindingly obvious right from day one ... a parent or a partner or a spouse or something" and "very often, in 90% of cases, it is obvious who the interested persons are". One demonstration of the blindingly obvious was the unanimously positive responses of my interviewees to the claims of the non-adopted daughter in Vignette 1. She was unquestionably an interested person in their responses because of caring links and reciprocity (Finch 1989; Douglas 2014), despite lacking the legal status of daughter. The emphasis is on a tacit, practised relationship, and her automatic involvement in the inquest illustrates an understanding of the inquest as a space open for engagement with alternative formulations of kinship, where those relationships mirror traditional forms of family.

Vignette 3 also revealed insights into framing and sequential decision making. The vignette was designed to provoke reflections about the treatment of a violent absent and otherwise unconnected biological father, contrasted with an informal father in the form of the new partner. Many of the answers reflected this, understanding his role through a lens of constraint, while adopting different approaches to the new partner. In a common approach, one Coroner reasoned that the new partner would see the papers anyway, going on to note that granting him interested person status would serve to antagonize the biological father. This framing positioned the new partner as engaged in the public proceedings as the mother's representative, as the Coroner decided that he would be allowed to ask questions, but it would be made clear that it was on the mother's behalf. This focus on public roles enables a gesture of justification towards a biological father unhappy with the involvement of the new partner, and simultaneously denies the substantive relationship between the new partner and the deceased child.

---

[2]   Contrast here Carol Smart's account of 'new kinship' in Smart (2009).

Another Coroner likewise felt there was no need for a formal decision about his status:

'Well now, there is no rush. Firstly, as they are partners, they are not in a situation in which she would want all the disclosure to be duplicated, it is going to go to her anyway, so I would expect my officers to just say further down the line we have got a PIR[3] and inquest, we can deal with these issues then. We would explain to her what rights she has and if what she is actually saying is she wants the father, the partner to be asking the questions of the witness rather than her, I have no problems with that at all, because she has asked for that, to be a representative, and it is likely as not that that will be in consultation with her. And therefore I would give him that status, but we may not come to that because if they are both going to appear in court, and I am helping them out, it may be he will give advice to the mother who will ask questions, and he will not need to be an IP, as he will have sight of the prior disclosures to the mother.' (Coroner)

This Coroner initially appears to be focused solely on questions of status and legal rights, only to dismiss them as unimportant. Instead, the emphasis is on enabling the effective participation of the family. This framing was even clearer when the same Coroner went on to explore the substance of the relationship between the new partner and the child, and reflected on the difficulty if the biological father objected to the new partner being involved:

'Which he is entitled to say. I am somewhat reluctant to allow other people to prevent others from becoming interested persons if it is around emotional personal reasons of their relationship, it needs to be on the relevance to the inquest. And if this has effectively been the father, it might be what we want to know for example is, how independent the child was, what were the circumstances in which she was allowed to walk home, well the real, the partner is far more likely to know that and ask relevant questions based on his knowledge of her character and behaviour.' (Coroner)

This response to a legitimate challenge by the biological father is not a reliance on legal status, but is instead an engagement in the substance of the relationship between the new partner and the child, with a (perhaps) telling near-reference to the new partner as 'the real' father.

---

[3]   A Pre-Inquest Review, or procedural hearing to resolve issues in advance of the substantive inquest hearing.

The Coroner's involvement of the new partner in the inquest is aimed at producing a meaningful account of what happened, and seeking to create a hearing which combines forms of accountability, but decisions about it will be avoided if possible and, if necessary, will be taken incrementally without rushing.

A decision of whether or not to approve a request by the new partner to be an interested person is at the discretion of the Coroner, as they will not fall into the automatic categories, but it was revealing, in discussion of the role of the missing sister in Vignette 4 (who would be automatically entitled to take part) that a similar concern with connection and kinship was part of the way in which her role was regarded. One example is the way in which, as quoted in Chapter 4, an informal 'de facto' sister was seen as entitled to be automatically involved, while, as another Coroner stated:

> 'I would be very happy for her to be involved, she is not going to be able to give an awful lot of information to help us, but she has every right to ask questions as the only representative. Indeed it is always difficult to do an inquest with nobody representing the family, unless I have reason to believe she has other interests if you see what I mean, on behalf of someone else or some other interest.' (Coroner)

She cannot provide any useful information, but the Coroner would be very happy for her to be involved, and it is always difficult if there is no one able to provide a kinship connection to the deceased. However, this quote also neatly demonstrates the shifting nature of framing: the Coroner is only very happy for her to be involved because she is family. They would not be so happy if she has "other interests", including someone else who is hiding behind her, seeking to gain entrance to the inquest illegitimately. The frame then shifts to one concerned with constraint, protecting both the inquest and the idea of kinship from opportunists seeking to misuse the forum and the office of family. The critical issue in framing this decision is therefore not the factual question required by law – as a matter of fact, does she fall into the category of people automatically entitled to take part? – but is instead directed to questions about the perceived purpose of her involvement, even though this is not an instance in which the law gives any discretion to the Coroner over whether or not she ought to be allowed to participate. Purpose, and in particular a perceived illegitimate purpose, is a factor to take into account and a potential prompt for understandings to shift.

Attending to purpose

Prior to the implementation of the Coroners and Justice Act 2009, those permitted involvement at the discretion of the Coroner were described in legislation as 'properly interested persons'. It was common for all participants to be described as properly interested persons, even after specific categories were added when 'properly' only applied to those outside the automatic categories, and although the 2009 Act changed the nomenclature to 'interested persons', it is not unusual for discussion to continue to preface the category of interested person with 'properly'. The requirement for propriety thus bled through to all participants, as illustrated by the earlier response to the missing sister – she may be an automatic entrant, but the properness or otherwise of her interest is perceived as remaining relevant. Many answers in my interviews reinforced this point – that while it is no longer either in the title of the discretionary category or a revealing tag for the automatically involved, the 'properness' of the nature of the interest remains an implicit and central concern of the inquest system.[4]

This attention to propriety and purpose is narrower when decisions about the role of family are framed through a concern to constrain, while a frame which understands their role as essential to an endeavour to combine forms of accountability is less concerned with identifying and excluding family on the basis of perceived illegitimate purposes. An example of this can be found in the different approaches of the High Court and the Coroner in the case of *Platts v HM Coroner for South Yorkshire*.[5] This case related to Madhi Al-Jaf, who died after he stepped in front of a lorry in April 2005. In the days before his death, as he exhibited 'increasingly bizarre behaviour',[6] he had made a series of implicit or explicit suicidal statements in interactions with the police, medical services and other state agents, and a central issue in the inquest was whether his death could have been prevented by those agents. In the inquest into his death, Ms Platts sought interested person status. She had been in a relationship with Mr Al-Jaf, but the Coroner found they had split up at the time of his death. When the Coroner refused her application to take part, she applied for judicial review of his decision. In the High Court, she did not pursue an argument that she was his partner and focused instead on the Coroner's general discretion to admit properly interested persons. Wilkie J held that despite 'the caution with which this court should approach an invitation to interfere with an exercise of judgment

---

4   However, as *Platts v HM Coroner for South Yorkshire* [2008] EWHC 2502 demonstrates the reasons given for wishing to be involved are matters which can be taken into account when Coroners exercise discretion.

5   *Platts v HM Coroner for South Yorkshire* [2008] EWHC 2502, a case which pre-dated the 2009/2013 reforms.

6   *Platts*, para 43.

which the rules impose on a Coroner',[7] the Coroner had been wrong to exclude Ms Platts.[8]

The differences in the approach of the Coroner and the High Court are stark and revealing. The Coroner's assessment was based on concerns with establishing legitimate formal categories and controlling the scope of the inquiry, and the first question he considered was one of traditional family. He found that Ms Platts had been the partner of the deceased for well over a year, but before Mr Al-Jaf's death, he had 'ended the existing family arrangement between himself and Ms Platts'.[9] Crucially, despite her protestations to the contrary, the Coroner found as a fact that she and the deceased were no longer partners and she was therefore 'a stranger to the inquest'.[10]

Having narrowly interpreted the meaning of 'partner' in the context of a relationship which clearly subsisted in some form,[11] the Coroner then framed Ms Platts' purposes for wanting to be involved, and dismissed them as irrelevant and illegitimate:

> 'First, it seems to me that Ms Platts seeks to participate in this inquest because she is concerned about how "the system" allegedly let down her former boyfriend, and because, in her words, she has "carried the guilt for three years". Whilst one may have considerable sympathy with Ms Platts as to the latter point, I am not satisfied that she has any reason for guilt, but, even if she does have any reason for guilt, in my view that is not sufficient to enable her to participate in this inquest.'

---

[7] *Platts*, para 43; the extent of discretion is highlighted by the reluctance of the court to intervene, as revealed by the fact that permission for judicial review of the Coroner's decision was initially denied, before the application was renewed (at para 2).

[8] The Coroner also found that Article 2 was not engaged in the particular circumstances of the case, and Ms Platts' application for judicial review challenged both of these decisions. In relation to the Article 2 point, Wilkie J held that, even within the considerable breadth of discretion available, the Coroner had been wrong to hold that Article 2 was not arguably engaged. See *Platts*, paras 33–37.

[9] Quote from the Coroner in *Platts*, para 40.

[10] *Platts*, para 42.

[11] Mr Al-Jaf had moved out of her home five weeks before his death, but he and Ms Platts continued to speak on the telephone every day in the weeks before he died, and there are numerous references to his 'girlfriend' (presumably Ms Platts) in the witness statements of the various professionals who engaged with the deceased in the hours before his death (see *Platts*, paras 17–32). As with some of my interviewees, the judgment suggests the Coroner may have conflated cohabitation with partnership (see discussion of this point in relation to the previous test of 'enduring family relationship' taken from adoption legislation and case law in Sloan (2011) and see also, inter alia, *Re E (A Child) (Adoption by One Person)* [2021] EWFC 45.

Ms Platts' concern with systemic failings is excluded as conspiracy theory using 'scare marks',[12] while her guilt is doubly dismissed as unwarranted and insufficient. Similarly, the second reason the Coroner identified – the possibility that Ms Platts wished to gather evidence for a civil claim – is further evidence of the threat she posed and the resulting need to protect the limited, technocratic, blame-free inquest.[13]

In contrast, the High Court emphasized the need to look at the whole of the relationship between Ms Platts and Mr Al-Jaf, including their very close connection, as well as the connection between their break-up and Mr Al-Jaf's behaviour and eventual death. The focus is on the substance of that relationship; where the Coroner saw bright lines and leapt from partner to stranger, the Court preferred nuance. Wilkie J's decision therefore represents an endeavour to reconcile legal right with the practices and complexities of kinship (Butler 2004) rather than a superimposition of the strictures of formal relationships. This framing is also attentive to purpose, removing the scare quotes and emphasizing the genuineness of Ms Platts' concern with systemic failings. It was legitimate for her to want to be involved, and any potential compensation claim does not make those concerns any less reasonable and substantial. Paying attention to judicial directives to exclude those with only trivial, contrived or idle curiosity meant that Ms Platts should be involved, and the Coroner's decision was therefore unreasonable.

Answers in my interviews similarly demonstrated this divide. Where actors understand their role as trying to combine technocratic and community forms of accountability, they adopt an expansive approach, attentive to the realities of emotional connections and the need to seek to establish meaningful outcomes. Effective participation is elevated, both in its own right and as a way of ensuring the inquest reaches a better outcome, and interviewees focus on the substance of inclusion, not on the formality of an obligation to include. In relation to disclosure and participation, a frame which understood the need to combine forms of accountability meant that actors sought to privilege explanation and interaction. This framing is of an account of law represented as having authority because of a blend of forms of accountability, including the participation of those closely connected to the deceased.

Where endeavours to combine forms of accountability are challenged or frustrated, or where the actor prioritizes concerns with control and order, a framing derived from a technocratic emphasis on neutrality and objectivity is

---

[12] Also known as sneer quotes; see Piety (2000) and Nacey (2012).

[13] The judgment of the Court is generous to the Coroner on this second point, accepting evidence from Ms Platts that the Coroner overstated her desire to be involved in order to seek compensation, but finding that the 'slip' by the Coroner could not be criticized.

deployed. Where risk and constraint give meaning to the situation, decisions focus on office and status, emphasizing formal legal categories, as well as a concern with protection and pre-emption. Interested persons are engaged with where required, and actors are concerned with privacy and limits to scope. Attention as to who could assist the inquiry is narrower, with a sole focus on relevant evidence, not on whether participation is effective from the perspective of the bereaved. In relation to questions of disclosure, this frame can be preoccupied with protecting the family from the risk of hurt, distress or indignity, or could emphasize minimum requirements and a presumption of family initiation.

As in the case of *Platts*, perceptions of the family's purpose for being involved is an important factor that is capable of being framed in different ways. This could also be seen in my interviews in the way in which some actors framed perceived attempts by kin to raise questions of liability, blame and compensation as improper,[14] as opposed to concerns not linked to personal gain. This approach was clearest among the officers I interviewed, who all mused on the impact of a perceived compensation culture (Lewis, Morris and Oliphant 2006; Morris 2007; Lewis and Morris 2012). As one officer volunteered, contrasting the biological father with the rest of the family in Vignette 3, the "family may be satisfied with an explanation, father might say, chi-ching,[15] you know, speaking callously".

The distinction is stark: a bereaved family might be entitled to compensation, but do not seek it, while the biological father is only interested because of the 'distasteful' pursuit of money (Douglas 2014, 231). The family are behaving properly, while the father is not.

However, in the alternative framing, blame is not necessarily improper; it can be wholly legitimate to seek blame and compensation and it can be a crucial part of accountability. One Coroner told me:

'I think it is unhelpful to simply trot out that the Coroner's court is not a court of blame [as] questions as to whether an act or omission caused or contributed to the death will properly arise in the course of some investigations. But a Coroner's court cannot make a conclusion apportioning blame to an individual.'

---

[14] See Hall-Tomkin (1999, 11–12), in which Brian Hall-Tomkin, Coroner for North Devon for over 30 years from 1967, describes how 'it is quite common to hear remarks indicative of our increasingly materialistic society. Almost always, after the conclusion of an inquest on a road traffic fatality, someone will ask, "well, is that it? Who is going to pay then?" Apart from the obvious failure to appreciate the purpose of the inquest, it is a sad reflection on modern society's wish to deal with death by reducing it to monetary terms.'

[15] Mimicking the sound of a cash register.

Although 'very cautious' at the start of their career, this Coroner argued that for wider reasons, there was potential benefits to examining these questions, noting that if there is civil litigation ongoing at the same time, the inquest can promote cost savings and settlement.

Even where there was acceptance of the role of blame, there was caution about seeking individual or systemic fault, and some Coroners expressed a particular aversion about the role of campaigning organizations in this context. One Coroner related a situation in which they were asked to approve an interested person who had been assisting the deceased in a care home, but who was also involved in a campaign group which had raised ongoing concerns about the institution. Describing their decision-making process, the Coroner reasoned that:

'if there is no other next of kin and she is the next best thing, then she would be an interested person, but if I have got a next of kin who is engaged, who is asking the questions on behalf of the family, I don't necessary need A N Other. The intention of being an interested person is about having people who are involved in it by virtue of the nature of their relationship. ... There is also another issue, that if the family aren't asking, you don't know the extent to which having this other interested person is desired or requested.'

This was a fine judgment, and the key to it is whether there were any engaged relatives. If there were not, and an individual was able to show they had caring links, the Coroner would grant interested person status. There is a hierarchy, with family at the top, but the system will construct 'the next best thing' as a form of 'fictive kinship' if necessary (Al-Haj 1995; Jacobs 2009 and 2012).[16] Framed narrowly, a reliance on a proper connection to the deceased may be a basis for excluding someone who presents as a threat to the system.[17] However, it is also important for a combining accountabilities framing because the role of kin is to make community accountability possible and, unless there was a relationship with the deceased, the interested person cannot be part of generating a contextual, nuanced and meaningful account.

This Coroner also highlights the possibility that the friend might raise questions the family do not want asking. Challenging the family's interests in this way is not framed as legitimate, whereas a friend raising blame with

---

[16] See the reference to permitting entry to interested persons who have a close similarity to those in the automatic categories in *R v Coroner of the Queen's Household ex p Al Fayed* (2001) 58 BMLR 205, [2000] Inquest LR 50.

[17] See, for example, the case of *Allman v HM Coroner for West Sussex* [2012] EWHC 534 (Admin).

the tacit or explicit approval of a family raised far fewer concerns, as another Coroner reflected:

> 'It depends ... they may say for example, well I visited him in hospital on a regular basis, his family lived a long way away, they didn't visit, but I have known him for years so I visited him in hospital, I'm not very happy with the way the nurses managed him, or something. You have got the family in court, they are clearly properly interested, they have come from miles away to be there on the day, but the friend was actually the one that was in the hospital and has relevant questions to put, so yeah, sure.'

In both accounts, the connection with the deceased is central, with both emphasizing a link founded on caring, but framed through concerns with combining accountabilities, and both demonstrating the importance of engaging with a broader tacit community and recognizing the possibilities of non-family kinship.

In the second account, the friend is critical in constructing and combining forms of accountability, while the family play a more passive role. Other Coroners reflected on an apparently quiescent family and, at the opposite end of the scale from a concern with blaming, the potential risks posed by such a family failing to live up to their proper role. Their purpose is again critical, as decisions here are concerned with encouraging outcomes which are meaningful, and actors expressed disappointment with family who frustrate endeavours to engage them, as one Coroner described:

> 'There are those where you can't make them engage though. Sometimes I think, get cross about this ... and I think my officers often say to them unofficially look, have you sought any legal advice. We can't point them to anybody, you can't make them go to anybody, but there are cases where families just want it finished, it is their way of getting closure, they don't want this running on for ages.'

Similarly, the focus can be on creating opportunities for an uninvolved family to participate, as one officer demonstrated, in an account of a father who was separated from the rest of the family:

Officer: Suddenly two months after the death the father appears on the scene and he is saying, what should I do? I said, you are making representations on behalf of your son, you are seeking assurances that this event is likely to have caused him to have done what he did. Then I say, have you had an opportunity to speak with the rest of the family? He said yes. I said, they have sought representation. He said, do you think I should? I said, it is a choice for you, but you should be reassured that that could be your best course of conduct, now there is nothing more that I can say.

Ed: And so is he now –?

Officer: He is going to see a solicitor.

The emphasis in this account is on responding to a directionless father to prompt him towards his proper role, endeavouring to make his engagement as full as possible, although the officer feels constrained by their role not to go beyond a clear indication of the best course of action. By contrast, a framing focused on the risks of an overly suspicious family does not actively seek to extend their role:

'It may well be that something hasn't gone quite right, but it is not our place to say to the family, are you getting a solicitor, the minute you say 'are you getting a solicitor?' – 'Well, do I need one?' It is not for us to say.' (Officer)

Solicitors create more work, and with a linked concern about families who are 'looking at pound signs', in the words of another officer, this account presents a thin form of family autonomy which does not seek to enable them to engage, and they are instead responsible for their own ability to interpret the circumstances which resulted in death. The role of the family may not be restricted, but it is not promoted, and as family are responsive to the actions of the officers, the system has the capacity to shape their purpose for involvement. Engaging with families in this way therefore appears to be an endeavour to resist the perceived illegitimacy of compensation which flows from the involvement of lawyers. It is also a concern with order, with preventing the perceived challenge of a family immediately picking up on potential failings. Rather than focusing on the fact that 'something hasn't gone right' and enabling those connected to the deceased to understand that context, it is an approach in which factors such as managing the hearing are organized into the decision-making frame. This can be seen in a Coroner response emphasizing the way in which rights to speak could be deployed to manage the hearing and prevent the new partner and the mother "both chipping in simultaneously"

Coroner: He doesn't need to be a properly interested person, she is a family member, we don't need another one, his interests are not going to be against the mother's, so I don't want to use the word 'superfluous', but he is not needed, I mean

	I have got no problem with him sitting next to her, and providing her with questions to ask if it is appropriate.
Ed:	And if he sought to ask the questions?
Coroner:	I would ask him on what basis he feels he needs to ask questions when she can. It is possible if she is so distressed that she can't then I might accept him, but it would be on her behalf, not him as a properly interested person.

Where decisions employed a combining accountabilities frame focused on the relationships of the new partner and the child, the attention here is instead on the mother. This focus on controlling the inquest does not look to any judicially mandated test for the possible involvement of the new partner, but rather rests on an understanding of pragmatism and necessity, adopting a 'natural emotional hierarchy' with the mother at the apex.

The hierarchy of family

In 2006, in evidence to a Commons Select Committee, Victor Round, former Honorary Secretary of the Coroners' Society and HM Coroner for Worcester, was asked how Coroners dealt with a number of potential interested persons. He stated: "We have the natural emotional hierarchy in a family, which tends to elect a boss, a leader, a family spokesman, and if it is a split family maybe two of them, but we cope with that regularly."[18]

As well as this natural emotional hierarchy, Mr Round emphasized associated legal regimes[19] and, in the context of a proposed extension to include friends of long standing,[20] argued that this emphasis on a hierarchy is important:

Otherwise you do, I am afraid, particularly with mental patients, have friends of long standing popping up all over the place, and nowadays

---

[18] See oral evidence attached to the report of the Constitutional Affairs Select Committee, 8th Report of Session 2005–2006, response to Q114, 13 June 2006, http://www.publi cations.parliament.uk/pa/cm200506/cmselect/cmconst/902/6061302.htm [Accessed 24 January 2022].

[19] Citing the Administration of Estates Act 1925, which deals with priority in relation to probate rules. See a critical discussion of the application of the probate rules and the way in which they can make will writing a political act in Monk (2011).

[20] The inclusion of 'friends of long standing' in the draft Bill was criticized by the Constitutional Affairs Select Committee during pre-legislative scrutiny, and was removed from the Bill as introduced; see para 139 of the 8th Report of Session 2005–2006, http:// www.publications.parliament.uk/pa/cm200506/cmselect/cmconst/902/90208.htm#a27 [Accessed 24 January 2022].

we say to them, 'Look, the family are in charge here, not you' and I would have hoped we would still be able to say that?[21]

The approach is bound up with concerns about constraining kin and seeks to deal with challenges through reliance on official status. As Mr Round's reference to the family being in charge makes clear, the hierarchy in this framing is necessary to exclude and control risk. Although the framing emphasizes family autonomy, it suggests that it is a matter of nature and fact where family stops. It ignores the ways in which family practices enact and simultaneously construct (Morgan 2011), and the recurrent cyclical interaction of that construction with both law and the range of informal decisions being made by officers and Coroners potentially deploying uncritical state thinking about the shape of family (Bourdieu 1996; Maclean and Eekelaar 2004; Cornford, Baines and Wilson 2013; Atkinson 2014). One Coroner reflected on this, stating that it was a question for the officers how far family extended, and officers didn't have training on it, they just "know enough about engaging with all of them, so it is funny isn't it, they know where to draw the line, some step son or I don't know, some great aunt or something like that".

To gain entrance to the inquest, the crucial factor is not necessarily a question of legal status, but is rather whether the individual falls within a negotiated social category of family (Finch and Mason 1993; Reimers 2011). This factor will be framed by reference to a concern with accountability or with constraint, and decisions which shape the process will be made before the Coroner engages with the case. An example is the way in which technocratic understanding frames the hierarchy of importance demonstrated by one officer in relation to scenarios like the new partner in Vignette 3. The idea of him asking to be granted interested person status "wouldn't arise. [The mother] is next of kin, she would be the interested party, he can come along as it is public but why would he need to be treated as the father?"

The framing is a limited conception of the inquest, with the dismissal of any substantive emotional connection between the child and the new partner who, presented with an officer who did not see any purpose in his involvement, would be excluded from interested person status without it even reaching the Coroner. It would appear naturally as if the family had elected a spokesperson. In such circumstances, the role of the officers is key and, as another officer explained, the "Coroner wouldn't ever say, right who

---

[21] See oral evidence attached to report of Constitutional Affairs Select Committee, 8th Report of Session 2005–2006, response to Q114, 13 June 2006, http://www.publicati ons.parliament.uk/pa/cm200506/cmselect/cmconst/902/6061302.htm [Accessed 24 January 2022].

is the mother, who is the father, at an inquest. It would just be, we would just say, the mother is sat here, she will be the one asking questions".

Similarly, this officer will have managed the question of who is an interested person in advance. In this context, it is important that some Coroners were suspicious of the possibility of perceived family overreach, emphasizing that it was for the Coroner to determine who was an interested person, but the operation of serial decision-making means that a formal decision may never be required by the Coroner, and where a decision is needed, it will be inevitably framed by information provided by family and decisions taken by family (see Davis et al (2002, 29) for a critical reflection on this). Family thus have a critical part to play in determining their own formation, in particular when decisions are framed through a concern with formal status, as two officers' reflections on the role of the girlfriend in Vignette 2 demonstrated:

Officer A: If they had a child together then we would probably treat it a bit different because they are joined by that child, so I would give them a bit more, but again you would liaise with the family. We wouldn't be giving out information to people without the family being aware, but if you just had boyfriend and girlfriend living together I don't think –

Officer B: We would involve the family and the boyfriend and girlfriend wouldn't we

Officer A: Yeah, a lot of the time we hope that they speak, touch wood, the majority of family would be aware of his girlfriend and they would be in contact.

The separation of the girlfriend and family, and the emphasis on liaising with family, even in a situation where the girlfriend would have a very strong argument to be an interested person, illustrates the application of a 'natural' hierarchy and the potential role of family in policing its own edges, as also suggested by another officer:

'I would say that we contact the family and ask them if they would like to contact the girlfriend ... we wouldn't be able to give her any information, we would suggest that right we'll contact the family and if you're happy for us to give the family your details then hopefully they can contact you and let you know what's happening.'

It is interesting to note that in relation to the responses by officers in this part, I also interviewed Coroners in those areas, who stated that the girlfriend would be granted interested person status. This illustrates the potential importance of serial decision making, as it is possible that while the Coroner would permit it, steps taken by the officers in this scenario might make it less likely that the girlfriend would have an opportunity to become an interested person. However, some officers interviewed also stated they would be likely to approach the Coroner with questions in this case, and in any event they would act with particular caution and sensitivity, not least because it was not unusual in their experience for deceased soldiers to have both a wife and a girlfriend. The example therefore also illustrates the importance of not overstating the officer's role and of understanding the importance of the Coroner–officer relationship, which can be very different across different areas (Davies 2002).

Another Coroner, who was not sure on the question of recognizing the girlfriend in Vignette 2 as an interested person, stated that she would be encouraged to be in contact with the family. This hierarchy also places family in a critical position in relation to managing privacy and communicating with those deemed outside family, as illustrated in a story told to me by another Coroner about a young man who had "taken his own life in unusual circumstances, and we had a letter from someone who went to school with him for many years, they had been very very close and had heard he had died in an accident, and would I write and tell him what the circumstances of the accident were?" The family were embarrassed by how he had died, and the Coroner "felt justified in the circumstances saying you are not a properly interested person" and told him he had to contact the family. The family informed the Coroner they would not attend any hearing and, when the inquest was held, nobody else attended. Sympathetic with their discomfort, this Coroner passed responsibility to the family for deciding how to engage beyond their own circle, and it was unsurprising that the investigation was able to be closed "on the basis of a written statement, in a public setting".

Resisting the natural emotional hierarchy

In contrast to this narrow risk framing of family as gatekeepers, some interviewees reflected on situations where, although they perceived family to have a key role in delineating their own 'edges', they would seek to subvert the natural emotional hierarchy, as with the girlfriend in Vignette 2:

'Say you have got someone, they have barely been going out with each other for any time at all but their relationship was very intense, and quite often, they are more distraught than the immediate family because they have got more invested in the relationship. We still have to go through the next of kin and what the Coroner says, but anyone can go to an inquest and as a final resort that is, we can keep in touch with them, and we can tell them when the inquest is going to be.' (Officer)

Rather than focusing on the need to constrain the distraught girlfriend, the officer is attentive to the substance of the intense relationship, and seeks to resist her exclusion and the perceived impositions of the law. They remain bound by the dual dictates of the family and the Coroner, but sympathy arising from recognition of the investment in the relationship frames their endeavour to seek to engage them and, as a final resort, enable their attendance at the inquest. A similar attention to the substance of the relationship was evident in the reflections of a Coroner in relation to how they would approach this vignette:

> 'Would she be counting as a partner within the meaning of section 47? It depends, I think at first blush I would probably say yes, I will call you interested if you really have been his girlfriend for ten months, if his parents popped up and said this woman led him astray etc and there is no way you should regard her then I might hold a pre-inquest hearing to say now come on, tell me why you think you should be interested when the parents say you have been a bad influence on him.'

The initial approach, oriented towards a broad tacit conception of kinship, is provisional and open to family challenge, in which case the Coroner will be obliged to make an explicit decision about the girlfriend's status. The basis for that challenge reveals the Coroner's opening presumption of a relationship built on reciprocity, because when it is queried, the relationship is evaluated against an ethic of care (Held 2005; Slote 2007). It is an account of the Coroner negotiating family and making decisions about status, but importantly the considerations are not those of law – the fact of a family relationship, or a reasonable and substantial interest. Instead, it is directed towards practices and the qualities of the relationship, exploring the wider context, aiming to reach a decision accessible to non-technocratic knowledges and seeking to make possible the construction of a contingent, individualized space, acknowledging and enabling a tacit community. The Coroner does not acknowledge the potential dangers in this delicate construction, including the danger of legal challenge. However, rather than adopting a risk framing and resorting to the protection of law, the approach gambles on contingency and openness. If this is not possible, then the court resorts in the last instance to a triadic form, making a decision, but not one in which legal categories are central (whether or not someone is a bad influence is not a criteria for determining interested person status), instead being focused on resolving the issue between those involved and reaching a decision which is comprehensible on those grounds.

Another example of the negotiation and possible subversion of the natural hierarchy of family in such cases was given by a Coroner in relation to the same vignette:

'I probably wouldn't recognize her as a PIP, but in effect, other than the provision of disclosure, and of course there will be sensitivity because of the army, there is not going to be very much difference, ok they wouldn't have the day to day contact with our office, but they would be advised of the hearing and she could come to the hearing, in fact we would suggest she comes to the hearing, we would go that far.'

Where law is perceived to conflict with centrality of kinship, the law is complied with, but a place for the importance of the relationship is found. In this account, in going as far as suggesting that she comes to the hearing, the importance of status – and interested person status in particular – is downplayed. The only significant difference noted relates to disclosure, and with this in mind, I now turn to consider the place of disclosure.

Disclosure

Examining documents – including medical and other records, medical and other expert reports, police and other investigator evidence, and witness statements – forms a significant part of the pre-hearing process from the perspective of the Coroner and interested persons. A key criticism of the pre-2009 Act was a lack of a requirement to provide disclosure of any such documents to families in advance of the hearing,[22] with widespread concerns that advance disclosure of documents was often non-existent or very limited.

This was addressed by the 2013 reforms, with the law now providing that on request, Coroners must provide relevant documents to interested persons.[23] A consistent theme in my interviews was a response that the centrality of the family in the contemporary inquest is reflected in the amended disclosure rules. Another was that the Coroners I interviewed stated that they had always provided disclosure anyway, although one went on to state that disclosure was wider now and, rather than selectively disclosing, they now disclosed everything.[24] However, my attention is not on whether

---

[22] Although from 2008 case law emphasized the need for the widest disclosure possible in cases where Article 2 was engaged; see, inter alia, *R (Smith) v Assistant Deputy Coroner for Oxfordshire* [2008] EWHC 694 (Admin) at 37. See Scraton and Chadwick (1986, 95) for a critical reflection on lack of disclosure in relation to deaths in custody.

[23] Coroners (Inquests) Rules 2013, r 13, which states that the Coroner can decide whether or not to provide copies or permit inspection of specific documents, including post-mortem reports, any other reports, recordings of hearings and 'any other document which the coroner considers relevant to the inquest'. These can be electronic or redacted (r 14), exceptions are set out in r 15 (including relating to unreasonable requests or irrelevant documents), and a restriction on charging a fee is given in r 16.

[24] Note the discussion in the introduction about selection of interviewees; as a convenient sample, it was a partly self-selecting group, but from a wide range of areas across England.

in practice disclosure is undertaken properly or at all (on which see Angiolini 2017, 208–209; Justice Committee 2021, 21–22), but rather on how the law represents disclosure and how the understanding of disclosure of those within the system illustrates the role of family.

Viewed through a jurisdictional lens, disclosure is an essential part of enabling the effective participation of the family, and is a critical part of the way in which law is represented and how the role of family is understood by those within the system. Interviewees emphasized the reciprocal nature of disclosure – that they "have got to make sure communication is exchanged" – and in that process it is again possible to distinguish the deployment of the two different frames.

The distinct place of family

One Coroner reflected on disclosure, stating there was an "entirely unsatisfactory state of affairs previously where they would turn up and hear this evidence about their loved one for the first time, sat there with everyone else, I would think that would be quite distressing in certain cases".

Hearing the evidence for the first time, the family could be caused double distress. Not only would they hear painful and personal details about the person lost, but they would hear them in a public forum with no time to prepare. Disclosure in this framing is thus directed towards recognizing and constructing the distinctly different place of family, with a focus on dignity and the family's primacy in grief.

As well as emotional preparation, decisions about disclosure are focused on procedural preparation. As one Coroner explained: "If you haven't done the prior preparation and you just busk it on the day then you are going to end up with egg on your face." It means that families have a chance to go through the papers carefully – "they do go through them with a fine tooth comb" – and officers were clear that "what we don't want is any nasty surprises, and any questions that can't be answered at the inquest leaving people feeling that they have missed their chance".

Framing decisions based on combining accountabilities emphasized the ways in which disclosure and communication are part of a more effective and meaningful investigation, with Coroners better able to focus the evidence collection process on the concerns of the family. In the contemporary inquest, interviewees suggested that communication by email and telephone were common, and a recurring theme in my interviews was an assertion that electronic communication meant that "it is much easier for there to be an information flow happening ... officers therefore have a lot more contact with the family day to day".[25]

---

[25] Although electronic disclosure was a particular issue for some interviewees, who felt they had inadequate systems to manage it properly.

Coroners and officers also discussed who this might exclude and how those people might be engaged, with positive reflections on the possibility of differential approaches. One Coroner described a recent case in which they offered institutional interested persons inspection and disclosure on request, but gave the family disclosure, without their request, "because I thought, I don't want them to be at a disadvantage, even though the law says you could've inspected, they weren't hugely educated they would have found it difficult, they probably needed to take it to people to get advice on its significance".

Questions about accessibility in relation to electronic communication also focused attention on the possibilities of broader meaningful engagement:

'There is certainly much more of a team effort now than was once the case. Some more mature family members may not be computer literate, which will now engage their younger family, who can prepare detailed letters or statements or queries or questions to be answered, so it is much more of a team effort now, and I would encourage that, because I think it means that people's understanding will be different.' (Coroner)

Disclosure in this account enables and encourages the participation and sharing of different understandings which are central to community forms of accountability. A framing which seeks to combine forms of accountability includes knowledges built from a tacit community grounded in a wide conception of kinship. However, the material of disclosure can act to crystallize that community, foregrounding pragmatic concerns with practicality and cost. Answers illustrating a combining accountabilities approach emphasized the ways in which disclosure is capable of being shared. As one Coroner reflected in relation to the new partner in Vignette 3, "what you would do is keep all the liaison with her, and if she chose to share it with the new partner, that is fine, but if he wanted to ask questions at the inquest I would say fine, he has brought her up hasn't he".

Liaising with the mother is a question of practical provision as the new partner had a caring parental relationship with the deceased child which legitimates his involvement. In an interesting comparison, this Coroner took a harder line compared to all the other Coroners I interviewed in relation to the involvement of the absent father. Where others considered themselves bound to recognize the biological father as an interested person, based on the mother's assertion that he is the father, this Coroner would not accept this as sufficient:

Coroner: It would be for the natural father to prove paternity, because he is not on the birth certificate.

Ed: But if [the mother] has said to you that he is the father, although he is not on the birth certificate, would you be telling your officers to take steps to –?

Coroner: No. No I wouldn't, not in this circumstance, because he is not on the birth certificate, if he was it would be a different matter.

While this Coroner went on to confirm that if the biological father was able to prove paternity otherwise, he would be entitled to interested person status, the deployment of legal technique to deny his engagement is in stark contrast to their framing of the decision in relation to the new partner. Where one scenario is understood and organized in relation to concerns with constraint, engaging in questions of order and status, the other is framed through a concern to create a meaningful outcome and engage with substantive relationships based on care.

The response also demonstrates the central place of technicality in the processes by which actors in the system reflect, shape and influence family practices. For this Coroner, the absence of the biological father's name from the birth certificate was key, and enabled the coalescence of family practices and law, producing a result which avoided the discordant inclusion of the unconnected biological father.

Disclosure, engagement of the family, and the community

Disclosure enables the identification or narrowing down of issues pre-hearing, but also carries the potential for the inquest to mirror settlement practices in civil litigation (Dingwall and Cloatre 2006; Prescott and Spier 2016). For some interviewees, identifying questions arising out of disclosure provided an opportunity to resolve issues raised in advance of the public hearing (as will be discussed further in Chapter 7). For example, an officer described how in

'straightforward [cases] often, once they have seen the disclosure, [families] don't feel they have to come to the inquest. I would say we get less families coming now that we do the advance disclosure. They have seen all there is to see. Some people come just as a mark of respect or to get a bit of closure [if the Coroner decides there is no need to hear any evidence]. But if the family come back and say, actually I have got some questions, the Coroner is very good and will try and get a witness if the family have a burning desire to, but it all runs a lot more smoothly now because they see they can, you know, we don't lie to our families.'

This response illustrates the range of reasons for family to attend, and the perceived crucial role of disclosure, with the system framed as responsive to their needs, whether that is seeking to close off the investigation or to interrogate the circumstances of death. This central place for the family, with the emphasis on identifying and potentially resolving issues in advance, dramatically illustrates the changed nature of the inquest as a public space, revealing the family's role as conduit to a wider public. Understood as providing a lay perspective and scrutinizing the investigative process, the family are responsible for ensuring transparency and oversight on behalf of the wider community. It is a framing which is entirely at odds with understandings of the inquest as a forum for solely expert technocratic accountability. The role is also revealed in the reflections of one Coroner in relation to non-family attendees at an inquest:

'What sometimes happens is you have got some people with the family who think they are being helpful by asking a question to clarify something and the problem is they haven't had the papers, so the answer's in the papers and that is why the family hasn't asked it, do you know what I mean, so that can be quite difficult to manage.' (Coroner)

In such a scenario, attention is not directed towards general public revelation, but rather towards a form of explanation which is meaningful for those engaged, excluding those who are outside that engagement in advance of the hearing. Non-family attendees seeking to clarify matters actually make the process more difficult, as their proper place is to both rely on and focus on the family's primacy in understanding. The impact of this is to make the threshold question of who family is and who gets to be an interested person even more critical.

Another Coroner reflected on how to respond to the risk of public misunderstanding through exclusion, describing how they would hold informal pre-inquest meetings which interested persons attended, but which were not open to the public.[26] Their concern was with evidence which might never be needed at the full hearing:

'If we had a whole hearing and the press and Joe Public have the right to attend they may ask why I am not hearing from Joe Bloggs, because Joe Bloggs says such and such, and there might be a good reason why Joe Bloggs is just not relevant, it might not be necessary

---

[26] It was not clear whether this Coroner was describing previous practice or current practice, but r 11 of the Coroners Inquests (Rules) 2013 now requires that all pre-inquest hearings be held in public.

for the purposes of the inquest. But of course Joe Public or the press go away thinking oh it was important.' (Coroner)

In contrast, the family, who would have had the disclosure and would have seen why Joe Bloggs was not relevant, did not present such a risk. The concern with maintaining a triadic, neutral form of accountability is central, as disclosure both presents and prevents risk to the effective operation of that forum, and the process must be carefully managed in response.

Disclosure and constraint

As well as managing the community, disclosure is a way of seeking to manage family expectations, but it is a technique with limitations, as people "will perhaps read them but not really digest them or understand, so they will come expecting me to do an inquiry into everything". Framed through concerns with constraining the family, disclosure could also present significant risks to the Coroner's management of information, as one Coroner reflected:

'What I do is I write to say, look this is made known to you on the basis that it can only be discussed with a legal representative or member of the family, it is not published, it is not copied or distributed, strictly it should be returned to me on closure, unless you wish to retain it at that stage and you should contact me then.'

Similarly, officers expressed concerns with privacy and preventing family members from "gaily transmitting medical information around". Another Coroner stated that they did not "like emails from non-professional email addresses". Web-based email was "just unreliable", after all "how would you like it if I was to give information about what happened to your mother to anybody who emailed in with initials and a Yahoo address?" The central concern is with a form of dignity based in office and defensive practice to resist challenge.

This framing could also focus on protection of the family from harm caused by contact with death (Dix 1998), with, for example, interviewees emphasizing that post-mortem reports were not sent out automatically – one officer stated "it is graphic and very medical" and a Coroner noted "it can be very distressing, so I wait until someone requests it" – and demonstrating the role of the officers in shaping the place of family:

Officer 1:   If they are asking about other things then we would mention that the pathologist will produce a full report that I can send to you ... if someone has no idea and they don't talk in a way that they are wanting to know any more then we wouldn't ultimately offer them anything. ... Otherwise I think we'd be there forever copying things, sending things out, but ultimately if they did request more information it would be down to the Coroner whether or not he would release that.

Officer 2: Post-mortem reports do not go to families unless they request it. So yes, unless they ask for something, we wouldn't send anything really.

Ed: How would they know if there was something that they could get?

Officer 2: They wouldn't to be perfectly honest would they? We don't offer it. Not unless we feel it might help them, but otherwise no.

Conclusion

Where the historical inquest had little in the way of formal process before the hearing, the inquest hearing as currently constructed is inseparable from the pre-hearing investigation and procedural requirements which shape that investigation, and cannot be understood without it. My central endeavour in this chapter has been to reveal and analyse the ways in which the family are engaged in the inquest investigation before the public hearing. Their decisions, and the tacit and sequential decisions, non-decisions and deferred decisions made by key actors in the inquest all shape the role of the bereaved in the investigation and the substance of the investigation itself.

One important aspect of this is disclosure. The responsibility to provide key documents in advance highlights the increased importance of the family's ability to engage with that material. As campaigners have long argued, and as some of my interviewees reflect in the following chapter, lawyers and advisers often play an essential role in ensuring disclosure is made explicable. For many families, the interpretation of complex evidence requires some form of assistance, but as the final quote in this chapter highlights, it is not solely about aiding comprehension, but can also be about assisting the bereaved to frame their concerns and request information.

The other impact of enhanced disclosure and of pre-hearing disposal is to make the threshold question of who family comprises even more important. The material possession of documentary evidence by the family underpins the possibility of critical engagement and opens up a space for resistance to injustice, but it also acts to formalize and privilege the family, shaping the proceedings, and potentially narrowing the possibility of the inquest as a site of wider meaningful public revelation, which I will turn to examine in the next chapter.

7

The Public(?) Hearing

Introduction

In this final substantive chapter I examine the ways in which my interviewees perceive the family's engagement with the construction of the public space of the inquest hearing. My contention is that the reforms of the inquest have produced a hearing which can be substantively more or less public in terms of what is covered and who is there to listen, and the family play a central role in determining how it is shaped. To explore this issue, I examine the different spaces in which inquests take place, before exploring order, disorder and the role of lawyers. I then move to discuss the ways in which the hearing can be more or less public in more detail, before concluding with a focus on the emphasis of meaningfulness in both the hearing and conclusions of the inquest. This conclusion (formerly verdict) receives a great deal of attention, particularly in doctrinal law, in relation to the appropriate legal tests for particular conclusions, as well as concerns with inconsistencies between areas in relation to conclusions (Mclean 2015a, 2015b, 2017; Harris and Walker 2019). Formal outcomes are undoubtedly important, including for the family, but as Davis et al note, 'arriving at a correct verdict is a small part of what goes on in the inquest' (Davis et al 2002, 60). Drawing on Scott Bray's insight that ' "facts" found by Coroners are not unproblematic findings' (2010, 574) and can only be understood in their wider social and legal context, my endeavour here is to reflect on that wider context. In particular, I explore questions of how those facts emerge from a process which concludes in a public hearing, and how family fit into that.

A public space

One of the aims of the 2009/2013 reforms was to have fewer inquests, with the ability to discontinue an investigation before the inquest where, for example, the death was a result of natural causes and there were no other concerns (CJA 2009, s 4). Where an inquest was to be held, the Chief Coroner has emphasized that the 'more modern look' of the inquest system is based on fewer delays and more hearings being held in public (see Chief Coroner 2013–14, 11). Inquests must now be opened in a public hearing wherever possible and dates for any future hearings must be announced.[1] Any pre-inquest hearings must be heard in public and there must be a final hearing within six months.[2] When it arose in my interviews, my interviewees were unanimous in their perception that no one (including family members) attended the public opening, and while many of them supported the idea of listing cases at that first hearing, some had difficulty with this. One Coroner summarized the problem: "I am lucky because I have got access to a court whenever I want one. The biggest problem is court access, so I can settle and run my own diary because I know when my court sessions are going to be."

Of my eight Coroner interviewees, four did not have a purpose-built courtroom, while the others had a court, in some cases attached to their offices and in other cases elsewhere.[3] These differences in provision are longstanding,[4] and Hurren (2010, 240–248) describes the battle of the late Victorian Coroner for Oxford to get his own court. His arguments, founded on the grounds of morality and public health, were unsuccessful. At the same time in the 1880s, his counterpart in Melbourne was having more success in obtaining a purpose-built court, a space which Trabsky (2015) argues was an exercise in community memorialization, bringing the bodies of the living and the dead into a forum of law (Trabsky 2015, 18). In the contemporary hearing, as Chapter 5 reflects, the dead body has disappeared from the

---

[1]   Coroners (Inquests) Rules 2013, SI 2013/1616, r 11. If the Coroner does not have access to a court, then they can be opened in private and announced at the next available juncture.

[2]   Coroners (Inquests) Rules 2013, r 8. In addition, where inquests last for over 12 months, the Chief Coroner has to include details of them in an annual report to the Lord Chancellor (CJA 2009, s 36). Lengthy delays between the death and a final hearing have been a longstanding criticism of the inquest system from the perspective of the bereaved (see, inter alia, Davis et al 2002, 26; Biddle 2003; Samuels 2011; Hawkes, 2014; Sense about Science 2014), and many of my interviewees expressed support in principle for the six-month rule, describing concerns about Coroners in other areas who were not progressing inquests quickly enough. However, many also emphasized that it could be difficult to meet this timescale in practice, particularly in complex cases when other inquiries were ongoing.

[3]   The legislation now provides that Coroners must have accommodation that is appropriate to their needs (CJA 2009, s 24) and some of my interviewees stated that a purpose-built court was in the process of being arranged.

[4]   See, for example, the discussion in Richardson (2001) of the picture of an inquest held by Thomas Wakley, in which he sat at a table surrounded by the jury. In relation to Coroner's courts and the use of other buildings see also, inter alia, Graham (1995); Burney (2000).

space of the inquest, and for some Coroners, the space for considering the circumstances of their death can vary considerably, as one told me:

'I personally have held inquests in a police club, where they switched off the bandit[5] and put a cover on the snooker table, and in the loft space of the community centre. My predecessor held them in what was not much more than a large broom closet at the old hospital. We hold them still in the lecture rooms of the hospital. I make use of the magistrates' court where they have a court which is relatively redundant, so I usually use that one without too much problem. Last week because it was a major one, I used a court in the Crown Court complex, which was very good. But otherwise I have to go all over the place.' (Coroner)

As the major case in the Crown Court indicates, the variety in space was not solely about availability, but was also a question of perceived suitability. As another Coroner stated,

'80% of cases are the straightforward you could do it round a table, in fact I do do it round a table in certain cases, there is no point bringing an 80 year old lady into a courtroom to hear her husband's inquest when in fact it is not disputed.'

At the other end of the scale, as a quote below illustrates, where there was a risk of disorder, a courtroom would be preferable. Further research on the staging, spacing and placing (Carlen 1976) of the contemporary inquest is needed (Davis et al 2002, 32 and 34; Tait and Carpenter 2013b, 96), but these responses show the potential adaptability of the public space of the hearing, and perhaps demonstrate the ways in which the ordering of this space can bring matters into the reach of the family or put them out of their reach (Keenan 2009, 187). These are accounts of a hearing partly shaped by, anticipating or in response to a bereaved family, but also by tensions between resourcing and concerns with dignity and effective participation, forced to remake cupboards and loft space into spaces for law and to situate dignity alongside the covered snooker table and the unplugged fruit machine. Such flexibility also risks unforeseen distress to families, as with one account I was told about a Coroner who shared a space with the Registrar:

'Another Coroner was telling me a while ago that it never really came home to him until a widow in front of him said rather wistfully "well

---

[5]   By which the Coroner meant a one-armed bandit or fruit machine (a gambling machine).

the last time I was in here was when I was getting married" – and that is distressing, you know, you can't but feel sympathy for the poor lady she has to say, been in this room twice, once to marry her husband and once to be at his inquest.'

The account is affecting, the circularity of events and restraint of the widow no doubt leading the Coroner to repeat it to me (the only story I was told of another Coroner's direct experience in an inquest). In retelling it, and highlighting the role of the other Coroner in previously failing to appreciate the impact of the use of the space, it gave emphasis to the importance of the room. At the same time, it gives weight to an account of the inquest as a place of significance, being framed as opposite to a wedding day, but likewise touched by law's ritual and authority. It is the combination of these contrasting moments of dignity and formality, moments in which family can be seen to be constructed by legal practices in the same public space, which gives the story poignancy, evincing particular sympathy from this Coroner.

One Coroner reflected explicitly on the public nature of the space of the public hearing, stating that

'I don't believe I have ever had a general member of the public come in and see what is going on, I have had people there who are properly interested persons or who have a link of some sort with the deceased, a friend or work colleague or something of that nature, member of the same organization, there is a link. I don't honestly think I have just had a general casual, I have an hour or two to kill, I will pop into the Coroner's court.'

It is a public space populated by those linked to the deceased, those in selected offices of the state – Coroner and staff, pathologist, police officer and doctor – and perhaps the media (Davis et al 2002, 72–73). Of the three publics identified by the Warwick Inquest Group (1985, 51) – the jury, the press and the public gallery – in most contemporary inquests it is only the media who are likely to attend. I asked one Coroner if they had a lot of press attendance:

'Surprisingly little. If they know of some particular death, they will say can you keep us advised of that, but I don't issue any sort of communiqué to the press saying this week I am going to deal with Fred Bloggs and Uncle Tom Cobley and all, if someone rings and asks we'll tell them where and when.'

In such an account, the press are not prevented from attending, but their help in creating a public space was not actively sought; instead, reliance was placed on the family to determine who, if anyone, ought to be aware of the proceedings. In contrast, other Coroners made information more readily available to the media, including details of their lists on websites: "There is a lot more information out in the public domain now, I have got a website, we are trying to upgrade it, we have got a list of our cases, we have got procedures."

However, this Coroner went on to note that this was so that people could take an interest, and contrasted with a situation "a few years ago [where] there was certainly a lack of provision of evidence to families". The attention of both is on constructing a hearing which seeks to enable those who had a connection to the deceased to attend and participate.

As in the case of Malcolm Burge, discussed in Chapter 1, and as highlighted in Davis et al's (2002) account of the inquest as obituary, the family play a critical role in media representations of the death. Butler describes the role of the media as critical in determining what amounts to a 'grievable death' (Butler 2006, 20), and there is an intimate relationship between the construction of a grievable death in the public forum of the inquest and the media reporting of that hearing, while the interaction between the media and the inquest process can also play a key role in a death being not grievable, particularly in relation to deaths in custody (see, inter alia, Scraton and Chadwick 1986; Pemberton 2008; Erfani-Ghettani 2015). In both cases, the individualizing, personalizing account of and by the family forms part of the framing of that narrative by the reporters in attendance.

Where the media are not in attendance, or where they are but strategies are deployed to limit their engagement (which will be discussed later on), and where there is no jury or public attendance, there is no audience unconnected to the deceased, and the inquest moves from 'theatre' (Warwick Inquest Group 1985) to 'a public laying to rest – almost, one might say, a state funeral' (Davis 2002, 71). Rehearsing the rhetoric of a still-public hearing in cases where "the little old lady is attending her husband's inquest on her own, and there is nobody else there but me and her" misses the ways in which such hearings are intimate and ceremonial, a mixture of the eulogical and the investigative. Critically, none of these potential formulations is fully realizable in the absence of family and, if framed through endeavours to combine accountabilities, without their effective participation.

Order

Most families in inquests are unrepresented, and I asked Coroners about their experiences of unrepresented family members asking questions in the hearing, including the purpose of the family asking questions. In discussion with one Coroner, I asked whether the objective of the family asking questions was to assist the Coroner in answering the four questions of who the person was, and how, when and where they died. The Coroner responded:

'I would like to think that I was going to get there by myself unaided, but they may have points which I wasn't aware of, in which case yes, it would be proper to ask them, but other than that, no, the principal reason for them being there is to ensure they leave satisfied that the system has operated properly.'

Adopting a technocratic frame, this is a limited role for family, who are responsible for oversight and maintaining public confidence in the system. They might assist in establishing the facts of a case, but the Coroner was not primarily focused on the quality of their participation. Instead, they focus on identifying the proper cause of death, and the absence of family in such circumstances would not affect the correctness of the outcome – as the same Coroner reflected in relation to a case where a family member had complained that they had not known about the date of a hearing: "I may well reopen it, we'll get the records and we'll go through it again, but it is not going to change anything."

In contrast, where interviewees understood their decision through a combined accountabilities framing, attention was focused on the family's legitimate interest and the effectiveness of their engagement in the hearing. This included encouraging them to ask questions, but also emphasized preparation and identifying concerns, in advance of the hearing or at the hearing itself, and the limits of the possibilities of preparation:

'Of course if you are skilful what you try to do, as it is an inquisitorial process, is to ask the questions in court before it is the turn of, gets to the family.' (Coroner)

'Sometimes you will turn up and you'll have a family who haven't said anything, they will turn up on the day with a long list of questions or who want to ask about all sorts of things and you have no idea where it is coming from.' (Coroner)

All interviewees commonly described holding hearings with unrepresented families who needed help. They could be "nervous" or could need help with "phrasing" a question, which included giving direction: "Is this what you are trying to ask?" Interviewees sometimes (but not always) focused on managing the risk of the family overstepping the bounds of the inquiry (Davis et al 2002), and I was particularly interested in the reflections of my interviewees on the difference between represented and unrepresented families. A common response was that they saw themselves as giving greater scope to unrepresented families. For example, in relation to whether questions put to witnesses had to be limited to the strict scope of the inquiry, one Coroner said not necessarily: "You do better with me possibly if you are a relative than if you are a legal representative." I asked why. They replied: "I think it is their only opportunity to ask these sort of questions and I don't think it is right that I should limit it."

One Coroner laughed when I asked this question, indicating it was almost a matter for some embarrassment:

> 'That is an interesting question, oh you have done your research haven't you, that is very interesting. Well, I think I choose these words; that I probably give family representatives more latitude. Where I might pull up a lawyer and say, I don't think this is appropriate or relevant, I might see where it is going with a family. That is partly because I don't want to create an image and a perception that I am unfriendly or they are inadequate, we need to build a relationship and a process. But I must be fair to all interested persons.'

The discomfort for this Coroner appeared to be a concern with the possible risk to their professional image, but they went on to explain how they would seek to cautiously intervene – it would "take a little longer", but the key is effective engagement with the family and the building of a meaningful account.

Another Coroner emphasized the cost and effort of organizing an inquest in support of their willingness to allow an unrepresented family a broader scope, and a common answer was that as long as questions were "within reason", they would be permitted. Where the line of "within reason" is drawn was not clear (Davis et al 2002, 50), but the role of other interested persons would play a role in determining it as

> 'if the hospital are fighting tooth and nail, that something is not relevant, then I am likely to take a slightly different line from if the hospital are completely relaxed about it, and I will give the family a greater degree of freedom and flexibility, so long as they are not getting silly about the boundaries of the inquiry.'

Another issue might be whether and whom to blame, and interviewees reflected on shifting to constrain family where they were seeking to assign blame, but this might also depend on how the questions were put:

> 'Obviously we are saddled with the fact that they should only ask appropriate questions and we should stop inappropriate questions but they are not lawyers, and I do always have in the back of my

mind that they need these answers, so I would probably only stop it if it was, well if it was aggressive, if it was about blame, although that is quite wide isn't it, you know if there is someone saying, you killed my Mum didn't you, that sort of thing I would stop. But if they were saying, well you didn't do this, that and the other, I would allow it, yes. I am not strict, I am probably a bit soft at times, I have more of a luxury of time than some of my colleagues in some of the more busy areas.'

Appropriateness acted as control, but it was a restraint which only exerted a pull on the progress of questions when the family were perceived to be hostile, causing a shift to emphasize the need to maintain order in the face of improper, disorderly conduct.

Disorder

'Sometimes family members can be quite abusive, quite personal, quite emotive, and quite adversarial – that is not often, occasionally they can be – and you have to protect the witnesses too, and I am trying to balance everything in court.' (Coroner)

Coroners described strategies for maintaining order when the cause of disorder is family. These included anticipating the possibility of disorder, and taking organizational and administrative steps to engage with the family, including having contact with them in advance "so it makes life easier to manage when it comes to the inquest", and making sure that correspondence was filed properly:

'The court originally organized case files with all communications in one file, and I said no, you file separately the interested persons communications, because the Coroner needs to see them in conducting any hearing. It is key to know what have they said and what have we said to them. And that is the backdrop to what you need to know in court; they have made a moan for 3 months about X, and how have we responded to it? If you know that you are in a better position of how to handle them in court. A Coroner must consider submissions of IPs on how to conduct the inquest and what evidence to call.' (Coroner)

The possible attendance of the biological father in Vignette 3 prompted some of my interviewees to reflect on the possibility of violence and disorder in the hearing, with one Coroner stating that "I would ensure that I had police presence. I have had these situations where have had to keep people apart in case there is trouble".

Another Coroner would emphasize the dignity of the deceased to counter unrest, as well as 'certainly' reflecting on an appropriate space for the hearing:

'We normally get the officer to go and meet them and say that, to respect the deceased we would want you to behave in an appropriate way. If she was saying, look there are going to be real problems then we might have to get the police there. Certainly we would have to think about where we are going to hold the inquest, we might try and arrange it in the magistrate's court.'

The selection of a magistrate's court emphasizes ordering and formality, a fixed official space in which it is easier to contain, separate and restrain. The answer also highlights the key role of the officer in advance management, which was a theme another Coroner raised:

'The officers here are very good, you have got a pretty good sense of the what the family's concerns are and how they have been reacting, of when you are going to have issues to deal with, or indeed when they are going to be so quiet that you are going to need to be more proactive, and so I would know at the outset usually of how to handle things, and what has been said before and been explained.'

Crucially in this account, disorder and the need to handle the family does not just arise in case of a family expressing agitation, but also a family who are too quiet and who need to be encouraged. Their passivity and reticence are perceived to put at risk efforts by the Coroner to create a space for combining accountabilities, meaning that there is a risk that the inquest will lack the contextual and contingent, undermining the prospect of combining both a meaningful and expert explanation of death. Finally, disorder was not limited to inappropriate questions, concerns with aggression and the risk of violence or the overly passive family; other accounts reflected on engagement, order, and control of a confident and potentially unruly family attending en masse, even where a spokesperson has been nominated to speak on their behalf. The following quotes set out two examples of these common narratives:

'It doesn't stop the others asking questions, that has happened, particularly with schoolteachers for some reason, one of them acts as the main advocate and usually you have several, and you'll find the brother, who is possibly another school teacher, still wants to ask questions, but I don't mind.' (Coroner)

'If they come mob-handed you know, lots of them, and they don't know any law, they can all start chipping in and if you are not careful you can lose control so you need to make clear, and I do this through my officers, make sure before they come that they know that they have got to choose a spokesman to put their questions. Then when you start you say right, and you take them through what an inquest is all about, it is a fact finding inquiry it is not a trial da-da-da, all the usual preamble, and you say and I hope that you've someone to be nominated and they will usually, yes it's him, but once you get going inevitably Uncle Joe, Uncle Bert and Auntie Joan and cousin Amanda will start chipping in and I'm afraid sometimes you have to say I am sorry remember what I said I will only hear one of you, or if you are generous, and I try to be generous, I might say well I will come to you in a minute but one at a time, you can't all chip in at once and we will take it in a logical sequence, it can't be all butting in and chipping in at the same time.' (Coroner)

In these accounts of a nominated single spokesperson and the limited engagement of others – a common theme in my interviews – the emphasis is on the engagement of the whole family. It is noticeable in the second quote that the Coroner refers to uncles, aunts and cousins, all of which are outside the automatic interested person categories. In both accounts, the limits to their involvement do not flow from questions of legal right or their status in inquest law, but from a concern over the ordering and management of the hearing. These Coroners understand their role as combining order with an effort to enable accountability founded on the engagement of a tacit community. That task is easier for the Coroner if one office holder acts for that community, but my interviewees did not understand their role as insisting on it. This task of management can be easier still when the office holder nominated on their behalf is not one of their own, but is instead a lawyer. They can free up the Coroner to do their job:

'If I am representing anyone I am representing the deceased, and if no one is there to represent [the family], I have to do my job harder. I am more likely to be difficult, I adjourned quite a testy inquest relatively recently to take more evidence, because I was dissatisfied with the questions I was being given, and there was nobody there to fight for this person who was unrepresented.'

A 'lawyered-up' hearing

Lawyers representing the family mean that someone other than the Coroner is going through records 'with a fine toothed comb' and while the Coroner sees themselves as engaged in a process which will combine forms of accountability and effectively enable family participation, lawyers can be a useful part of the team. One Coroner used other lawyers in attendance to check if there were any legal issues or advice that the unrepresented family needed, asking: "Is there a matter, even if it is not the interests of your client, that should be drawn to their attention?" Another Coroner emphasized the importance of the perspective of lawyers for the family in a complex case:

> 'The best inquests in the more complex cases are in fact a bit of a team effort, the better the representation, the better the quality of the inquiry. It may be impossible for me to see or recognize a particular issue or a piece of information which you may be privy to and which I may not be privy to. I have always thought, and this is a personal view, in what we might describe as the Article 2 cases, there truly should be no issue about means — the family should be publicly funded if the State has any involvement, if not you are getting a completely unbalanced line of inquiry, and they always say well it is up to the Coroner, but it is just not fair because how are they going to participate properly? It is becoming more and more of a problem for those trying to seek funding.'

Without lawyers for the family in those Article 2 cases, it is an unbalanced team — a situation described by Walsh as the state represented by 'an army of lawyers while the family sits alone' (Walsh 2015, 1).[6] Obtaining legal aid for families is increasingly challenging in the context of 'austerity justice' (Hynes 2012) with indications of errors in decisions which could lead to eligible families not getting legal aid (Nicholls 2014, 24). One interviewee highlighted that a potential civil claim can be a way of families obtaining legal representation,[7] but suggested that for most families, this was a route to obtaining funding so that they could meaningfully engage in the inquest.

---

[6] Peter Walsh, the Chief Executive of AvMA, critiques a Ministry of Justice assertion that families do not need representation in inquests, arguing that 'our own experience … which overwhelmingly suggests that the outcomes of inquests from the families' point of view are very significantly improved when they have been represented than when they have not' (Walsh 2015, 1).

[7] As lawyers can reclaim some inquest costs as costs preparatory for a civil claim if they are awarded inter partes costs in a subsequent claim. See *Roach v Home Office* [2009] EWHC 312; and *Fullick v Commissioner of Police of the Metropolis* [2019] EWHC 1941 (QB).

In contrast, another Coroner framed the factor of subsequent litigation as a risk which undermined the inquest hearing:

'Quite often I have barristers in front of me, which makes my inquests last longer, makes them more complex, makes them cost more money, and you can tell there is an eye to litigation at the end, that is happening increasingly, cases that eight years ago I would have dealt with in an hour will now take half a day.'

In this framing it is the lawyers who make the inquest more complex, taking up more time and money without improving that hearing. Comments which understood the role of family in terms of a more limited inquiry also suggested that family representation specifically could be the cause of problems, as "if a family is represented and are seeking answers to difficult questions, it is bound to put people on a defensive mode and it is bound to have a knock-on effect".

Thus, representation is part of constructing the hearing and the way in which the inquest proceeds (see also Warwick Inquest Group 1985, 47). While lawyers for the family may be asking the same questions and are likely to be asking them so that a family can engage in the process, they will be held to a higher standard of relevance and are more likely to be restrained from pursuing a line of questioning than if the family was unrepresented. This may be because the involvement of lawyers forces a narrower focus by all involved on technical questions, because of a concern with subsequent litigation, and because there is less need with lawyers representing the family to build a process and a relationship (although, as mentioned earlier, some Coroners saw lawyers as part of a team generating a meaningful and thorough inquiry). It was also revealing that where there were lawyers and the possibility of blame, the lawyer for the family could be deployed as an ally to help to constrain the family

'if you have got a particularly, difficult is not the right word for the family, but a family that don't quite understand what it is all about and want to have a trial and hang someone out to dry, then it is helpful to have a lawyer who is familiar with inquest work who can help you to say to the family look I'm sorry that really isn't a matter for the inquest.'

The lawyer here acts as buffer, helping the Coroner. However, in contrast, there are also instances in which it is not the family but the competence of their representative which is perceived to cause problems for the system. Many Coroners made comments to the effect that poor representation "increases the pressure on the Coroner and officer", and one Coroner expressed concern with changes in rules which "mean that anyone could be representing the family, it doesn't have to be a lawyer, it could be the office cat if you want".

Whether the family has a poorly qualified representative or none, a concern focused on a technocratic form of accountability emphasizes formal legal equality and the difficulties that can arise for the Coroner:

'If everyone else comes to the inquest with a lawyer and if the family doesn't, it puts the family and the Coroner into a difficult position. The Coroner is supposed to be neutral conducting a fact-finding inquiry, and yet is expected to assist the family to tease out the real issues in the case, and there is a real danger that he or she will be seen to be partisan by the lawyers for the police or the prison service or whomever.'

Partisanship on the part of the inquest system is a longstanding concern from the perspective of those engaged with deaths in custody (see, inter alia, Warwick Inquest Group 1985, 43–44), but some of my interviewees expressed concern with appearing partisan in favour of the bereaved rather than the state. One Coroner described how "I went to watch one of my assistant deputies and it made me step back and think about how I approached it because [they were] gushing all over the family trying to be nice, but for somebody watching it, it didn't look fair".

The representation of technocratic neutral objectivity was perceived to be at risk, as the Coroner went on to describe:

'It looked as though possibly there was some obvious bias towards the family, and I think you have got to be careful with that. I know they are there to find out why their child or husband or wife died, and we are all there to support them in that, but I think people can do it, whilst still making them the focus, approaching it in a professional way as well.'

Lawyers for the family help to insulate the Coroner from suggestions they are not neutral and impartial, and if they are not there, it makes it harder for the Coroner to maintain this neutral stance. In contrast, a framing oriented towards combining accountabilities is less concerned with the appearance of bias and is instead focused on a concern with making sure that the family can participate properly. In complex cases, this means they should have lawyers, but if they do not, there is an acknowledgement that while the family do not have any more rights than anyone else, their understanding of what is going on is a central concern of the inquest. This framing focuses on seeking to enable them to bring their account into the law:

'I will say to the family, this is the process in which you can make submissions about conclusions. What I am going to do is to go to the lawyers first, see what they say, and then I will come to you – so they see how it is done – and I will say, you can make submissions, but what has been said by X seems to me to be the sort of things that you might be saying in this instance, and I might help them through with it, so that they understand.' (Coroner)

The Coroner needs the family to understand the process, to understand their role in the process and to understand what the conclusion can achieve. The emphasis on channelling their understanding might be framed as an endeavour to restrain and constrain them, but is also a recognition of the need of the system for the family. Thus the Coroner is going through the process of training and enabling the family because the system needs the family to be engaged with understanding how the deceased died. Reflections on ways in which the hearing is made more or less public, involving the jury and the family further, illustrate this theme.

A more public hearing: the family and the jury

In the contemporary inquest, inquests with juries are rare, occurring in around 1–2 per cent of cases (Chief Coroner 2020, 9). A jury must be called in certain circumstances[8] and there is also a discretion open to the Coroner to call a jury if there is 'sufficient reason for doing so'.[9] One Coroner told me: "I tend to use my discretion quite freely to sit with a jury." I asked whether they would exercise a discretion when people don't request it, and the Coroner paused, before stating "I have, but it would have been very infrequent".[10] The implication, even with a Coroner who perceives themselves as often choosing to sit with a jury, is that where there is discretion, it is family who will initiate the process which leads to a jury being empanelled. Another Coroner expanded on this: "There are sometimes applications, I mean no Coroner in their right mind would have a jury for fun, I know we have the discretion to do it, it is just so much work."

That additional work includes the need to take detailed notes for their summing up, but it is not only this:

---

[8]   Detailed in CJA 2009, s 7(2), including violent or unnatural deaths or death from an unknown cause in custody or state detention, deaths resulting from an act or omission of the police in the execution of their duty, or from a notifiable accident, poisoning or disease (for example, a health and safety breach).

[9]   CJA 2009, s 7(3).

[10] Although not always; see Tweedie and Ward (1989).

'As soon as you make a case a jury case it takes three times as long, the amount of effort I have to put in is enormous.' (Coroner)

'I have to consider their breaks, you can't do so much evidence in a day, I have to make sure they are understanding the issues.' (Coroner)

Critically, just having a jury is inherently risky:

'I have to be very careful that any statement I have made is supported, and that my directions are absolutely water-tight because I am going to be judicially reviewed if I am directing the jury wrongly, so there is a lot more work for me. It is exhilarating, it is exciting, it is a huge challenge, it is exhausting, it is legally more risky.' (Coroner)

In relation to a framing concerned with constraining the ambit of the hearing, one Coroner was very clear that changes which meant that deaths in mental health secure units had to be heard with a jury would significantly undermine the inquest into those deaths:

'I am an expert in this field and I genuinely think I really don't need a jury and I am running a deeper, fuller and more complex inquiry without them because I can really explore the evidence in ways that you don't have to simplify when you have a jury. It inhibits me. I am really really fed up about it, and I really don't believe it is going to deliver any better service in this jurisdiction.'

The framing is concerned with the specific risk that the shift undermines technocratic accountability. The necessity of making the information accessible to a jury inhibits effective expert interrogation, investigation and rule setting. In contrast, Pannick argues that the presence of an inquest jury ensures public confidence in the rule of law and, critically, opens up the case to public scrutiny, refuting possible allegations of a cover-up (Pannick 2010, 31–32). It is a perspective which links closely to scholarship on an active jury, which argues that jury note taking and question asking means a greater opportunity to minimize 'inaccurate juror decision making' (Friedland 1990, 192; see also Scott 2017). More controversially, in the US context, Friedland also argues that 'an active jury model would fulfil the conceptual role of the jury as an important democratic participant in the American trial process' (Friedland 1990, 220; see also Heuer and Penrod, 1990). Outside an individual courtroom, his claim has been supported by research on what Harris (1995) describes as the 'communitarian' function of the jury. This is the idea that 'by obliging men to turn their attention to affairs which are not exclusively their own [the jury] rubs off that individual egotism which is the rust of society' (De Tocqueville 1945, 295). The jury room provides a 'constitutional teaching moment' (Ferguson 2013a, 2013b), and extensive scholarship by Gastil and others which focuses on civic participation has included the striking finding that taking part in a jury results in an increased propensity to vote (Gastil 2008b).[11] Examining case law in which courts have implicitly considered the communitarian function of the jury, Harris contends that the US Supreme Court has given tacit support for it. In particular, he notes that the Court gives weight to the importance of the jury for community participation and education, as well as the symbolic importance of the jury in a ritualized display which maintains societal faith in the administration of justice (Harris 1995, 805).

Another Coroner emphasized this concern with ensuring faith in the process, but – linking the family to that analysis – framed the role of the jury through a concern to create a space for meaningful revelation for the family:

'Where it is a matter of a public interest, and the family, and this is not one of the criteria under the Coroners and Justice Act, it just all comes within my discretion, I sometimes find that it is important in certain cases where the family are very hung up about what's happened, to the extent that, they would feel better with the case being judged by their peers, and I know it is not judging is it – but do you know what I mean – the facts judged by their peers rather than from some perhaps case hardened Coroner.'

This Coroner told a story about a complex case which involved mental health treatment and multiple agencies, and concluded that it was "a classic example of where the jury deciding on the facts, looking at whether or not there was systemic problems in the different agencies; to me it would have been an appropriate case in any event, even if I hadn't had to do it under statute anyway".

The complexity of the case and the concern with revealing systemic issues are factors in both accounts. In one, the simplification needed in jury cases means that the need to achieve technocratic accountability organizes public interest concerns in a very different way from the second, for whom accountabilities are combined by the engagement of the jury. In a similar vein, another Coroner told me a story about a case in which a jury member asked a critical question that the Coroner and six sets of lawyers had missed,

---

[11] See, for example, Gastil, Deess and Weiser 2002; Gastil and Weiser 2006; Gastil et al 2008; Gastil et al 2010; Dzur 2012.

arguing that "jurors have a quaint ability to see something afresh and ask something that is very helpful. Of course it goes the other way, and you may get irrelevant questions".

The jury combine irrelevant questions with penetration through a fresh perspective, but they also require the Coroner to think more carefully about the exposure of evidence:

Ed: Do you prefer to sit with a jury?

Coroner: (*Pause*) From a personal point of view it breaks it up a bit, but that is not a good reason. It makes you think sometimes more deeply about the questions you ask, because of course, in the Coroner's court as you know, the Coroner starts by basically dealing with the evidence in chief. When there is a jury present, it needs greater attention to detail, because when they are not there, people know most of the facts in any event, but a jury has seen nothing, and I think in certain cases that is an area where Coroners could improve on. You get into a pattern of how you ask questions, and we need to turn it up a notch when it comes to dealing with a jury.

Ed: So is the implication of that that certain things would be assumed if there is not a jury?

Coroner: Yeah.

Ed: And it would be a quicker process?

Coroner: Yes, we push on, we can't push on with a jury, or if you do, you soon know about it because the jury will then ask questions, because of course they can ask questions.

Ed: And will the family play that role in circumstances where there isn't a jury?

Coroner: The difference there is that the family have, now they have got disclosure, they have got an understanding about the case, so you know very often I will say to a witness, 'we are aware of the background', but a jury aren't going to know that.

The role of the jury is therefore critical in bringing evidence out at the hearing.[12] An inquest might be heard in public, but facts can be assumed and evidence abridged unless the jury is present to force the hearing to go slowly and from the beginning. The family's role in the investigation before

---

[12]   With interesting parallels to Duff et al's discussion of juries and communicative participation; see Duff et al (2007, 220–223).

the hearing makes their role fundamentally different. They are aware of the background, and disclosure to them is an integral part of enabling the inquest to abbreviate the evidence. In a hearing without a jury, 98–99 per cent of hearings, it is thus the family who enable the conjoining of efficient truncation of evidence with a narrative of public justice. It is their meaningful interaction that matters, and their actions can result in making the public hearing less of a public event.

A less public hearing

At the opposite end of the scale, Coroners discussed the possibilities of resolving concerns away from the public hearing, with the emphasis on the role of disclosure in answering questions. One Coroner stated that questions which were "not too wide or difficult" could be answered before the inquest "and that saves the need for the witness to come to court". Sometimes, as was discussed in Chapter 6, these are resolved through disclosure to the family, while in other cases, Coroners described the way they sought to enable family to resolve issues:

'In this area we arrange for the hospital to meet with the family in advance of the inquest, and it is minuted. Most of the problems in the hospital death are around communication and not understanding, and they suddenly feel that the hospital has buttoned down the hatches as soon as the person has died, and they can't get the answers, so we waste a lot of time at inquest, them finding out things that they could have easily found out prior to the inquest had the hospital been open with them. So we have this agreement with [the hospital] that they will meet with the family if the family want to, with the senior staff involved and as I say it is minuted. In 80% of the cases it does help the inquest.' (Coroner)

The focus is on time saving and efficiency, but an underlying concern with the needs of procedural justice remains, leading the Coroner to emphasize the formality of the meeting, the minutes providing protection and holding those present to account. A different Coroner was less concerned with the risks of impropriety and contradictory understandings, and saw the meeting as a linked but separate process, engendering flexibility and the possibility of a more amicable approach:

'I will often encourage families to have a meeting with the consultants beforehand if they want to or indeed afterwards so that they can sit around the table and actually have a slightly more friendly discussion and explanation, which sometimes can be terribly helpful to clarify things which they previously thought were set in stone which were never set in stone.'

In both cases, the effect is to take issues out of the inquest, and another Coroner also highlighted this possibility, stating that a family may have had concerns, but: "The thing to remember is, it may well be that all the concerns they may have had have been dealt with outside of the inquest process." The framing seeks to promote the meaningful engagement of the family, and also emphasizes the role of the pre-hearing decisions in determining the community around the deceased. Instead of evidence and engagement in a publicly accessible hearing, the ability to engage is determined away from the public gaze, potentially reinforcing formal family ties and so potentially excluding other forms of kinship (Reimers 2011), undermining the possibility of community forms of accountability.

This is further illustrated by the role of family in enabling what one Coroner described as an "office inquest", in which no witnesses attend and evidence is read out by the Coroner. One Coroner explained that they would write to a family who had said they did not propose to attend and would tell them they would only be reading out written evidence: "But if any other member of the family wants to attend, then will you please let me know because it may be necessary to set another date when I know I will have the physical presence of a witness."

Witnesses introduce cost and can make arranging the date of an inquest more difficult. They also introduce formality and ceremony, and the possibilities of surprise, revelation and spectacle. Their presence makes an inquest a more accessible and substantive public event. Therefore, in the preceding account of the Coroner, it is important that it is not simply the fact that family have concerns which provokes calling witnesses, but the very possibility of any family attending. Another Coroner provided a specific account of a case in which they suggested that had the family been involved, witnesses would have been called. The story related to an investigation into a death in a care home, when an elderly person had rolled out of bed when the side of the bed was down. The Coroner collected evidence and "I looked at that file and had slight concerns about risk assessments and how this could have happened, but on seeing these reports had been undertaken subsequently, I was satisfied that whatever steps needed to be taken had been taken", so in the end the Coroner read out the evidence and did not call witnesses.

It is not solely the approach of family which determines the decision to call witnesses and, as with the Coroner's initial concerns in the earlier case, one Coroner emphasized that in cases of "public interest" witnesses would have to be called. In other cases, the approach of family is key, particularly where the death was "let's say a suicide. Husband is found hanging in the garage, we investigate it, we provide them with facts, disclosure if they want it, and then we do a summary and that is read out".

Media reporting, particularly sensationalist or inaccurate reporting of suicides, can cause great distress to the bereaved (see, inter alia, Barraclough and Shepherd 1977; Harwood et al 2002; Biddle 2003), and attempts have been made to reduce this distress, with, for example, the Wright Committee recommending that the press should be prohibited from publishing an account of the inquest in cases of suicide, and that suicide should be replaced by a verdict that the deceased died by their own hand, with no enquiry into the state of mind of the deceased (Wright Report 1936, 65). In the current system, an attending family may have the impact of reducing the prospect of a suicide conclusion (Tait and Carpenter 2013b),[13] and in suicide cases, Coroners are often sympathetic to the desire for bereaved families to keep information from a intrusive media (Davis et al 2002, 33–34), with evidence of Coroners adopting strategic approaches to the management of publicly available information in suicide cases (Gregory 2014, 10–11; see also Binns and Arnold 2020). As the preceding account indicates, one way in which the information which is available can be limited is if the family "don't want to engage in the process of an inquest".

As well as a concern with privacy, that lack of engagement might be because the family don't see any need for the inquest, and one Coroner sympathized with that:

'In quite a lot of my cases, the family have said it is absolutely straightforward, there is no issues in the case, quite often they will say please Coroner get on and deal with it on the documents alone, we don't want to come, I have quite a lot of those. Sometimes I sit thinking to myself this is a complete waste of time, occasionally because no one is making a fuss, family is happy, but I have to do the inquest for technical reasons, what for? To what purpose?'

The death is unambiguous and uncomplicated, the family are not fussed and consequently the Coroner is left with a rump technical duty with dubious purpose, open but not accessible, public in only the most formal terms. In such cases, it is the family – who are unhappy and who are making a fuss – who shift the inquest from perfunctory tedium to meaningful investigation. One Coroner reflected on this impact of the family in relation to all of their cases:

---

[13] Although it is interesting to contrast my (not necessarily representative) interviewees' assertions that family members now attended more hearings with the rise in suicide verdicts since 2007; see Coroners Statistics (2014, 9).

'Families differ, don't they, greatly, and the truth is, depending on the nature of the family, it can certainly influence the length and comprehensive nature of the inquest. Apart from the family obviously I have a statutory duty to determine those four facts and I do that, but if it is a very active family who have got lots of questions, that can expand the nature of the evidence at the inquest, so it does make a difference. If the family show no interest, have no issues, then it can be a more swift inquest.'

The family's attitude was a "very big determining factor" in the comprehensiveness of the inquest for this Coroner, affecting the detail, the focus, the range and the length of the inquest hearing.

The significant influence of the family on what will be heard in the public space mirrors similar developments in civil procedure (Fiss 1984; Luban 1995), which have been criticized by scholars for undermining public justice. Reflecting on these developments, for example, Hadfield and Ryan argue that the civil courtroom provides 'an arena in which the experience of democratic equality is made available' (Hadfield and Ryan, 2013, 93).[14] The contemporary emphasis on pre-court settlement fails to recognize the importance of the court space for lived experience of democracy, reducing the possibility that 'conflicts do not belong exclusively to the disputants or to the government; [but] give the public a place in which to interpret, own, or disown what has occurred' (Resnik and Curtis 2011, 302). However, the public and the public space in these accounts needs to be carefully picked apart (on which, see, for example, Hynes, Gill and Tomlinson et al 2020), and risks being presented as detached from kin. What the involvement of family in pre-hearing processes potentially holds out is the generation of a more contextual explanation for those linked to the deceased, who are able to play a role in the dissemination of wider narratives. Not limited to their ability to close the hearing down, this also includes their ability – from the perception of the Coroner – to construct an inquest as a place in which an engaged family will receive explanation and understanding.

A hearing with meaningful revelation, explanation and closure?

The need for family to understand was a key theme in my interviews (see also Davis et al 2002, 47). My interviewees were keen for family to attend the hearing, with one stating that since the new Rules, "it is more common

---

[14] For alternative perspectives on the role of the trial, see also Jaconelli (2002) and Duff et al (2007).

practice that people are almost encouraged to come to the inquest". As Chapter 6 suggested, if they are not there, it causes a problem for the inquest:

Coroner: We do have a number of deaths where there isn't anyone. That's not to say family don't exist, but because of breakdowns in relationships and marriages etc, it may be that the family are there but have absolutely no interest in the death, for all I know they are organizing a dance for the occasion, there can be that degree of antipathy. It is a bit unkind but it exists.

Ed: Commonly?

Coroner: No, happily no, it is uncommon.

Ed: Is that something you have noticed any change?

Coroner: It has always been there, it is just a bit sad when we have to deal with it because it makes it difficult to know who, if anybody, we are trying to satisfy, as an individual. I mean obviously the registrar wants to know, general records office have an interest, everyone who acts on the statistics we generate does.

As this Coroner sees it, it is a bit unkind to note situations where a family has broken down and has no interest in a death; happily, such a scenario is uncommon. Where it does occur, families can be seen to be resisting endeavours by the system to construct a frame in which forms of accountability are combined, leaving the inquest asking the question of who, if anybody, it is seeking to satisfy. Critically, in relation to questions of dignity, the actions of such a family leave the dignity of the inquest thinned out, falling back upon a framing of law-as-risk-avoidance, a technocratic formulation, focused on legal requirements and official statistics, and silent as to meaningful revelation. Focused on the public status of the dead, it 'is a bit sad' to be separated from the attachments of an involved family, office holders refusing to take up their office, leaving the inquest dissatisfied. If there is no one there to represent the family, then, as one Coroner explained, "I have got to think what is it that that person would ask, so that actually I am conducting it fairly, and it is more difficult with nobody there, at least I have got somebody who can ask those questions".

The involvement of family makes the inquest fairer. This Coroner was discussing the long-lost sister in Vignette 4, and it was not the sister's knowledge which is key, but rather her connection to the deceased and her resultant ability to help create a space where accountabilities can be combined, to think about and ask the types of questions which the system needs family to ask.

Where family do attend, all my interviewees emphasized that they sought to enable them to understand what happened to the deceased. For one Coroner, this included 'translation' of complex evidence and putting their own expertise to one side: "In court I am as naïve as possible. I will ask the simplest of questions, because I need to get the family to understand it."

As this quote re-emphasizes, the production of family understanding is obligatory, a foundational requirement of the inquest. This task was often expressed in therapeutic terms, with an emphasis on closure, and, as noted earlier, often meant permitting questions which went beyond the question of cause of death. One Coroner related how they would go further and act in expectation of such questions, as

> 'this is their opportunity to ask questions of the witnesses themselves, so it could be something as simple as, do you think he suffered before he died, and we have to anticipate that kind of question because that is so common, and I often ask that to the doctor who has certified death and I think they are sometimes, not lying to you, because that is too strong a word, but for the sake of the family they may be being a little economical with the truth, so they will say something along the lines of "I am pretty sure this was instantaneous, they would have known nothing about it" but they don't know that, the doctor, but it is a nice thing for the family to go away with, not worrying about that aspect.'

The anticipation of the Coroner and the 'not lying' response of the doctor are oriented towards protection of the family from the risk of further distress. They demonstrate the ways in which attention to risk can shift the inquest from a jurisdiction focused on enabling family engagement and understanding to a focus on a paternalistic well-intentioned granting of understanding. The intention is pro-therapeutic, but the impact can be anti-therapeutic and can undermine therapeutic engagements with the law (Dix 1998; Freckelton 2007, 593). As Davis et al note, for family members 'the inquest can be an event of enormous symbolic significance', and contemporary Coroners have to respond to a wide range of feelings from bereaved individuals (Davis et al 2002, 70). However, as Howarth argues, rather than devising and imposing a model of grief, it is essential that engagement with grieving recognizes the differentiated experiences of the bereaved, the aim being to 'amplify the whispered communication across the boundary between the living and the dead that has hitherto been muffled by the noisy, dominant discourse and prescriptive professional rituals of modernity' (Howarth 2000, 136; see also Howarth 2007). An approach to the family's understanding which seeks to manage and protect can drown out this whispered communication, whether the risk is perceived to be hurt to the family or whether, as in the next quote, the risk appears to arise from the family's approach to the investigation:

> 'I have done well over a thousand inquests of all types and most people just want to know what happened. Even if someone has done something dreadful, doctors are really good at this, they will get in the stand, they will say, "I did this this and this, I am so sorry, I should have realized I wish I had read the notes better, I should have realised they were allergic to penicillin, I can't believe I prescribed it I am so sorry", and that is often all the family wants actually. Doctors are really good at it, or even if they have not done anything wrong, they will get to the end of their evidence and then they'll turn round and they'll say, "excuse me, I'd just like to address the family, I am really sorry, I give you my sympathy for your loss", and it is devastating, it works really well in court.' (Coroner)

The apology is devastating, from the Latin *devastare*, to lay waste completely. From the approving perspective of the onlooking Coroner, the complete laying of waste is a martial move specific to the court, leaving any perceived family strategy in the room desolate and empty. It is perceived as a feint which works really well, leaving the family disarmed, their objectives simultaneously achieved and apparently destroyed (although it is important to note that the apology and the acceptance of that apology may be no less genuine for that perception by the Coroner). The interpretation of the apology thus frames the family as inherently antagonistic, despite just wanting to know, and a risk to be managed.

The devastating apology here is an adjunct to the main business of the inquest, occurring at the end of the gathering of the witness' evidence. In contrast, a framing which is engaged in combining forms of accountability takes the meaningfulness of the hearing as its focal point, creating space for the family to generate their own understandings, as one Coroner described, as quoted in Chapter 1:

> 'There are a range of simple inquests that I could just read, but I feel if an interested person needs to understand an explanation, it is right that they have somebody to ask the questions to, even though I understand it all, because I can't give the answer, and nor can I explain what is down there. Probably the best example is a cot death. In many cases I don't need to call a witness, the pathologist and clinician give the expected results and I could read the whole thing, but how terribly unsatisfactory is that for some families? The family may want to ask questions like, 'did it matter that I put them on their side?' and that is part of closure, so depending on the case

I would try to call either the pathologist or the clinician, it depends a bit on the case and circumstances but I would try to have a witness for them to question if the family want. Occasionally the family are too distressed and don't want it. I suppose that increases my backlog doesn't it, because it adds another hour, a bit more work, but I think that is right.' (Coroner)

These questions and answers may not be needed for the Coroner's purposes, but their exclusion, when they are desired, is terribly unsatisfactory. This Coroner is again engaged in the language of therapy and closure, but the emphasis is on creating a space for family's differentiated experiences of bereavement. However, this space can be risky. One Coroner described a road traffic inquest in which a child had been killed. The driver who had run over the child was very distressed at what had happened, and at the end of the hearing, the family asked to say something. The Coroner acceded to their request nervously

'and of course, I don't know what they are going to say, but they say something like, could you make it clear to the driver of the car that we don't blame him in any way and we hope he has not been adversely affected – I remember being considerably affected by it – they said it's not his fault, no blame on him at all.'

In addition, as the rise in narrative conclusions illustrates,[15] it is the creation of a space out of which a contextual conclusion can be produced (Scott Bray 2010, 587). Importantly, the 2009/2013 amendments, which turned the inquest verdict into the inquest conclusion, left the contents of that conclusion unprescribed, beyond a direction that 'straying from the list [of approved short form conclusions] will usually be unwise' (Chief Coroner 2015, 6). Coroners and juries can thus use a short-form conclusion of their own choice, or replace or supplement a short form with a narrative conclusion.[16] Many of my interviewees described the conclusion as important for constructing the family's understanding of what happened, and the Chief Coroner emphasizes this, along with the importance of 'clarity', describing the importance of reaching a conclusion

---

[15] Narrative verdicts/conclusions are included with other non-standard conclusions in the unclassified category, which has risen from 1 per cent of verdicts in 1995 to 21 per cent of conclusions in 2020 (see Coroners Statistics 2020).

[16] With some limitations and directions for the use of such conclusions, see Matthews (2014, 311–347) and Chief Coroner (2015). It should also be noted that even a short-form conclusion will include the inquest's answer to the question of 'how' a person died with a short summary of their findings of fact.

which is 'accessible for bereaved families and public alike, and also clear for statistical purposes'.[17]

In relation to establishing this conclusion, Tait and Carpenter (2013a, 2013b; see Carpenter et al 2015b) have highlighted the role of the family in influencing conclusions, and while my focus was on the hearing and not on the conclusion, one Coroner did reflect on this in detail in my interview:

> '[C]losure is important so that is partly about addressing the issues and worries as far as we can do it through the process of the inquest, and it is partly about reaching conclusions that seem appropriate to that. One of the ways I do that is I have a lower threshold for doing a narrative conclusion. If the family appear to need an explanation, or if there are complexities, my worry is if I provide a short form conclusion of natural causes, and button it all up, that it looks as if I have just dismissed everything. I know in law I might be entitled to do that, but if there are recorded one or two relevant circumstances, I think that the family are often happy that they have been listened to and it is there. The statisticians don't like it, I don't know if the Chief Coroner likes it, but I think that sometimes that's appropriate.'

The approach of the Coroner dismisses arguments concerned with contingency and complexity, and their attention is instead on a meaningful conclusion which recognizes the participating family. As the Coroner notes, the rise has left statisticians concerned about accurately coding deaths (Hill and Cook 2011), but may be helpful for more nuanced contextual studies of death (see Brown 2014), and has to be considered in the context of other critiques of the accuracy of death statistics, particularly in relation to suicide (see, inter alia, Atkinson 1978; Cooper and Milroy 1995; Tait and Carpenter 2013b; Palmer et al 2015). However, concerns about statistical accuracy and the function of death statistics are not limited to suicide (see Prior 1985; Pemberton 1988), and it was revealing that in another set of reflections on conclusions, a Coroner demonstrated two sides of this debate. Firstly, reflecting on the importance of statistics coming out of inquests in relation to deaths from asbestos, the Coroner stated that the key was that "suddenly we get some reliable statistics on how prevalent it is" and this enabled action to be taken against widespread use of asbestos. The same Coroner later stated that over the past decade, they had witnessed a "considerable uplift"

---

[17] Chief Coroner 2015, 6. The Chief Coroner emphasizes that this means that 'wherever possible Coroners should conclude with a short-form conclusion' and that long narrative verdicts in comparison 'achieve neither clarity nor accessibility [and] make it difficult to assess for statistical purposes' (at 6 and 8).

in criticism of doctors where individuals had undergone elective surgery which had gone wrong and resulted in death. The Coroner's concern was that "I suppose misadventure would cover it, as willing acceptance of a known risk, but misadventure doesn't clarify it to a lot of bereaved people, who think misadventure means someone has done something wrong". The attention of the Coroner was therefore not on the collation of statistics, but was rather directed to making sure the outcome avoided the risk of blame. They described their practice in such circumstances of crafting a conclusion "to make it clear" to the family that the death was a result of medical intervention, but that the doctor was blameless.

Conclusion

The inquest hearing needs family; their attendance may arouse concerns with ordering, but the absence of kin poses a greater threat to the undertaking. They may embody, connect and channel a wider tacit community, and they can precipitate the transformation of the hearing from formally public into a substantively public space, expanding the focus of the hearing, provoking the need for the presence of witnesses or a jury, and connecting the death to concerns of dignity and a narrative of an individual lived life. However, perhaps paradoxically, opening up to family can simultaneously act to limit the public nature of the hearing itself, meaning that families do not see the need to attend, or enabling the curtailing of evidence made available in the public space.

This public space is one ostensibly directed towards reaching a conclusion, but as Davis et al argue, the conclusion of an inquest is only a small part of the purpose of the investigation.[18] Nevertheless, it can be a very important part from the perspective of the family, and my interviewees highlighted many of those reasons, including a risk that families blamed themselves for the circumstances resulting in death. One Coroner felt it was important that

> 'where someone is blaming themselves, by having an inquest where they are exonerated, I am not saying that an inquest is there to exonerate people, but where it is so clear and it is said to them that they would have died anyway, then it brings them that bit of closure.'

---

[18] For Davis et al (2002, 59–60), this is a point particularly powerfully made in relation to road traffic accidents; they argue that it is 'implausible' to regard inquests into deaths on the roads as being directed towards a verdict, as they will invariably result in a conclusion of road traffic accident (now changed to collision, unless the high threshold of unlawful killing is met; see Matthews 2020, Chapter 13, paragraphs 46–59 and paragraph 65).

This quote encapsulates the wider ambiguity of the inquest. It is a space which can be presented as required only to answer four limited questions and record the details required by the Births and Deaths Registration Act 1953 but this is only the starting point for a jurisdiction which can be understood as playing a much more substantial role in explaining, revealing and requiring justifications for an individual death.

8

Reimagining the Inquest

Introduction

The key conceptual link between the theoretical resources in which I have drawn in my analysis – jurisdiction, systemic decision making, kinship and family – is the ways in which they are continually constituted and reconstituted through practices. I have argued that the inquest can be conceptualized through these practices as a process of accountability – of communicating the circumstances of death, where the circumstances of death are revealed and explained, and justifications are explored. However, the current system can be characterized as containing two competing perspectives: an understanding of the role of the Coroner and inquest, and the family within that process, as limited, serving a neutral expert accounting for death, and an emergent framing in which the participation of those connected to the deceased is conceived as essential to a meaningful accounting. The distinction lies in different representations of the law and different understandings of who participates in the development of that communication, how they participate and what the process produces. Family have to be involved, but this can be understood – as the former Chief Coroner suggested – as part of a system in which they listen to a medico-legal explanation for death or as a process in which the bereaved participate in the production of that explanation. In relation to either, it is a critical conceptual development. Where Prior (1989) argues that the inquest individualizes death, I suggest that the current system is represented as a forum which re-affirms, refashions and reveals interconnectedness, acknowledging the ways in which we are 'socially constituted bodies, attached to others [and] at risk of losing those attachments' (Butler 2006, 20). In this context, who is permitted to enter and is recognized as grieving is of vital importance (McIntosh 2016).

This role for the bereaved reveals a potential recalibration of the politics of death, in a shift in which kinship, connection and context is represented and understood as central to state responses to death. It is not inevitable, and the role for family can be sharply contested, in a system which, as evidence has shown,[1] can shut the bereaved out and focus solely on technocratic forms of accountability (see, for example, Aitken 2021) or exclude kin through a narrow interpretation of 'family'. It is also a shift with particular consequences in a case where kinship is absent or refuses the duties imposed upon it, or which might be critiqued as the state delegating responsibilities to family, or which might be transformed into a faux-therapeutic framing in which closure is purportedly granted to the attentive bereaved.

In this chapter, I draw together the threads from my preceding chapters into two parts. In the first part I reflect on policy and potential future directions of the inquest, before turning to provide concluding reflections on academic scholarship and the role and construction of kinship in the system, considering the ways in which practices interlink in the inquest process.

Future directions

Burney (2000) argues that the 20th-century inquest was a result of a productive interplay between narratives of scientific and legal expertise on the one hand and popular sovereignty on the other. Drawing on this, one way to reflect on future directions for the inquest is to conceive the contestation between forms of accountability as a productive tension which is in the process of generating a new forum for investigating death.

In this context, it is instructive to consider how other scholarship has considered ways to conceive of underlying tensions in the system. A compelling account is provided by Tait and Carpenter, who examine a tension in the Coronial role between understanding in the individual case as opposed to attention to governmental aims, suggesting there is a 'relative disregard for the governmental aspects of the Coronial role' (Tait and Carpenter 2013a, 8, 200). They query whether this means that Coroners have 'allocated themselves a role within' a 'therapeutic community', which Miller and Rose argue is enacted through a process of problematization, diagnosis and intervention (Miller and Rose 2008, 142–143). An analysis of the inquest founded on this would frame the Coroner as acting in a calculated way to resolve the psychological trauma caused by death. Drawing on their interviews with Coroners, Tait and Carpenter query whether the focus on closure means the inquest is part of 'the governance of subjective experience' (Tait and Carpenter 2013b, 101), but go on to counsel against simple binaries, concluding that: 'The English Coronial inquest appears to

---

[1] See, most recently, evidence submitted to the 2021 Justice Select Committee report (Justice Committee 2021).

have an equally complex relationship between its bureaucratic and pastoral functions, a relationship that has yet to be fully, or even partially, resolved' (Tait and Carpenter 2013b, 102).

Their account is provocative, but when viewed through a lens of accountability, the discord between pastoral and bureaucratic functions is not the critical productive tension in the contemporary jurisdiction. This is because they can be aligned in an individual case, with the system seeking to construct an outcome which responds to both functions, or they can be seen to be in direct contestation in a case. In relation to either, the approach to them (either as functions in tension with each other or complementing each other) can be characterized as essentially part of a technocratic formulation. In an individual case, this narrow conception of accountability can encompass both functions, as care is taken of the bereaved, and they are given – they listen to – explanations, and the inquest produces expert findings into death. Equally, they could be in tension with the Coroner choosing to privilege one over the other, as Tait and Carpenter suggest. In either case, the pastoral role is conceived as giving closure to the family and is tied up with their obedience (Foucault 2007; Biebricher 2011).

Instead, the productive tension at the core of the construction of the contemporary inquest – the competing relations which can be seen to be the cause of the (re)production of the jurisdiction and which points to future directions for the inquest – is that between representations and understandings of the inquest which seek to combine forms of accountability and those which frame the process as essentially technocratic. These two opposing perspectives compete, but can also be conceived as producing a system in which it is hard to see how some formerly central aspects of the system can be coherently sustained. These include the idea that a lack of adversarialism means that state funding for legal representation for bereaved kin is not necessary, even in contested hearings.

The limited access to legal representation for the bereaved is a longstanding concern for many (see, inter alia, Stone 1986, 21–22; Scraton and Chadwick 1987, 38; Green and Green 1992; Angiolini 2017, 213–217; Owen 2020, 79–83). The response from the state to arguments for more funding for advocacy has been to emphasize the inquisitorial nature of the inquest. However, as was discussed in Chapter 7, representatives for other interested persons[2] have an impact, and this is particularly impacted by representatives acting on behalf of the state. As the Justice Select Committee described, "it can be difficult for coroners to maintain an inquisitorial approach, particularly for complex inquests that involve many people and organizations, some of

---

[2]   And it is notable that such persons are regularly referred to as 'parties' – see, for example, the quote from *Joseph* in Chapter 4 and the Coroner quoted in Chapter 6.

whom may be seeking to limit their civil (or criminal) liability with the assistance of legal representation".

While the government has long resisted the extension of funding for lawyers for the bereaved, this is an increasingly difficult position to defend. It is telling that both understandings of the inquest outlined in this book point towards an extension of representation, as advocates are either needed to address what the Coroners' Society – in a triadic formulation – describes as an 'inequality of arms' (Justice Committee 2021, 22), or else are seen as essential for the effective participation of the bereaved who can otherwise be left 'feeling lost and unsupported and that their questions are not being considered' (Justice Committee 2021, 22; see also McIntosh 2016).

Another challenge for the system is to the conception of the inquest as a local service. This has been repeatedly criticized, including by the Chief Coroner (Chief Coroner 2020) and the Justice Select Committee (Justice Committee 2021), and can be contrasted with the development of a national medical examiner system (Harris 2017b; Department for Health and Social Care 2021). From a perspective of combined forms of accountability, the community is that of the bereaved and those connected to the deceased, not the area in which the Coroner sits, while a triadic framing would suggest that it is an anachronism that the Coroner remains a locally appointed and funded office.

While, as with representatives for the bereaved, a critical concern for central government is the cost of change, many local authorities are struggling financially following post-2010 austerity measures that have impacted on the system (Wheatley 2012; Angiolini 2017, 205; Chief Coroner 2020, 9). At the same time, moves to shift officers from police to local authority employment raise concerns about the independence of the investigation in relation to deaths linked to local authority responsibilities, including deaths in care homes (Mahoney 1997; Head and Taft 2007; McGovern and Cusak 2014). As one Coroner interviewee reflected,

> 'unless local authorities brought in an independent investigator for deaths in residential care homes etc, I would be greatly troubled to think that they would be employing the officers, because sooner or later there would be well, we pay you, what the hell do you think you are doing investigating and criticizing or eliciting evidence that enables the Coroner to criticize etc. In my view there is a real risk of lack of independence, and perception of bias.'

Powerful financial considerations may act to hamper calls for change, particularly in relation to representation, but it is hard to see a clear conceptual basis for resisting such reforms. It would therefore be unsurprising if the pressure resulted in much-needed further change in the system. At the same time, this research suggests other aspects of the contemporary system which require close attention. While – as will be discussed later on – there is the potential for fluidity and openness in understandings of family in the inquest, it is not always framed in these terms. There is always a risk that kinship can be understood in narrow, limited terms, with, for example, an emphasis on cohabitation in relation to partners. While courts have repeatedly emphasized in family law proceedings that an enduring family relationship does not require 'intimacy, conjugality, or co-habitation',[3] there has been little case law on the issue in the inquest context. More broadly, there is the prospect that narrow understandings of family, and suspicion that the bereaved wish to be involved in the inquest for purportedly improper purposes, could act to exclude bereaved individuals from involvement. In this context, my analysis highlights the importance of the system engaging with kinship in context rather than relying on formal categories of family. Returning to the approach in Chapter 6, it is a call for the inquest to understand itself as a jurisdiction of conscience, not one of civility.

Constructing a place for kinship in the inquest

The account of the inquest as an official process, centred on a Coroner whose purpose is 'to promote an understanding of the medical cause of death and to reach a legal verdict' (Howarth 2007, 172), dominated the 20th century. It is an account which, in 'social or public terms', Howarth suggests

> plays a pivotal role in constructing a narrative of life which places the deceased on a unique and inexorable trajectory towards their death. Sudden death threatens chaos and the notion that death may be random suggests lack of control. The ordered public ritual of the inquest, with its aim of classifying and explaining mortality, attempts to give it a more predictable veneer. (Howarth 2007, 160)

Like Howarth, Langer sees the inquest as an endeavour to establish control over an unpredictable death, but emphasizes the role of agency in that endeavour. She suggests that during an inquest, 'those affected by the death will present their own agency as compromised by other forces' (Langer 2010, 89) and argues that '[s]uccessful inquests ... are about the transformation of [agency] because commonly they present the death as the inescapable consequence of the intersection of a multitude of events' (Langer 2010, 86).

It is provocative to reflect on what it means for an inquest to be successful. For Langer, focused on suicide and drawing on an anthropological perspective

---

[3]   *Re E (A Child) (Adoption by One Person)* [2021] EWFC 45, para 58(vi).

in which the inquest is a response to the 'havoc' caused by deaths which challenge 'deeply held assumptions' about a good death, 'inquests serve to – albeit temporarily and partially – reassert culturally specific notions about persons and about death' (Langer 2010, 85–86). Perceptions of success necessarily depend on perspective and what is seen as a desirable objective, and a contrast can be made with scholarship which identifies the way in which an emphasis on inevitability and pathology hides wider structures of injustice (Razack 2011b, 2015). However, even where the state is not implicated in the death, I suggest that notions of success, victory or triumph – as with the devastating apology in Chapter 7 – do not sit comfortably with a process which involves uncovering loss and pain (see, for example, Spillane et al 2019). In addition, I suggest that the changes I have discussed introduce further complexity to the roles that agency and inevitability play in the current system.

Returning to the death of Malcolm Burge discussed in Chapter 1, for example, it is a story in which agency is denied to Malcolm at the expense of inevitability, as seen in the account of the Coroner who describes a 'tragic tale', in which Malcom was 'caught up' in 'changes to the government benefit system'. Meanwhile, his family emphasized their own lack of agency: they were powerless to prevent what happened to him because they were not aware of the problem until it was too late.

However, the contemporary inquest is not simply a process in which mortality is classified and in which the Coroner's purpose is always solely directed towards medico-legal explanation. It is possible instead to see ways in which the law and the system resist a framing of themselves as producing explanations which solely classify and order death in neutral, medical terms, amendable to aggregation and statistical evaluation, and rather see themselves as engaging with the production of a more contextual, nuanced, individualized account (Tait et al 2016). It is also a site in which agency and inevitability can be seen to play out in different ways. My account is of a family, at least from the perspective of the law and actors within it, with agency. While the agency of his family may have been constrained before his death, Malcolm Burge's sister and niece are clearly active in the investigation of his death, and their words emphasize the contingent nature of the circumstances; they would have helped him, this could have been prevented, it was not inescapable and it was a consequence of decisions actively taken by the state. It is therefore a re-assertion of contingency which enables a potent critique of the state, and is linked to other deaths associated with austerity and the withdrawal of social welfare support (Traynor 2013; Antonakakis and Collins 2014; Coope et al 2014; Mills 2018) in which inquests provided a critical forum for families to have their concerns raised publicly. For example, in February 2014, an inquest into the death of Mark Wood in Oxford heard evidence that he had died from malnourishment, and that his decline and death were due in part to a decision by the Department for Work and Pensions that he was capable of working. Following the inquest, his sister wrote to Mark's MP, David Cameron, and made statements to the media: 'We worked for years to create a place for him to live safely. But that stopped when his benefits were stopped. He tried so hard to survive' (Gentleman 2014).

While, as Morgan describes, a triadic form of accountability seeks to 'mute raw politics' (Morgan 2006, 257), an approach to accountability which emerges from a tacit community can provide space for that critique to emerge, 'creating a space for frank debate about values' (Morgan 2006, 259). A combined approach to accountability represents the inquest as a system which seeks to provide this space, in the hearing and in the public attention that the process generates. It also represents itself as providing a space for that tacit community of family to define itself.

In relation to this process, my analysis of the categories of next of kin (Chapter 4) and interested persons (Chapter 6) develops Bourdieu's account of the production of family. His endeavour is to understand family as a realized category, which Atkinson describes as meaning the ways in which 'individuals are thrown into a world in which this category, and its associated vocabulary, is simply there from the start, that is, infused in all the injunctions and sayings framing the expectations and practices of everyday life' (Atkinson 2014, 226). In relation to the realization of this category, Bourdieu's analysis describes a decision maker who, when presented with a decision to make relating to kinship, draws on their own understanding of family. Their decision, based in their subjective conception of family, remakes an objective form of family, which is part of a cycle, acting to create further subjective understandings of family. However, a question for this account (Morgan 2011) is how it explains changes in the field of family, and this is something which Atkinson focuses on in particular, albeit not in the context of official decision makers, but rather on changes within the field of family itself. His suggestion is that there is 'a dialectical relation between material conditions and representations, or, more accurately, between objective structures and subjective schemas' (Atkinson 2014, 226). That dialectical relation means that, rather than a perfect reproduction, 'domestic, private, everyday, "ordinary" familial struggles' (Atkinson 2014, 226) mediate larger structural changes and have caused the family to change form over time. These struggles are part of the reproduction of family through practices, legitimizing the division of the world into families, and providing a basis for seeking strategies to support other family members.

It is here, in an understanding of family members as having a strategic aim to support their own, that the family in the inquest fits. Decision makers in the inquest have an understanding of family themselves, and are also presented with forms of family in the process of undertaking their investigation and are called to make choices about the reproduction of the category of family. The reproduction of family which takes place may cycle perfectly through objective material structures and subjective understandings, but other external conditions can be inserted into the dialectic, as decisions can also be seen to defer to and draw from those domestic and private struggles within the field of family. Family may be obvious, but also – tacit, contingent, implicit, provisional – it has space to shape itself, determining its own 'natural' hierarchy. In that process, formal relations or the legal rules are represented as less important than foundations based on practices of family and support, although this can shift where family is framed as a threat to be constrained.

This cycle of production is not simply an exercise undertaken at a single point by a single decision maker, but occurs throughout the process and is shaped by prior decisions taken (or not taken). Throughout, family is being realized, as they are notified, engaged with the investigation and called to take part in hearings. In this process, formal status may protect, from the perspective of kin, the enabling of automatic involvement, but this has limits, because it is also subverted and seen as secondary to ideas of purpose – the perceived purposes of family (see my earlier criticism of this) and understandings of the purposes of an inquest.

These understandings are acutely important in the inquest because of the relative freedom which the legislation and courts grant to the system and to the Coroner in particular. In the context of that broad space to act, the devices and practices which represent the law are closely linked to the ways in which actors in the system organize their understanding of the decisions they are called upon to make. Where law is represented as requiring – and the process understood by decision makers as including – a place for participating kin in a meaningful accounting of death, then it may be that formal family can give way to alternative conceptions of kinship. The alternative is that family are conceived as a potential threat to be contained and accounting assumes a solely triadic form. Even in this case, someone is needed to represent connection so that the Coroner can sit independently above the process and produce a neutral, objective, expert explanation. The family role will be more limited, but the system needs them, and so, as my Coroner interviewee stated in Chapter 6, 'goodness gracious you would want someone there' – as someone needs to represent kinship.

However, they have to behave appropriately – an assessment which can be tied up with implicit understandings relating to race, culture and class, and conceptions of dignity, politeness and reasonableness.[4] There is a risk to possible outcomes if they do not respond properly; a risk that the approach

---

[4] See, for example, *R (Joseph) v Director of Legal Aid Casework* [2015] EWHC 2749.

of family will undermine the objectivity and neutrality of the forum, or that their absence will fail to ensure the investigation produces a robust outcome. Viewed from the perspective of a framing which seeks to combine the two forms of accountability, the risk is greater still: that they will not play their part in the production of a meaningful explanation for death.

This is a final paradox of the contemporary system – that kinship must be given space for their own accounting of death, but for the system to succeed in a representation in which it seeks to combine forms of accountability, that space cannot extend to a rejection of the process itself. Kin are there for their own purposes, to protect their own interests, but those purposes must be achieved through engagement, through meaning making, and through showing that death is loss of a relational tie. It is a new paradox for a system undergoing significant change, sitting uncomfortably alongside those other paradoxes and contradictions which are integral to the inquest and the roles it plays: producing family and kinship, representing the law and explaining sudden death.

Bibliography

Aitken, D. (2021). Investigating prison suicides: the politics of independent oversight. *Punishment & Society*, https://doi.org/10.1177/146247452 1993002.

Al-Haj, M. (1995). Kinship and modernization in developing societies: the emergence of instrumentalized kinship. *Journal of Comparative Family Studies*, 26(3), 311–328.

Amadei, G. L. (2014). The evolving paradigm of the Victorian cemeteries: their emergence and contribution to London's urban growth since 1833. PhD thesis, School of Architecture, Canterbury: University of Kent.

Ambade, V. N., Keoliya, A. N., Deokar, R. B. and Dixit, P. G. (2011). Decomposed bodies: still an unrewarding autopsy? *Journal of Forensic and Legal Medicine*, 18(3), 101–106.

Angell, S. (2007). Moore's 'The History of the Life of Thomas Ellwood Written by Himself' – book review. *Quaker Studies*, 11(1), 135–136.

Angiolini, E. (2017). *Report of the Independent Review of Deaths and Serious Incidents in Police Custody*. London: HM Government.

Anonymous. (1841). The law of deodands. *Monthly Law Magazine*. 10.

Anthony, T. (2013). *Indigenous People, Crime and Punishment*. Abingdon: Routledge.

Antonakakis, N. and Collins, A. (2014). The impact of fiscal austerity on suicide: on the empirics of a modern Greek tragedy. *Social Science and Medicine*, 112, 39–50.

Arendt, H. (2006 [1954]). *Between Past and Future: 8 Exercises in Political Thought*. Harmondsworth: Penguin (2006 edition).

Aries, P. (1981). *The Hour of Our Death*. New York: Vintage Books.

Atkinson, J. M. (1978). *Discovering Suicide: Studies in the Social Organisation of Sudden Death*. Basingstoke: Macmillan.

Atkinson, W. (2010). Phenomenological additions to the Bourdieusian toolbox: two problems for Bourdieu, two solutions from Schutz. *Sociological Theory*, 28(1), 1–19.

Atkinson, W. (2014). A sketch of 'family' as a field: from realized category to space of struggle. *Acta Sociologica*, 57(3), 223–235.

Aubry, T. and Travis, T. (eds) (2015). *Rethinking Therapeutic Culture*. Chicago: University of Chicago Press.

Baker, D. (2016a). *Deaths after Police Contact*. Basingstoke: Palgrave Macmillan.

Baker, D. (2016b). Deaths after police contact in England and Wales: the effects of Article 2 of the European Convention on Human Rights on Coronial practice. *International Journal of Law in Context*, 12(2), 162–177.

Bano, S. (2005). 'Standpoint', 'Difference' and Feminist Research. In R. Banakar and M. Travers (eds) *Theory and Method in Socio-Legal Research*. London: Bloomsbury Publishing. Kindle Edition, 91–112.

Barker, N. (2012). *Not the Marrying Kind: A Feminist Critique of Same-Sex Marriage*. Basingstoke: Palgrave Macmillan.

Barnes, M., Kirkegaard, A. and Carpenter, B. (2014). Intake rigour: ensuring only 'reportable deaths' become Coroners' cases. *Journal of Law and Medicine*, 21, 572–583.

Barraclough, B. M. and Shepherd, D. M. (1977). The immediate and enduring effects of the inquest on relatives of suicides. *British Journal of Psychiatry*, 131(4), 400–404.

Barter, C. and Renold, E. (1999). The use of vignettes in qualitative research. *Social Research Update*, 25(9), 1–6.

Bartrip, P. W. (1987). *Workmen's Compensation in Twentieth Century Britain: Law, History, and Social Policy*. Farnham: Gower.

Bartrip, P. W. and Burman, S. (1983). *The Wounded Soldiers of Industry: Industrial Compensation Policy, 1833–1897*. New York: Oxford University Press USA.

Beckett, C. (1999). Deaths in custody and the inquest system. *Critical Social Policy*, 19(2), 271–280.

Berman, P. S. (1999). An anthropological approach to modern forfeiture law: the symbolic function of legal actions against objects. *Yale Journal of Law and Humanities*, 11(1), 1–45.

Bevir, M. (2011). Why historical distance is not a problem. *History and Theory*, 50(4), 24–37.

Biddle, L. (2003). Public hazards or private tragedies? An exploratory study of the effect of Coroners' procedures on those bereaved by suicide. *Social Science and Medicine*, 56(5), 1033–1045.

Biebricher, T. (2011). Faith-based initiatives and pastoral power. *Economy and Society*, 40(3), 399–420.

Binns, A. and Arnold, S. (2020). Death of a watchdog: reduced coverage of Coroners' inquests by local media. *Journalism Practice*, 1–19.

Black, J. (2008). Constructing and contesting legitimacy and accountability in polycentric regulatory regimes. *Regulation & Governance*, 2(2), 137–164.

Bourdieu, P. (1977). *Outline of a Theory of Practice* (trans. R. Nice). Cambridge: Cambridge University Press.

Bourdieu, P. (1996). On the family as a realized category. *Theory, Culture and Society*, 13(3), 19–26.

Bremenstul, M. E. (2013). Victims in life, victims in death: keeping burial rights out of the hands of slayers. *Louisiana Law Review*, 74(1), 213–253.

Broderick Report (1971). *The Royal Commission into Coroners and Coronership*. London: HMSO, Cmnd 4810.

Brogdon, B. G. (2013). Forensic imaging of the living: a short stab at long distance. *Journal of Forensic Radiology and Imaging*, 1(1), 19–21.

Brown, R. (2014). *Avoidable Mortality in Cumbria: A Case File Review of 78 Suicides*. Liverpool: Centre for Public Health, Liverpool John Moores University.

Bryman, A. (2012). *Social Research Methods*. Oxford: Oxford University Press.

Buchanan, D. R. and Mason, J. (1995). The Coroner's office revisited. *Medical Law Review*, 3(2), 142–160.

Burke, E. W. (1929). Deodand: a legal antiquity that may still exist. *Chicago-Kent Law Review*, 8, 15–32.

Burney, I. A. (1994). Viewing bodies: medicine, public order, and English inquest practice. *Configurations*, 2(1), 33–46.

Burney, I. A. (2000). *Bodies of Evidence: Medicine and the Politics of the English Inquest, 1830–1926*. Baltimore: JHU Press.

Buss, D. and Herman, D. (2003). *Globalizing Family Values: The Christian Right in International Politics*. Minneapolis: University of Minnesota Press.

Butler, J. (2002). Is kinship always already heterosexual? *Differences: A Journal of Feminist Cultural Studies*, 13(1), 14–44.

Butler, J. (2004). *Undoing Gender*. London: Psychology Press.

Butler, J. (2006). *Precarious Life: The Powers of Mourning and Violence*. New York: Verso.

Butler, S. M. (2014). *Forensic Medicine and Death Investigation in Medieval England*. Abingdon: Routledge.

Canetto, S. S. (1993). She died for love and he for glory: gender myths of suicidal behavior. *OMEGA: Journal of Death and Dying*, 26(1), 1–17.

Carlen, P. (1976). The staging of magistrates' justice. *British Journal of Criminology*, 16, 48–55.

Carpenter, B. and Tait, G. (2009). Health, death and Indigenous Australians in the Coronial system. *Australian Aboriginal Studies*, 1, 29–41.

Carpenter, B. and Tait, G. (2010). The autopsy imperative: medicine, law, and the Coronial investigation. *Journal of Medical Humanities*, 31(3), 205–221.

Carpenter, B. Tait, G. and Quadrelli, C. (2013). Arguing the autopsy: mutual suspicion, jurisdictional confusion and the socially marginal. In *Crime, Justice and Social Democracy: Proceedings of the 2nd International Conference*, Crime and Justice Research Centre, Queensland University of Technology, Gardens Point, Brisbane, Australia, 10–18.

Carpenter, B., Tait, G. and Quadrelli, C. (2014). The body in grief: death investigations, objections to autopsy, and the religious and cultural 'other'. *Religions*, 5(1), 165–178.

Carpenter, B., Harris, M., Jowett, S., Tait, G. and Scott Bray, R. (2021). Coronial inquests, indigenous suicide and the colonial narrative. *Critical Criminology*, 1–19, https://doi.org/10.1007/s10612-021-09578-w.

Carpenter, B., Tait, G., Adkins, G., Barnes, M., Naylor, C. and Begum, N. (2009). Increasing the information available to Coroners: the effect on autopsy decision-making. *Medicine, Science, and the Law*, 49(2), 101–108.

Carpenter, B., Tait, G., Adkins, G., Barnes, M., Naylor, C. and Begum, N. (2011). Communicating with the Coroner: how religion, culture, and family concerns may influence autopsy decision-making. *Death Studies*, 35(4), 316–337.

Carpenter, B., Tait, G., Quadrelli, C. and Drayton, J. (2015a). Scrutinising the other: incapacity, suspicion and manipulation in a death investigation. *Journal of Intercultural Studies*, 36(2), 113–128.

Carpenter, B., Tait, G., Stobbs, N. and Barnes, M. (2015b). When Coroners care too much: therapeutic jurisprudence and suicide findings. *Journal of Judicial Administration*, 24(3), 172–183.

Carr, H. (2012). Rational men and difficult women: *R (on the Application of McDonald) v. Royal Borough of Kensington and Chelsea* [2011] UKSC 33. *Journal of Social Welfare and Family Law*, 34(2), 219–230.

Casey, D. and Scott, C. (2011). The crystallisation of regulatory norms. *Journal of Law and Society*, 38(1), 76–95.

Castellano, U. (2009). Beyond the courtroom workgroup: caseworkers as the new satellite of social control. *Law and Policy*, 31(4), 429–462.

Cawthon, E. (1986). Thomas Wakley and the medical Coronership: occupational death and the judicial process. *Medical History*, 30(02), 191–202.

Cawthon, E. (1989). New life for the deodand: Coroners' inquests and occupational deaths in England, 1830–46. *American Journal of Legal History*, 33, 137–147.

Cawthon, E. A. (1997). *Job Accidents and the Law in England's Early Railway Age: Origins of Employer Liability and Workmen's Compensation*. Edwin Lewiston; Queenston; Lampeter: Mellen Press.

Chapple, A. and Ziebland, S. (2010). Viewing the body after bereavement due to a traumatic death: qualitative study in the UK. *BMJ (Clinical Research Ed.)*, 340, c2032, 1–11.

Chapple, A., Ziebland, S. and Hawton, K. (2015). A proper, fitting explanation? *Crisis*, 33(4), 230–238.

Chattopadhyay, S. (2014). Partial autopsy: a second thought. *International Journal of Forensic Science & Pathology*, 2(2), 1–2.

Chief Coroner (2013–2014). *First Annual Report*.

Chief Coroner (2013a). *Guidance Note 3: Oaths and Robes*.

Chief Coroner (2013b). *Summary of Reports to Prevent Future Deaths* (formerly Rule 43 Reports) (First Report: For Period 1 April 2013–30 September 2013).

Chief Coroner (2013c). *Guidance Note 5: Reports to Prevent Future Deaths.*

Chief Coroner (2014–2015). *Second Annual Report.*

Chief Coroner (2014a). *Law Sheet No. 3: The Worcestershire Case.*

Chief Coroner (2014b). *Guidance Note 16: Deprivation of Liberty Safeguards (DoLS).*

Chief Coroner (2016). *Third Annual Report.*

Chief Coroner (2017). *Fourth Annual Report.*

Chief Coroner (2018). *Fifth Annual Report.*

Chief Coroner (2020). *Sixth Annual Report: 2018–2019; Seventh Annual Report: 2019–2020.*

Christman, J. (2004). Relational autonomy, liberal individualism, and the social constitution of selves. *Philosophical Studies*, 117(1), 143–164.

Clarke, E. and McCreanor, T. (2006). He wahine tangi tikapa 1…: statutory investigative processes and the grieving of Maori families who have lost a baby to SIDS. *Kōtuitui: New Zealand Journal of Social Sciences Online*, 1(1), 25–43.

Coke, E. (1809). *The Third Part of the Institutes of the Laws of England: Concerning High Treason, and Other Pleas of the Crown, and Criminal Causes.* Vol. 1. W. Clarke and Sons.

Coles, D. and Shaw, H. (2006). Comment: deaths in custody – truth, justice, and accountability? The work of INQUEST. *Social Justice*, 136–141.

Conaghan, J. (2014). Celebrating Duncan Kennedy's scholarship: a 'crit' analysis of *DSD and NBV v Commissioner of Police for the Metropolis*. *Transnational Legal Theory*, 5(4), 601–621.

Condren, C. (2006). *Argument and Authority in Early Modern England: The Presupposition of Oaths and Offices.* Cambridge: Cambridge University Press.

Constitutional Affairs Select Committee. (2006). *Reform of the Coroners' System and Death Certification, 8th Report of Session 2005–2006.*

Conway, H. (2003). Dead, but not buried: bodies, burial and family conflicts. *Legal Studies*, 23(3), 423–452.

Conway, H. (2016). *The Law and the Dead.* Abingdon: Routledge.

Coope, C., Gunnell, D., Hollingworth, W., Hawton, K., Kapurc, N., Fearnd, V., Wells, C. and Metcalfe, C. (2014). Suicide and the 2008 economic recession: who is most at risk? Trends in suicide rates in England and Wales 2001–2011. *Social Science and Medicine*, 117, 76–85.

Cooper, P. N. and Milroy, C. M. (1995). The Coroner's system and under-reporting of suicide. *Medicine, Science and the Law*, 35(4), 319–326.

Cornford, J., Baines, S. and Wilson, R. (2013). Representing the family: how does the state 'think family'? *Policy and Politics*, 41(1), 1–18.

Coroners Statistics (2020). Available from: https://www.gov.uk/governm ent/statistics/coroners-statistics-2020/coroners-statistics-2020-england-and-wales [Accessed 1 August 2021].

Coroners' Officers and Staff Association. (2013). Training Materials. *Investigations: Putting the NEW Law into Practice.*

Courts and Tribunals Judiciary (2015). Coroner's Report to Prevent Future Death for Malcolm Burge. Available from: https://www.judiciary.uk/publications/malcolm-burge/ [Accessed 18 May 2022]

Cowan, V. (2014). Last rites and death duties. *Criminal Law and Justice Weekly,* 178(44), 657–658.

Cowburn, D. (1929) The Metropolitan policeman as Coroner's officer. *Police Journal,* 2, 397–405.

Cowburn, J. (2013). Cuts have seen rapid suicide increase in Islington – says psychologist. *Islington Gazette* [online], 26 December. Available from: http://www.islingtongazette.co.uk/news/cuts_have_seen_rapid_suicide_increase_in_islington_says_psychologist_1_3146730 [Accessed 24 January 2022].

Cross, C. and Garnham, N. (eds) (2016). *The Inquest Book: The Law of Coroners and Inquests.* London: Bloomsbury Publishing.

Davies, A. C. (2001). *Accountability: A Public Law Analysis of Government by Contract.* Oxford: Oxford University Press.

Davis, G., Lindsey, R., Seabourne, G. and Griffiths-Baker, J. (2002). *Experiencing Inquests.* Home Office Research Study 241.

Dawson, N. M. (2014). The double life of *Duke of Somerset v Cookson,* or a legal excavation of the Corbridge Lanx. *Journal of Legal History,* 35(3), 258–280.

Day, H. G. (1849). *A Brief Sketch of the 'Hounslow Inquest' and of the late trial 'Wakley versus Cook and Healey'.* London: Simpkin, Marshall and Co. Available from: https://wellcomecollection.org/works/u9k6xaft.

Day, P. and Klein, R. (1987). *Accountabilities: Five Public Services.* Vol. 357. London: Taylor & Francis.

De Tocqueville A (1945). *Democracy in America* (trans. Henry Reeve). New York: Knopf.

Department of Communities and Local Government response to Lakanal House fire Rule 43 letter (2013, 20 May). Available from: http://www.lambeth.gov.uk/sites/default/files/ec-letter-from-rt-hon-eric-pickles-mp-20May2013.pdf [Accessed 24 January 2022].

Department of Health and Social Care (2021). *Working Together to Improve Health and Social Care for All.* White Paper, CP 381. Available from: https://www.gov.uk/government/publications/working-together-to-improve-health-and-social-care-for-all [Accessed 24 January 2022].

Dingwall, R. and Cloatre, E. (2006). Vanishing trials: an English perspective. *Journal of Dispute Resolution,* 51–70.

Dix, P. (1998). Access to the dead: the role of relatives in the aftermath of disaster. *The Lancet,* 352(9133), 1061–1062.

Donzelot, J. (1979). *The Policing of Families.* New York: Pantheon Books.

Dorries, C. P. (2004). *Coroners' Courts: A Guide to Law and Practice* (2nd edn), Oxford: Oxford University Press.

Dorries, C. P. (2014). *Coroners' Courts: A Guide to Law and Practice* (3rd edn), Oxford: Oxford University Press.

Dorsett, S. and McVeigh, S. (2012). *Jurisdiction*. Abingdon: Routledge.

Douglas, G. (2014). Family provision and family practices: the discretionary regime of the Inheritance Act of England and Wales. *Oñati Socio-Legal Series*, 4(2), 222–242.

Douglas, G., Woodward, H., Humphrey, A., Mills, L. and Morrell, G. (2011). Enduring love? Attitudes to family and inheritance law in England and Wales. *Journal of Law and Society*, 38(2), 245–271.

Douzinas, C. (2007). *Human Rights and Empire: The Political Philosophy of Cosmopolitanism*. Abingdon: Routledge.

Dowdle, M. (2006). Public accountability: conceptual, historical, and epistemic mappings. In M. W. Dowdle (ed) *Public Accountability: Designs, Dilemmas and Experiences*. Cambridge: Cambridge University Press, 1–32.

Drayton, J. (2011). Organ retention and bereavement: family counselling and the ethics of consultation. *Ethics and Social Welfare*, 5(3), 227–246.

Drayton, J. (2013). Bodies-in-life/bodies-in-death: social work, Coronial autopsies and the bonds of identity. *British Journal of Social Work*, 43(2), 264–281.

Duff, R. A., Farmer, L., Marshall, S. and Tadros, V. (2007). *The Trial on Trial: Volume 3: Towards a Normative Theory of the Criminal Trial*. London: Bloomsbury Publishing.

Dupré, C. (2012). Dignity, democracy, civilisation. *Liverpool Law Review*, 33(3), 263–280.

Dying Matters (2014). Millions leaving it too late to discuss dying wishes. Available from: http://dyingmatters.org/news/millions-leaving-it-too-late-discuss-dying-wishes [Accessed 24 January 2022].

Dyregrov, A. and Kristensen, P. (2020). Information to bereaved families following catastrophic losses. Why is it important? *Journal of Loss and Trauma*, 25(5), 472–487.

Dzur, A. W. (2012). *Punishment, Participatory Democracy, and the Jury*. Oxford: Oxford University Press.

Easton J. (2020) *Death in Custody: Inquests, Family Participation and State Accountability*. Bingley: Emerald Group Publishing.

Emerson, R. M. (1991). Case processing and interorganisational knowledge: detecting the 'real reasons' for referrals. *Social Problems*, 38(2), 1101–1115.

Epstein, L. and Martin, A. D. (2014). *An Introduction to Empirical Legal Research*. Oxford: Oxford University Press.

Erfani-Ghettani, R. (2015). The defamation of Joy Gardner: press, police and Black deaths in custody. *Race and Class*, 56(3), 102–112.

Explanatory Memorandum to Coroners (Inquests) Rules 2013, SI 2013/ 1616.

Explanatory Memorandumto Coroners (Investigations) Regulations 2013 SI 1629/2013.

Explanatory Memorandumto Coroners Rules 1984, SI 1984/552.

Fellows, R. (1930). *History of the Canterbury and Whitstable Railway.* Canterbury, Jennings.

Ferguson, A. G. (2013a). Jury instructions as constitutional education. *University of Colorado Law Review,* 84, 233–304.

Ferguson, A. G. (2013b). The jury as constitutional identity. *University of California at Davis Law Review,* 47, 1105–1172.

Figueiredo, A. E. B., Silva, R. M. D., Vieira, L. J. E. S., Mangas, R. M. D. N., Sousa, G. S. D., Freitas, J. S., Conte, M. and Sougey, E. B. (2015). Is it possible to overcome suicidal ideation and suicide attempts? A study of the elderly. *Ciência & Saúde Coletiva,* 20, 1711–1719.

Finch, J. (1987). The vignette technique in survey research. *Sociology,* 105–114.

Finch, J. (1989). *Family Obligations and Social Change.* Cambridge: Polity Press.

Finch, J. and Mason, J. (1993). *Negotiating Family Responsibilities.* London: Routledge.

Fincham, B., Langer, S., Scourfield J. and Shiner, M. (2011). *Understanding Suicide: A Sociological Autopsy.* Basingstoke: Palgrave Macmillan.

Finkelstein, J. J. (1972). The Goring Ox: some historical perspectives on deodands, forfeitures, wrongful death and the Western notion of sovereignty. *Temple Law* Quarterly, 46, 169–290.

Fiss, O. M. (1984). Against settlement. *Yale Law Journal* 93(6): 1073–1090.

Fletcher, A. K. (2011). Coroners' Rule 43 reports. *Clinical Risk,* 17(6), 217–219.

Foote, C. E. and Frank, A. W. (1999). Foucault and therapy: the disciplining of grief. In A. S. Chambon, A. Irving and L. Epstein (eds) *Reading Foucault for Social Work.* New York: Columbia University Press, 157–187.

Foucault, M. (2007). *Security, Territory, Population: Lectures at the Collège de France, 1977–78.* Dordrecht: Springer.

Freckelton, I. (2007). Death investigation, the Coroner and therapeutic jurisprudence. *Journal of Law and Medicine,* 15(2), 242–253.

Freckelton, I. (2008). Therapeutic jurisprudence misunderstood and misrepresented: the price and risks of influence. *Thomas Jefferson Law Review,* 30, 575–596.

Freckelton, I. (2016). Minimising the counter-therapeutic effects of Coronial investigations: in search of balance. *Queensland University of Technology Law Review.,* 16, 4–29.

Freckelton, I. and Ranson, D. (2006). *Death Investigation and the Coroner's Inquest.* Oxford: Oxford University Press.

Friedland, S. I. (1990). Competency and responsibility of jurors in deciding cases. *Northwestern University Law Review*, 85, 190–220.

Frisby, H. (2015). Drawing the pillow, laying out and port wine: the moral economy of death, dying and bereavement in England, c. 1840–1930. *Mortality*, 20(2), 103–127.

Gallagher, S. (2010). Museums and the return of human remains: an equitable solution? *International Journal of Cultural Property*, 17, 65–86.

Garland, D. (2019). Reading Foucault: an ongoing engagement. *Journal of Law and Society*, 46(4), 640–661.

Gastil, J. and Weiser, P. J. (2006). Jury service as an invitation to citizenship: assessing the civic value of institutionalized deliberation. *Policy Studies Journal*, 34(4), 605–627.

Gastil, J., Deess, E. P. and Weiser, P. (2002). Civic awakening in the jury room: a test of the connection between jury deliberation and political participation. *Journal of Politics*, 64(2), 585–595.

Gastil, J., Deess, E. P., Weiser, P. J. and Simmons, C. (2010). *The Jury and Democracy: How Jury Deliberation Promotes Civic Engagement and Political Participation*. Oxford: Oxford University Press.

Gastil. J, Black, L. W., Deess, E. P. and Leighter, J. (2008a). From group member to democratic citizen: how deliberating with fellow jurors reshapes civic attitudes. *Human Communication Research*, 34(1), 137–169.

Gastil, J., Deess, E. P., Weiser, P. and Meade, J. (2008b). Jury service and electoral participation: a test of the participation hypothesis. *Journal of Politics*, 70(2), 351–367.

Gentleman, A. (2014). Vulnerable man starved to death after benefits were cut. *The Guardian* [online], 28 February. Available from: http://www.theg uardian.com/society/2014/feb/28/man-starved-to-death-after-benefits-cut [Accessed 24 January 2022].

Gilboy, J. A. (1991). Deciding who gets in: decision-making by immigration inspectors. *Law and Society Review*, 571–599.

Gilleard, C. (2008). A murderous ageism? Age, death and Dr. Shipman. *Journal of Aging Studies*, 22(1), 88–95.

Glasgow, G. H. (2004a). The campaign for medical Coroners in nineteenth-century England and its aftermath: a Lancashire focus on failure. Part I. *Mortality*, 9(2), 150–167.

Glasgow, G. H. (2004b). The campaign for medical Coroners in nineteenth-century England and its aftermath: a Lancashire focus on failure. Part II. *Mortality*, 9(3), 223–234.

Glasgow, G. H. (2007). The election of County Coroners in England and Wales circa 1800–1888. *Journal of Legal History*, 20(3), 75–108.

Glennon, L. (2005). Displacing the 'conjugal family' in legal policy: a progressive move? *Child and Family Law Quarterly*, 17(2), 141–163.

Gloppen, S., Gargarella, R. and Skaar, E. (2004). *Democratization and the Judiciary: The Accountability Function of Courts in New Democracies.* Vol. 8. London: Psychology Press.

Goffman, E. (1974). *Frame Analysis: An Essay on the Organization of Experience.* Cambridge, MA: Harvard University Press.

Government Response to Constitutional Affairs Select Committee (2006). *8th Report of Session 2005–2006*, Cm 6943, November.

Graham, C. (1995). Sudden death and the LCC: accommodation for inquests in London before the First World War. *Architectural Research Quarterly*, 1(2), 60–69.

Gray, A. (2011). A Review of transport and the law of deodand. *Journal of the Railway and Canal Historical Society* (212), 26–33.

Green, J. (1999). From accidents to risk: public health and preventable injury. *Health, Risk and Society*, (1)1, 25–39.

Green, M. and Green, J. (1992). *Dealing with Death: A Handbook of Practices, Procedures and Law.* London: Jessica Kingsley.

Greer, S. (2010). Anti-terrorist laws and the United Kingdom's 'suspect Muslim community': a reply to Pantazis and Pemberton. *British Journal of Criminology*, 50(6), 1171–1190.

Gregory, M. J. (2014). Managing the homicide-suicide inquest the practices of coroners in one region of England and Wales. *International Journal of Law, Crime and Justice*, 42(3), 237–250.

Greiling, D. and Spraul, K. (2010). Accountability and the challenges of information disclosure. *Public Administration Quarterly*, 338–377.

Grimm, P. (2010). Social desirability bias. *Wiley International Encyclopedia of Marketing.*

Guide to Coroner Services (2014). Ministry of Justice, February.

Guide to Coroners and Inquests and Charter for Coroner Services (2012). Ministry of Justice, March.

H. B. [full name not given] (1845). Art. II – law of deodands. *Law Magazine and Review: A Quarterly Review of Jurisprudence.* 3, n.s. 188.

Hacker, D. (2010). The gendered dimensions of inheritance: empirical food for legal thought. *Journal of Empirical Legal Studies*, 7(2), 322–354.

Hacker, D. (2014). Disappointed 'heirs' as a socio-legal phenomenon. *Oñati Socio-Legal Series*, 4(2), 243–263.

Haddleton, R. E. (2006). What to do with the body: the trouble with postmortem disposition. *Property & Probate*, 20, 55–59.

Hadfield, G. K. and Ryan, D. (2013). Democracy, courts and the information order. *European Journal of Sociology/Archives Européennes de Sociologie*, 54(1), 67–95.

Hale, B. (2009). Dignity. *Journal of Social Welfare and Family Law*, 31(2), 101–108.

Hale, S. M. (1800). *The History of the Pleas of the Crown*. E. Rider, Little-Britain.

Hall-Tomkin, B. with Hilliard, B (1999). *West Country Coroner: The Notable Cases and Absorbing Career of North Devon's Coroner*. Newbury: Countryside Books.

Harlow, C. and Rawlings, R. (2006). Promoting accountability in multi-level governance: a network approach. *European Governance Papers* (EUROGOV) No. C-06-02.

Harris, A. (2017a). 'Natural' and 'unnatural' medical deaths and Coronial law: a UK and international review of the medical literature on natural and unnatural death and how it applies to medical death certification and reporting deaths to coroners: natural/unnatural death: a scientific review. *Medicine, Science and the Law*, 57(3), 105–114.

Harris, A. (2017b). Department of Health consultation on medical examiners and death certification reforms: a commentary on the criteria for notification to be laid down in regulation. *Medicine, Science and the Law*, 57(3), 152–157.

Harris, A. and Walker, A. (2019). Interpretation of 'unnatural death' in Coronial law: a review of the English legal process of decision making, statutory interpretation, and case law. *Medical Law Review*, 27(1), 1–31.

Harris, G. C. (1995). The communitarian function of the criminal jury trial and the rights of the accused. *Nebraska Law Review*, 74, 804–842.

Harris, N. (2014). Unsuitable arrangements: funeral expenses and the benefits system. *Journal of Social Security Law*, 21(3), 126–150.

Harwood, D., Hawton, K., Hope, T. and Jacoby, R. (2002). The grief experiences and needs of bereaved relatives and friends of older people dying through suicide: a descriptive and case-control study. *Journal of Affective Disorders*, 72(2), 185–194.

Havard, J. D. J. (1960). *The Detection of Secret Homicide*. London: Palgrave Macmillan.

Hawkes, N. (2014). Why the delays in counting the dead? *British Medical Journal*, 349, g4305.

Hawkins, K. (2002). *Law as Last Resort: Prosecution Decision-Making in a Regulatory Agency*. Oxford: Oxford University Press.

Hawton, K. and Simkin, S. (2003). Helping people bereaved by suicide: their needs may require special attention. *Bereavement Care*, 22(3), 41–42.

Hawton, K., Linsell, L., Adeniji, T., Sariaslan, A. and Fazel, S. (2014). Self-harm in prisons in England and Wales: an epidemiological study of prevalence, risk factors, clustering, and subsequent suicide. *The Lancet*, 383(9923), 1147–1154.

Head, S. and Taft, A. (2007). Keeping older adults safe: what happens when things go wrong? *PSIGE Newsletter*, 101, 48.

Held, V. (2005). *The Ethics of Care: Personal, Political, and Global*. Oxford: Oxford University Press.

Hempel, S. (2014). John St John: quackery and manslaughter. *The Lancet*, 383(9928), 1540–1541.

Henley Standard (2012). Priest's grave moved at night. *Henley Standard* [online], 10 September. Available from: http://www.henleystandard.co.uk/news/news.php?id=1162657 [Accessed 22 January 2022].

Hernandez, T. K. (1998). The property of death. *University of Pittsburgh Law Review*, 60, 971–1028.

Heslop, P., Blair, P., Fleming, P., Hoghton, M., Marriott, A. and Russ, L. (2013). *Confidential Inquiry into Premature Deaths of People with Learning Disabilities (CIPOLD)*. Bristol: Norah Fry Research Centre.

Heuer, L. and Penrod, S. D. (1990). Some suggestions for the critical appraisal of a more active jury. *Northwestern Law Review*, 85, 226–239.

Hill, C. and Cook, L. (2011). Narrative verdicts and their impact on mortality statistics in England and Wales. *Health Statistics Quarterly*, 49, Spring (ONS), 81–100.

Hill QC, M. (2013). Grave concerns. *Solicitors Journal*, 157/28, 21–22.

Hobsbawm, E. J. (1983). Introduction: Inventing traditions. In T. O. Ranger and E. J. Hobsbawm (eds) *The Invention of Tradition*. Cambridge: Cambridge University Press, 1–14.

Hogan, T. B. (1979). Crime, punishment and responsibility. *Villanova Law Review*, 24, 690–705.

Hogle, L. F. (2003). Life/time warranty: rechargeable cells and extended lives. In S. Frankin and M. Lock (eds) *Remaking Life and Death: Toward an Anthropology of the Biosciences*. Oxford: James Currey, 61–96.

Home Affairs Select Committee. (2013). *Independent Police Complaints Commission. Eleventh Report of Session 2012–13*.

Home Office Position Paper (2004). *Reforming the Coroner and Death Certification Service*. CM 6159.

Hopkins, H. (1977). *The Strange Death of Private White: A Victorian Scandal That Made History*. London: Weidenfeld & Nicolson.

Howarth, G. (1997). Death on the road: the role of the English Coroner's court in the social construction of an accident. In M. Mitchell (ed) *The Aftermath of Road Accidents: Psychosocial, Social, and Legal Consequences of an Everyday Trauma*. London: Routledge, 15–32.

Howarth, G. (2000). Dismantling the boundaries between life and death. *Mortality*, 5(2), 127–138.

Howarth, G. (2007). *Death and Dying: A Sociological Introduction*. Cambridge: Polity Press.

Hunnisett, R. (1958). The origins of the office of Coroner. *Transactions of the Royal Historical Society (Fifth Series)*, 8, 85–104.

Hunnisett, R. (1961a). *The Medieval Coroner*. Cambridge: Cambridge University Press.

Hunnisett, R. (1961b). *Bedfordshire Coroners' Rolls.* Vol. 41. Streatley: Bedfordshire Historical Record Society.

Hurren, E. T. (2010). Remaking the medico-legal scene: a social history of the late-Victorian Coroner in Oxford. *Journal of the History of Medicine and Allied Sciences*, 65(2), 207–252.

Hynes, J., Gill, N. and Tomlinson, J. (2020). In defence of the hearing? Emerging geographies of publicness, materiality, access and communication in court hearings. *Geography Compass*, 14(9), e12499, 1–11.

Hynes, S. (2012). *Austerity Justice.* London: Legal Action Group.

Impey, J. (1817). *The practice of the office of sheriff and under sheriff: … also the practice of the office of Coroner, shewing the mode of his appointment, with the powers and duties of taking inquisitions and mode of holding court, andc.: to each of which works are added copious appendixes of useful precedents.* London: W. Clarke.

INQUEST. (2013) *Written evidence to Home Affairs Select Committee Report.* Independent Police Complaints Commission. Eleventh Report of Session 2012–2013. [IPCC 26]. Available from: https://publications.parliament.uk/pa/cm201213/cmselect/cmhaff/494/494we12.htm [Accessed 11 April 2022].

Inquisition and Narrative Verdict – Catherine Hickman (2013, 28 March). Available from: http://www.lambeth.gov.uk/sites/default/files/ec-inquisition-and-narrative-verdict-catherine-hickman.pdf [Accessed 24 January 2022].

IRR (Institute for Race Relations) (2015). *Dying for Justice.* Available from http://www.irr.org.uk/news/dying-for-justice/ [Accessed 24 January 2022].

Jacob, M. (2009). The shared history: unknotting fictive kinship and legal process. *Law and Society Review*, 43(1), 95–126.

Jacob, M. (2012). *Matching Organs with Donors: Legality and Kinship in Transplants.* Philadelphia: Pennsylvania University Press.

Jaconelli, J. (2002). *Open Justice: A Critique of the Public Trial.* Oxford: Oxford University Press.

Jameson, F. (1976). Review article: on Goffman's frame analysis. *Theory and Society*, 3(1), 119–133.

Jamieson, P. (1988). Animal liability in early law. *Cambrian Law Review*, 19, 45–68.

Jassal, L. K. (2015). Necromobilities: the multi-sited geographies of death and disposal in a mobile world. *Mobilities*, 10(3), 486–509.

Johnson, J. (1994). Coroners, corruption and the politics of death: forensic pathology in the United States. In M. Clark and C. Crawford (eds) *Legal Medicine in History*, Cambridge: Cambridge University Press, 268–289.

Jones, D. (2014). The relationship between homicide rates and forensic post-mortem examinations in England and Wales. *Journal of Homicide and Major Incident Investigation*, 9(2), 58–72.

Jones, I. (2018). 'It's all about justice': bodies, balancing competing interests, and suspicious deaths. *Journal of Law and Society*, 45(4), 563–588.

Jupp, P. C. (1999). A history of the cremation movement in Great Britain: the first 125 years. *Pharos International*, 65(1), 18–25.

Jurasinski, S. (2014). Noxal surrender, the deodand, and the laws of King Alfred. *Studies in Philology*, 111(2), 195–224.

Justice Committee (House of Commons Select Committee) (2021). *The Coroner Service. First Report of Session 2021–2022*. HC 68.

Kapelańska-Pręgowska, J. (2019). Medical negligence, systemic deficiency, or denial of emergency healthcare? Reflections on the European Court of Human Rights Grand Chamber Judgment in Lopes de Sousa Fernandes v. Portugal of 19 December 2017 and previous case-law. *European Journal of Health Law*, 26(1), 26–43.

Kasstan, B. (2017). Haredi (material) cultures of health at the 'hard to reach' margins of the state. In T. Carroll, D. Jeevendrampillai, A. Parkhurst and J. Shackelford (eds) *The Material Culture of Failure*. Abingdon: Routledge, 95–111.

Keenan, S. (2009). Australian legal geography and the search for postcolonial space in Chloe Hooper's *The Tall Man: Death and Life on Palm Island*. *Australian Feminist Law Journal*, 30(1), 173–199.

Kellehear, A. (2009). Dying old: and preferably alone? Agency, resistance and dissent at the end of life. *International Journal of Ageing and Later Life*, 4(1), 5–21.

Kennedy, D. (1976). Form and substance in private law adjudication. *Harvard Law Review*, 1685–1778.

Kennedy, D. (1997). *A Critique of Adjudication (Fin de Siècle)*. Cambridge, MA: Harvard University Press.

Kennedy, D. (2008). *Legal Reasoning: Collected Essays*. Contemporary European Cultural Studies. Aurora: Davies Group Publishers.

Kennedy, I. (2001). *The Report of the Public Inquiry into Children's Heart Surgery at the Bristol Royal Infirmary 1984–1995: Learning from Bristol*, Cm 5207.

Kidner, R. (1999). A history of the Fatal Accident Acts. *Northern Ireland Legal Quarterly*, 50, 318–335.

King, M. (2008). Restorative justice, therapeutic jurisprudence and the rise of emotionally intelligent justice. *Melbourne University Law Review*, 32, 1096–1126.

Kirton-Darling, E. (2018). Safe and sound: precariousness, compartmentation and death at home. In H. Carr, B. Edgeworth and C. Hunter (eds) *Law and the Precarious Home: Socio-legal Perspectives on the Home in Insecure Times*. London: Bloomsbury Publishing, 181–200.

Klinenberg, E. (2001). Dying alone: the social production of urban isolation. *Ethnography*, 2(4), 501–531.

Klinenberg, E. (2015). *Heat Wave: A Social Autopsy of Disaster in Chicago*. Chicago: University of Chicago Press.

Kostal, R. W. (1994). *Law and English Railway Capitalism, 1825–1875*. Oxford: Clarendon Press.

Langer, S. (2010). Distributed personhood and the transformation of agency: an anthropological perspective on inquests. In J. Hockey, C. Komaromy and K. Woodthorpe (eds) *The Matter of Death: Space, Place and Materiality*. Basingstoke: Palgrave Macmillan, 85–99.

Langer, S., Scourfield, J. and Fincham, B. (2008). Documenting the quick and the dead: a study of suicide case files in a Coroner's office. *Sociological Review*, 56(2), 293–308.

Larner, W. (2000). Neo-liberalism: policy, ideology, governmentality. *Studies in Political Economy*, 5–25.

Larner, W. (2003). Neoliberalism? *Environment and Planning D: Society and Space*, 21(5), 509–512.

Latour, B. (2005). *Reassembling the Social*. Oxford: Oxford University Press.

Law Commission of Canada (2001). Beyond Conjugality: Recognizing and Supporting Close Personal Adult Relationships. Available from: http://ssrn.com/abstract=1720747 [Accessed 24 January 2022].

Lee, L. (2015). Presidential address: will victims see justice at last? *Medico-Legal Journal*. doi:10.1177/0025817215581579.

Leiboff, M. (2005). A beautiful corpse. *Continuum*, 19(2), 221–237.

Leichtentritt, R. D., Shamir, M. M., Barak, A. and Yerushalmi, A. (2014). Bodies as means for continuing post-death relationships. *Journal of Health Psychology*, 1–12. doi: 1359105314536751.

Lemke, M. (2014). From putrescence to post-mortem: aesthetic transformations in Victorian burial reform. MA thesis, Ottowa: Carleton University. Available from: https://curve.carleton.ca/system/files/theses/31856.pdf [Accessed 24 January 2022].

Leslie, M. (2016). 'I can't put that on paper': how medical professional values shape the content of death certificates. *International Journal of Law in Context*, 12(2), 178–194.

Leslie, M. B. (1996). The myth of testamentary freedom. *Arizona Law Review*, 38, 235–290.

Leslie, M. B. (2014). Frustration of intent in the wealth transmission process. *Oñati Socio-Legal Series*, 4(2), 283–305.

Lewis, R. and Morris, A. (2012). Tort law culture: image and reality. *Journal of Law and Society*, 39(4), 562–592.

Lewis, R., Morris, A. and Oliphant, K. (2006). Tort personal injury claims statistics: is there a compensation culture in the United Kingdom? *Torts Law Journal*, 14(2), 158–175.

Linsley, K. R., Schapira, K. and Kelly, T. P. (2001). Open verdict v. suicide – importance to research. *British Journal of Psychiatry*, 178, 465–468.

Lipsky, M. (2010). *Street-Level Bureaucracy, 30th Anniversary Edition: Dilemmas of the Individual in Public Service*. New York: Russell Sage Foundation.

Luban, D. (1995). Settlements and the erosion of the public realm. *Georgetown Law Journal*, 83(7), 2619–2662.

Luce, T. (2003). *The Report of the Fundamental Review of Death Certification and Coroner Services* (The Luce Review), Cm. 5831, June.

Luce, T. (2010). Coroners and death certification law reform: the Coroners and Justice Act 2009 and its aftermath. *Medicine, Science, and the Law*, 50(4), 171–178.

Lukes, S. (1974). *Power: A Radical View*. London: Macmillan Education

MacCormack, G. (1984). On thing-liability (Sachhaftung) in early law. *Irish Jurist*, 19, 322–349.

Mackenzie, C. (2008). Relational autonomy, normative authority and perfectionism. *Journal of Social Philosophy*, 39(4), 512–533.

Mackenzie, C., and Stoljar, N. (eds) (2000). *Relational Autonomy: Feminist Perspectives on Autonomy, Agency, and the Social Self*. Oxford: Oxford University Press.

Maclean, M. and Eekelaar, J. (2004). The obligations and expectations of couples within families: three modes of interaction. *Journal of Social Welfare and Family Law*, 26(2), 117–130.

MacMahon, P. (2014). The inquest and the virtues of soft adjudication. *Yale Law and Policy Review*, 33(2), 275–322. Available from: http://online.wsj.com/public/resources/documents/inquest.pdf

Mahoney, E. (1997). Disabling tenants' rights. *Osgoode Hall Law Journal*, 35, 711–720.

Manning, P. and Hawkins, K. (1990). Legal decisions: a frame analytic perspective. In S. H. Riggins (ed) *Beyond Goffman: Studies on Communication, Institution and Social Interaction*. Berlin: Mouton De Gruyter, 203–233.

Manthorpe, J. and Mantineau, S. (2009). *Serious Case Reviews in Adult Safeguarding (Final Report)*. London: Social Care Workforce Research Unit, King's College.

Manthorpe, J. and Martineau, S. (2010). Serious case reviews in adult safeguarding in England: an analysis of a sample of reports. *British Journal of Social Work*, 41, 224–241.

Maple, M., Cerel, J., Jordan, J. R. and McKay, K. (2014). Uncovering and identifying the missing voices in suicide bereavement. *Suicidology Online*, 1–12.

Martin, G. and Scott Bray, R. (2013). Discolouring democracy? Policing, sensitive evidence, and contentious deaths in the United Kingdom. *Journal of Law and Society* 40, 624–656.

Marvell, A. (c. 1650). The nymph complaining for the death of her fawn. Available from: http://www.poetryfoundation.org/poem/173953 [Accessed 24 January 2022].

Mashaw, J. L. (2006). Accountability and institutional design: some thoughts on the grammar of governance. In M. W. Dowdle (ed) *Public Accountability: Designs, Dilemmas and Experiences*. Cambridge: Cambridge University Press, 115–127.

Mason, J. K. and Laurie, G. T. (2001). Consent or property? Dealing with the body and its parts in the shadow of Bristol and Alder Hey. *Modern Law Review*, 64(5), 710–729.

Matheson, R. (2014). *Death, Dynamite and Disaster: A Grisly British Railway History*. Stroud: History Press.

Matthews, D. (2017). From jurisdiction to juriswriting: at the expressive limits of the law. *Law, Culture and the Humanities*, 13(3), 425–445.

Matthews, P. (2014). *Jervis on Coroners* (13th edn). London: Sweet & Maxwell.

Matthews, P. (2020). *Jervis on Coroners* (14th edn). London: Sweet & Maxwell.

McBain, G. (2014). Modernising the law on the unlawful treatment of dead bodies. *Journal of Politics and Law*, 7(3), 89–98.

McEvoy, K. and Conway, H. (2004). The dead, the law, and the politics of the past. *Journal of Law and Society*, 31(4), 539–562.

McGovern, C. and Cusak, D. A. (2014). The case for a cost-effective central Coronial database following an analysis of Coronial records relating to deaths in nursing homes. *Journal of Forensic and Legal Medicine*, 25, 21–25.

McGowan, C. R. and Viens, A. M. (2010). Reform of the Coroner system: a potential public health failure. *Journal of Public Health*, 32(3), 427–430.

McGuinness, S., and Brazier, M. (2008). Respecting the living means respecting the dead too. *Oxford Journal of Legal Studies*, 28(2), 297–316.

McGuinness, S., and Thomson, M. (2020). Conscience, abortion and jurisdiction. *Oxford Journal of Legal Studies*, 40(4), 819–845.

McIntosh, S. (2012). Fulfilling their purpose: inquests, Article 2 and next of kin. *Public Law*, 3, 407–415.

McIntosh, S. (2016). Taken lives matter: open justice and recognition in inquests into deaths at the hands of the state. *International Journal of Law in Context*, 12(2), 141–161.

McKeough, J. (1983). Origins of the Coronial jurisdiction. *University of New South Wales Law Journal* 6, 191–210.

Mclean, M. (2015a). The Coroner in England and Wales: Coronial decision-making and local variation in case outcomes. Doctoral thesis. Huddersfield: University of Huddersfield.

Mclean, M. (2015b). Coroner consistency: the 10-jurisdiction, 10-year, postcode lottery? *Medicine, Science and the Law*, 55(2), 102–112.

Mclean, M. (2017). Contradictory coroners? Decision-making in death investigations. *Journal of Clinical Pathology*, 70(9), 787–791.

McVeigh, S. (ed) (2007). *Jurisprudence of Jurisdiction*. Abingdon: Routledge

McVeigh, S. (2014). Law as (more or less) itself: on some not very reflective elements of law. *UC Irvine Law Review*, 4, 471–491.

McVeigh, S. (2015). Office and the conduct of the minor jurisprudent. *UC Irvine Law Review*, 5, 499–511.

McVeigh, S. and Pahuja, S. (2009). Rival jurisdictions: the promise and loss of sovereignty. In C. Barbour and G. Pavlich (eds) *After Sovereignty: On the Question of Political Beginnings*. Oxford and New York: Routledge-Cavendish, 104–121.

Melsheimer, R. E. (1888). *Jervis on the Office and Duty of Coroners* (5th edn). London: Sweet, Maxwell and Stevens and Sons.

Metters, J. (2003). The Anatomy Act and cremation. *Pharos International*, 69(1), 3–7.

Miller, P. and Rose, N. (2008). *Governing the Present: Administering Economic, Social and Personal Life*. Cambridge: Polity Press.

Miller, T., Birch, M., Mauthner, M. and Jessop, J. (eds) (2012). *Ethics in Qualitative Research*. London: Sage.

Mills, C. (2018). 'Dead people don't claim': a psychopolitical autopsy of UK austerity suicides. *Critical Social Policy*, 38(2), 302–322.

Milmo, C. (2015). The appalling death of a man caught up in benefits nightmare. *The Independent* [online], 6 February. Available from: http://www.independent.co.uk/news/uk/home-news/the-tragic-tale-of-the-pensioner-who-killed-himself-after-begging-for-help-over-benefit-cuts-10029754.html [Accessed 24 January 2022].

Ministry of Justice (2013). *Implementing the Coroner reforms in Part 1 of the Coroners and Justice Act 2009*, Consultation Paper, CP2/2013.

Mok, E. (2014). Harnessing the full potential of Coroners' recommendations. *Victoria University of Wellington Law Review*, 45, 321–366.

Monk, D. (2011). Sexuality and succession law: beyond formal equality. *Feminist Legal Studies*, 19(3), 231–250.

Monk, D. (2014). Writing (gay and lesbian) wills. *Oñati Socio-Legal Series*, 4(2), 243–263.

Moore, J. (2016). *Coroners' Recommendation and the Promise of Saved Lives*. Cheltenham: Edward Elgar.

Morgan, B. (2006). Technocratic v. convivial accountability. In M. W. Dowdle (ed) *Public Accountability: Designs, Dilemmas and Experiences*. Cambridge: Cambridge University Press, 243–268.

Morgan, D. (1999) Risk and family practices. In E. Silva and C. Smart (eds) *The New Family?*. London: Sage, 13–30.

Morgan, D. H. (2011). Locating 'family practices'. *Sociological Research Online*, 16(4), 174–182.

Morgan, D. H. (2011). *Rethinking Family Practices*. Basingstoke: Palgrave Macmillan.

Morris, A. (2007). Spiralling or stabilising? The compensation culture and our propensity to claim damages for personal injury. *Modern Law Review*, 70(3), 349–378.

Mowll, J. (2007). Reality and regret: viewing or not viewing the body after a sudden death. *Bereavement Care*, 26(1), 3–6.

Murphy, G. E. (1998). Why women are less likely than men to commit suicide. *Comprehensive Psychiatry*, 39(4), 165–175.

Nacey, S. (2012). Scare quotes in L2 English and British English. Available from: http://brage.bibsys.no/xmlui/bitstream/handle/11250/134546/Nacey.pdf?sequence=1 [Accessed 24 January 2022].

NCEPOD Report (2006). *The Coroner's Autopsy: Do we deserve better? National Confidential Enquiry into Patient Outcome and Death.* Available from: https://www.ncepod.org.uk/2006Report/Downloads/Coronial%20Autopsy%20Report%202006.pdf [Accessed 15 July 2015].

Ngo, M., Matthews, L. R., Quinlan, M., and Bohle, P. (2019). Information needs of bereaved families following fatal work incidents. *Death Studies*, 478–489.

Ngo, M., Matthews, L. R., Quinlan, M. and Bohle, P. (2021). Bereaved family members' views of the value of coronial inquests into fatal work incidents. *OMEGA – Journal of Death and Dying*, 82(3), 446–466.

Nicholls, J. (2014). Inquest judicial review and civil claims arising from death – Part 1. *Legal Action*, November, 21–24.

Oliphant, K. (2013). Tort law, risk, and technological innovation in England. *McGill Law Journal*, 59, 819–845.

O'Malley, P. (2000). Risk societies and the government of crime. In M. Brown and J. Pratt (eds) *Dangerous Offenders: Punishment and Social Order*. London and New York: Routledge, 17–33.

O'Malley, P. (2002) Imagining insurance: risk, thrift and life insurance in Britain. In T. Baker and J. Simon (eds) *Embracing Risk: The Changing Culture of Insurance and Responsibility*. Chicago and London: University of Chicago Press, 97–115.

Owen, R. (2020). *When Things Go Wrong: The Response of the Justice System.* London: Justice. Available from: https://files.justice.org.uk/wp-content/uploads/2020/08/06165913/When-Things-Go-Wrong.pdf [Accessed 24 January 2022].

Owens, C., Lambert, H., Lloyd, K. and Donovan, J. (2008). Tales of biographical disintegration: how parents make sense of their sons' suicides. *Sociology of Health and Illness*, 30(2), 237–254.

Palmer, B. S., Bennewith, O., Simkin, S., Cooper, J., Hawton, K., Kapur, N. and Gunnell, D. (2015). Factors influencing Coroners' verdicts: an analysis of verdicts given in 12 Coroners' districts to researcher-defined suicides in England in 2005. *Journal of Public Health*, 37(1), 157–165.

Pannick, D. (2010). Inquests without a jury: the government needs to think again. *Inter Alia*, 31–33.

Pantazis, C. and Pemberton, S. (2009). From the 'old' to the 'new' suspect community: examining the impacts of recent UK counter-terrorist legislation. *British Journal of Criminology*, 49(5), 646–666.

Pantazis, C. and Pemberton, S. (2011). Restating the case for the 'suspect community': a reply to Greer. *British Journal of Criminology*, 51(6), 1054–1062.

Partington, M. (2004). *Salvaging the Sacred: Lucy, My Sister*. London: Quaker Books.

Pavlich, G. C. (2005). Experiencing critique. *Law and Critique*, (16), 95–112.

Pavlich, G. C. (2007). *Governing Paradoxes of Restorative Justice*. London: Psychology Press.

Pavlich, G. C. (2011). *Law and Society Redefined*. Oxford: Oxford University Press.

Pemberton, J. (1988). Are hip fractures underestimated as a cause of death? The influence of Coroners and pathologists on the death rate. *Journal of Public Health*, 10(2), 117–123.

Pemberton, S. (2008). Demystifying deaths in police custody: challenging state talk. *Social and Legal Studies*, 17(2), 237–262.

Pervukhin, A. (2005). Deodands: a study in the creation of common law rules. *American Journal of Legal History*, 47(3), 237–256.

Piety, T. R. (2000). Critique of adjudication: fin de siecle: confession without avoidance. *Cardozo Law Review*, 22, 947–969.

Pietz, W. (1997). Death of the deodand: accursed objects and the money value of human life. *RES: Anthropology and Aesthetics*, 31, 97–108.

Post-Mortem,Forensic and Disaster Imaging Group (PMFDI) (2012). NHS Implementation Sub-Group of the Department of Health Post-mortem, Forensic and Disaster Imaging Group. *Can Cross-Sectional Imaging as an Adjunct and/or Alternative to the Invasive Autopsy be Implemented within the NHS?* Available from: https://www.gov.uk/government/news/strategy-for-implementation-of-a-national-less-invasive-autopsy-imaging-serv ice-within-the-nhs [Accessed 11 August 2015].

Pottage, A. (2014). Law after anthropology: Object and technique in Roman law. *Theory, Culture and Society*. doi: 0263276413502239.

Powell, R., Weber, L. and Pickering, S. (2013). Counting and accounting for deaths in Australian immigration custody. *Homicide Studies*, 17(4), 391–417.

Prescott, J. J. and Spier, K. E. (2016). A comprehensive theory of civil settlement. *New York University Law Review*, 91, 59–143.

Prior, L. (1985). Making sense of mortality. *Sociology of Health and Illness*, 7(2), 167–190.

Prior, L. (1989). *The Social Organisation of Death: Medical Discourse and Social Practices in Belfast*. Basingstoke: Palgrave.

Prisons and Probation Ombudsman (2013). *PPO Thematic Report: Learning from PPO Investigations*. Available from: https://www.ppo.gov.uk/app/uplo ads/2014/07/Recommendations_thematic.pdf [Accessed 31 July 2013].

Pylkkänen, A. (2007). Liberal family law in the making: Nordic and European harmonisation. *Feminist Legal Studies*, 15(3), 289–306.

Rankin, J., Wright, C. and Lind, T. (2002). Cross sectional survey of parents' experience and views of the postmortem examination. *British Medical Journal*, 324(7341), 816–818.

Razack, S. H. (2011a). The space of difference in law: inquests into aboriginal deaths in custody. *Somatechnics*, 1(1), 87–123.

Razack, S. H. (2011b). Timely deaths: medicalizing the deaths of Aboriginal people in police custody. *Law, Culture and the Humanities*, 9, 352–374.

Razack, S. H. (2015). *Dying from Improvement: Inquests and Inquiries into Indigenous Deaths in Custody*. Toronto: University of Toronto Press.

Reimers, E. (2011). Primary mourners and next-of-kin: how grief practices reiterate and subvert heterosexual norms. *Journal of Gender Studies*, 20(3), 251–262.

Resnik, J. and Curtis, D. (2011). *Representing Justice: Invention, Controversy, and Rights in City-States and Democratic Courtrooms*. New Haven: Yale University Press.

Ribbens, J. (1989). Interviewing: an 'unnatural situation'? *Women's Studies International Forum*, 12(6), 579–592.

Richardson, R. (2001). Coroner Wakley: two remarkable eyewitness accounts. *The Lancet*, 358(9299), 2150–2154.

Riles, A. (ed) (2006). *Documents: Artifacts of Modern Knowledge*. Ann Arbor: University of Michigan Press.

Robb, B. and Sullivan, J. (2004). The past and the present: listening to parental experiences of autopsy practice. *Grief Matters: The Australian Journal of Grief and Bereavement*, 7(2), 39–43.

Roberts, W. P. (1844). *The Haswell Colliery Explosion, 28th September, 1844. Narrative, report of the proceedings at the Coroner's Inquest, and plan of that part of the colliery in which the accident occurred. Compiled … for and revised by W. P. Roberts*. Newcastle upon Tyne.

Roche, D. (2003). *Accountability in Restorative Justice*. Oxford: Oxford University Press

Rogers, N. (2020). *Law, Fiction and Activism in a Time of Climate Change*. Abingdon: Routledge.

Rose, N. (1990). *Governing the Soul: The Shaping of the Private Self*. London: Taylor & Francis/Routledge.

Roseneil, S. and Budgeon, S. (2004). Cultures of intimacy and care beyond 'the family': personal life and social change in the early 21st century. *Current Sociology*, 52(2), 135–159.

Roseneil, S., Crowhurst, I., Hellesund, T., Santos, A. C. and Stoilova, M. (2013). Changing landscapes of heteronormativity: the regulation and normalization of same-sex sexualities in Europe. *Social Politics: International Studies in Gender, State and Society*, 20(2), 165–199.

Royal Liverpool Children's Inquiry, Redfern, M., Keeling, J. W. and Powell, E. (2001). *The Royal Liverpool Children's Inquiry: Return to an Address of the Honourable the House of Commons Dated 30 January 2001 for an Inquiry into the Removal, Retention and Disposal of Organs and Tissue Following Post-mortems at Royal Liverpool Children's NHS Trust (Alder Hey)*. London: HMSO.

Ruder, T. D. and Ampanozi, G. (2013). Can cross-sectional imaging as an adjunct and/or alternative to the invasive autopsy be implemented with the NHS? *Journal of Forensic Radiology and Imaging*, 1, 28–29.

Ruder, T. D. and Rutty, G. N. (2013). The first Leicester post-mortem computed tomography imaging course. *Journal of Forensic Radiology and Imaging*, 1, 38.

Rugg, J. (2000). Defining the place of burial: what makes a cemetery a cemetery? *Mortality*, 5(3), 259–275.

Rugg, J. (2013a). Choice and constraint in the burial landscape: re-evaluating twentieth-century commemoration in the English churchyard. *Mortality*, 18(3), 215–234.

Rugg, J. (2013b). Constructing the grave: competing burial ideals in nineteenth-century England. *Social History*, 38(3), 328–345.

Ryan, M. (1996). *Lobbying from Below*. London: UCL Press.

Ryan, S. (2017) *Justice for Laughing Boy: Connor Sparrowhawk – A Death by Indifference*. London and Philadelphia: Jessica Kingsley Publishers.

Samuels, A. (2011). Deaths and Coroners: Coroners Act 2009. *Medico-Legal Journal*, 79(1), 26–28.

Scott, C. (2000). Accountability in the regulatory state. *Journal of Law and Society*, 27, 38–60.

Scott, J. (2017). From presence to participation: the role of the juror reimagined. *Law and Humanities*, 11(2), 286–308.

Scott Bray, R. (2006). Fugitive performances of death and injury. *Law Text Culture*, 10, 41–71.

Scott Bray, R. (2010). Death scene jurisprudence: the social life of Coronial facts. *Griffith Law Review*, 19(3), 567–592.

Scott Bray, R. (2012). Executive impunity and parallel justice? The United Kingdom debate on secret inquests and inquiries. *Journal of Law and Medicine*, 19(3), 569–592.

Scott Bray, R. and Martin, G. (2016). Exploring fatal facts: current issues in Coronial law, policy and practice. *International Journal of Law in Context*, 12(2), 115–140.

Scott Bray, R., Carpenter, B. and Barnes, M. (2018). Southern death investigation: theorizing Coronial work from the Global South. In K. Carrington, R. Hogg, J. Scott and M. Sozzo (eds) *The Palgrave Handbook of Criminology and the Global South*. Cham: Palgrave Macmillan, 139–161.

Scourfield, J., Fincham, B., Langer, S. and Shiner, M. (2012). Sociological autopsy: an integrated approach to the study of suicide in men. *Social Science and Medicine*, 74(4), 466–473.

Scraton, P. (1999). Policing with contempt: the degrading of truth and denial of justice in the aftermath of the Hillsborough disaster. *Journal of Law and Society*, 26(3), 273–297.

Scraton, P. (2002). Lost lives, hidden voices: 'truth' and controversial deaths. *Race and Class*, 44(1), 107–118.

Scraton, P. (2007) *Power, Conflict and Criminalisation*. London and New York: Routledge.

Scraton, P. (2013). The legacy of Hillsborough: liberating truth, challenging power. *Race and Class*, 55(2), 1–27.

Scraton, P. and Chadwick, K. (1986). Speaking ill of the dead: institutional responses to deaths in custody. *Journal of Law and Society*, 13(1), 93–115.

Scraton, P. and Chadwick, K. (1987). *In the Arms of the Law: Coroners' Inquests and Deaths in Custody*. London: Pluto Press.

Scraton, P., Jemphrey, A. and Coleman, S. (1995). *No Last Rights: The Denial of Justice and the Promotion of Myth in the Aftermath of the Hillsborough Disaster*. Liverpool: Liverpool City Council.

Seale, C. (1995). Dying alone. *Sociology of Health and Illness*, 17(3), 376–392.

Select Committee on the Inquiries Act (2014). *Post-legislative assessment of the Inquiries Act 2005, Report of Session 2013–14, House of Lords* (26 February).

Selket, K., Glover, M. and Palmer, S. (2015). Normalising post-mortems: whose cultural imperative? An indigenous view on New Zealand post-mortem policy. *Kotuitui: New Zealand Journal of Social Sciences Online*, 10(1), 1–9.

Sense about Science (2014). Open letter to David Cameron re late registration of the dead in England and Wales, 18 June. Available from: http://www.rss.org.uk/Images/PDF/influencing-change/rss-open-letter-to-late-registration-deaths-18-june-2014.pdf [Accessed 22 January 2022].

Sharp, D. (2012). Thomas Wakley (1795–1862): a biographical sketch. *The Lancet*, 379(9829), 1914–1921.

Sharpe, R. R. (1913). *Calendar of Coroners Rolls of the City of London, AD 1300–1378*. London: R. Clay and Sons, Limited.

Shaw, H. and Coles, D. (2007). *Unlocking the Truth: Families' Experiences of the Investigation of Deaths in Custody*. London: INQUEST.

Sim, J. and Ward, T. (1994). The magistrate of the poor? Coroners and deaths in custody in nineteenth-century England. In M. Clark and C. Crawford (eds) *Legal Medicine in History*. Cambridge: Cambridge University Press, 245–267.

Simon, J. (2005). Edgework and insurance in risk societies: some notes on Victorian lawyers and mountaineers. In S. Lyng (ed) *Edgework: The Sociology of Risk Taking*. London and New York: Routledge, 203–226.

Simor, J. (ed) (2015). *Human Rights Practice*. London: Sweet & Maxwell.

Sloan, B. (2011). Enduring families, enduring the adoption process, *LQR*, 127, 173–176.

Slote, M. (2007). *The Ethics of Care and Empathy*. Abingdon: Routledge.

Smart, C. (2007). *Personal Life*. Cambridge: Polity Press.

Smart, C. (2009). Making kin: relationality and law. In A. Bottomly and S. Wong (eds) *Changing Contours of Domestic Life, Family and Law: Caring and Sharing*. Oxford: Hart Publishing, 7–23.

Smith, H. (1967). From deodand to dependency. *American Journal of Legal History*, 11, 389–403.

Smith, J. (2003). *Shipman Inquiry (Third Report) (2003)*, Cm. 5854.

Spalding, N. J. and Phillips, T. (2007). Exploring the use of vignettes: from validity to trustworthiness. *Qualitative Health Research*, 17(7), 954–962.

Speed, C. (2012). Self-inflicted deaths in prison: an exploration of INQUEST's challenges to state power. *Internet Journal of Criminology*. Available from: http://www.antoniocasella.eu/archipsy/Speed_2012.pdf [Accessed 24 January 2022].

Spillane, A., Matvienko-Sikar, K., Larkin, C., Corcoran, P. and Arensman, E. (2019). How suicide-bereaved family members experience the inquest process: a qualitative study using thematic analysis. *International Journal of Qualitative Studies on Health and Well-Being*, 14(1), 1563430, 1–10.

Sprigge, S. S. (1897). *The life and times of Thomas Wakley: founder and first editor of the 'Lancet', Member of Parliament for Finsbury, and Coroner for West Middlesex*. London, New York and Bombay: Longmans, Green and Co (republished by General Books LLC, 2012).

Stanley, N. and Manthorpe, J. (eds) (2004). *The Age of the Inquiry: Learning and Blaming in Health and Social Care*. London: Routledge.

Stein, M. A. (2008). Victorian tort liability for workplace injuries. *University of Illinois Law Review*, 3, 933–984.

Stone, E. (1986). *Coroners Courts in England and Wales*. London: Justice.

Sullivan, J. and Monagle, P. (2011). Bereaved parents' perceptions of the autopsy examination of their child. *Pediatrics*, 127(4), e1013–e1020.

Sutherland, G., Kemp, C., Bugeja, L., Sewell, G., Pirkis, J. and Studdert, D. M. (2014). What happens to Coroners' recommendations for improving public health and safety? Organisational responses under a mandatory response regime in Victoria, Australia. *BMC Public Health*, 14(1), 732–739.

Sutton, T. (1997). The deodand and responsibility for death. *Journal of Legal History*, 18(3), 44–55.

Sutton, T. (1999). The nature of the early law of deodand. *Cambrian Law Review*, 30, 9–20.

Tait, G. and Carpenter, B. (2010). Firearm suicide in Queensland. *Journal of Sociology*, 46(1), 83–98.

Tait, G. and Carpenter, B. (2013a). Regulating bereavement: inquests, family pressure and the gate keeping of suicide statistics. *Proceedings of the 2nd International Conference on Crime, Justice and Social Democracy*. Available from: http://eprints.qut.edu.au/61392/ [Accessed 22 January 2022].

Tait, G. and Carpenter, B. (2013b). Suicide and the therapeutic Coroner: inquests, governance and the grieving family. *International Journal for Crime, Justice and Social Democracy*, 2(3), 92–104.

Tait, G. and Carpenter, B. (2014). Suicide, statistics and the Coroner: a comparative study of death investigations. *Journal of Sociology*. doi: 10.1177/ 1440783314550058.

Tait, G., and Carpenter, B. (2016). The continuing implications of the 'crime' of suicide: a brief history of the present. *International Journal of Law in Context*, 12(2), 210–224.

Tait, G., Carpenter, B. and Jowett, S. (2018). Coronial practice, indigeneity and suicide. *International Journal of Environmental Research and Public Health*, 15(4), 765. https://doi.org/10.3390/ijerph15040765

Tait, G., Carpenter, B., Quadrelli, C. and Barnes, M. (2016). Decision-making in a death investigation: emotion, families and the coroner. *Journal of Law and Medicine*, 23(3), 571–581.

Taylor, S. (ed) (2002). *Ethnographic Research: A Reader*. London: Sage.

Thomas, L. (2020). Does the state really care when it kills you? Lecture for Gresham College series *Death, the State and Human Rights*, 1 October. Available from: https://www.gresham.ac.uk/series/death-state/ [Accessed 22 January 2022].

Thomas, L., Straw, A. and Friedman, D. (2008). *Inquests: A Practitioner's Guide* (2nd edn). London: Legal Action Group.

Thomas, L., Straw, A., Machover, D. and Friedman, D. (2014). *Inquests: A Practitioner's Guide* (3rd edn). London: Legal Action Group..

Thornton, P. (2012a). The Coroner system in the 21st century. Parmoor Lecture, 25 October, Howard League for Penal Reform.

Thornton, P. (2012b). Speech at the Annual Conference of the Coroners' Society of England and Wales, 21 September.

Thornton, Q. C. P. (2014). Coroner reform: 25 years in the making. *Medico-Legal Journal*, 82(3), 88–96.

Thurston, G. (1962). The Coroner and the police. *Police Journal* 35, 12–22.

Thurston, G. (1969). A queer sort of thing. *Medico-Legal Journal*, 37(4), 165–171.

Thurston, G. (1976). *Coronership*. London: B. Rose.

Timmermans, S. (2005). Death brokering: constructing culturally appropriate deaths. *Sociology of Health and Illness*, 993–1013.

Timmermans, S. (2006). *Postmortem: How Medical Examiners Explain Suspicious Deaths*. Chicago: University of Chicago Press.

Tomlins, C. (2016). 'Be operational, or disappear': thoughts on a present discontent. *Annual Review of Law and Social Science*, 12, 1–23.

Toulmin Smith, J. (1852). *On the Constitution and Functions of the Coroner and Coroner's Inquest and their relation to Municipal Self-Government, A Letter to Edward Herford Esq, Coroner of Manchester*. Charing Cross: Trelawney Saunders.

Trabsky, M. (2015). The custodian of memories: Coronial architecture in nineteenth-century Melbourne. *Griffith Law Review*, doi:10.1080/10383441.2015.1051209.

Trabsky, M. (2016). The Coronial manual and the bureaucratic logic of the Coroner's office. *International Journal of Law in Context*, 12(2), 195–209.

Trabsky, M. (2019). *Law and the Dead: Technology, Relations and Institutions*. Abingdon: Routledge.

Traynor, L. (2013). Benefit cuts blind man committed suicide after Atos ruled him fit to work. *Daily Mirror* [online], 28 December. Available from: http://www.mirror.co.uk/news/uk-news/benefit-cuts-blind-man-committed-2965375#ixzz35Ti06Ika [Accessed 24 January 2022].

Troyer, J. (2008). Abuse of a corpse: a brief history and re-theorization of necrophilia laws in the USA. *Mortality*, 13(2), 132–152.

Tuffin, R., Quinn, A., Ali, F. and Cramp, P. (2009). A review of the accuracy of death certification on the intensive care unit and the proposed reforms to the Coroner's system. *Journal of the Intensive Care Society*, 10(2), 134–137.

Tweedie, J. and Ward, T. (1989). The Gibraltar shootings and the politics of inquests. *Journal of Law and Society*, 16(4), 464–476.

Vines, P. E. (2007). The sacred and the profane: the role of property concepts in disputes about post-mortem examination. *Sydney Law Review*, 29(2), 235–261.

Walsh, P. (2015). Is access to justice becoming a lost cause? *Clinical Risk*, 2(1), 1–2.

Ward, I. (2014). *Sex, Crime and Literature in Victorian England*. Oxford: Hart Publishing.

Warwick Inquest Group (1985). The Inquest as a theatre for police tragedy: the Davey case. *Journal of Law and Society*, 12(1), 35–61.

Weeks, J., Heaphy, B. and Donovan, C. (2001). *Same Sex Intimacies: Families of Choice and Other Life Experiments*. London: Psychology Press.

Wellington, R. H. (1905). *The King's Coroner: Being a Complete Collection of the Statutes Relating to the Office Together with a Short History of the Same*. Vol. 1. W. Clowes.

Wells, C. (1991). Inquests, inquiries and indictments: the official reception of death by disaster. *Legal Studies*, 11(1), 71–84.

Weston, K. (2013). *Families We Choose: Lesbians, Gays, Kinship.* New York: Columbia University Press.

Wheatley, N. (2012). 'The Emperor's New Clothes?' Are adequate resources for Coroners services not really there? A review of the resourcing of Coroners services in England and Wales in 2012 with particular reference to Coroners officers. MSc thesis. Centre for Death and Society, Bath: University of Bath.

White, S. D (2002). A burial ahead of its time? The Crookenden burial case and the sanctioning of cremation in England and Wales. *Mortality*, 7(2), 171–190.

White, S. D. (2003). The Cremation Act 1902: from private to local to general. *Pharos International*, 69(1), 14–18.

Will Aid (2014). Will Aid research 2014: key findings. Available from: http://www.willaid.org.uk/press/research [Accessed 22 January 2022].

Wilson, A. R. (2007). With friends like these: the liberalization of queer family policy. *Critical Social Policy*, 27(1), 50–76.

Wilson, A. R. (2009). The 'neat concept' of sexual citizenship: a cautionary tale for human rights discourse. *Contemporary Politics*, 15(1), 73–85.

Wolmar, C. (2005). *The Subterranean Railway.* London: Atlantic Books.

Woods, S. (2014). Death duty: caring for the dead in the context of disaster. *New Genetics and Society*, 33(3), 333–347.

Woodthorpe, K., Rumble, H. and Valentine, C. (2013). Putting 'the grave' into social policy: state support for funerals in contemporary UK society. *Journal of Social Policy*, 42(3), 605–622.

Wright Report (1936). *Departmental Committee on Coroners*, Cmnd 5070.

Yin, R. K. (1994). *Case Study Research: Design and Methods* (2nd edn). Vol. 5. London: Sage.

Index

Lord Campbell's Act *see* Fatal Accidents Act
Luce, Tom 26, 27, 55, 56, 97

M

McVeigh, Shaun 21–22, 29, 56, 93, 100–104
media, the role of 1, 5, 31, 66, 87, 89,
    124–125, 145–146, 151–152,
    167–168, 182
methods 8–10, 78–80
Morgan, Bronwen 13, 16, 17, 53, 182
Morgan, David 74, 79, 137, 182

N

newspapers *see* media
next of kin *see* law; family

O

office 114, 132, 137–138, 146, 169
officers and their specific role 20, 79, 83,
    89, 97, 119, 123, 127, 134, 138–139,
    146–147, 156
order 131, 135, 144, 150–157

P

periodisation 2, 49–50, 54, 97
post-mortem 3, 57–60, 93–95, 107–114,
    141, 146–147
practices of family *see* family
pre-inquest hearing 127, 140, 145, 149
Pre-Inquest Review *see* pre-inquest hearing
press *see* media
Prevention of Future Death reports, Rule 43
    reports 14, 15, 55
Prior, Lindsay 52–54, 108, 173, 176
privacy 110, 132, 139, 146, 167
procedure
    implicit and provisional decision-making 21
    importance of 18–20
public – inquest hearing as a public space 7,
    19, 53, 106, 110, 124–125, 139, 144,
    145, 151, 164–168
public health 30–31, 42, 52–53, 105,
    112, 149
purpose of inquest *see* inquest

R

Razack, Sherene 2, 11, 181
representatives *see* lawyers
representing the law 22, 70, 97, 142, 183
ritual 18, 105, 151, 163, 170, 180

routinisation *see* decision-making
Rule 43 reports *see* Prevention of Future
    Deaths reports

S

scope of inquest 20, 68–69, 122, 132, 154
Scott Bray, Rebecca 11, 18, 26, 52, 111,
    148, 172
Scraton, Phil 11, 90
    with Kathryn Chadwick 11, 27–29, 32, 52,
    54, 141, 152, 178
sequential decision-making *see*
    decision-making
settlement 133, 144, 165–168
Shipman Report *see* Smith, Janet
Smith, Janet 27, 55, 56
social welfare *see* Coroner
solicitors *see* lawyers
space, geography, offices *see* courtrooms;
    locality; public space
state responsibility *see* Article 2 ECHR
statistics 173–174

T

therapeutic jurisprudence 1, 69–70, 170,
    177–178
therapy *see* therapeutic jurisprudence
Trabsky, Marc 29, 53, 61, 105, 149
typification *see* decision-making

V

verdict *see* conclusions
vignettes
    use of vignettes 10
    vignette 1 (the non-adopted daughter and
        missing wife) 80–81, 83, 88, 117, 126
    vignette 2 (the girlfriend) 81, 86, 110, 125,
        138, 139, 140, 141
    vignette 3 (the mother, new partner and
        biological father) 81, 83, 87, 126–128,
        132, 135–137, 143–144, 155
    vignette 4 (the long-lost sister) 82, 89,
        91–92, 114, 128–129, 169

W

Wakley, Thomas 16, 30–32, 41–44, 149
welfare *see* Coroner
woodwork, coming out of the 88–89,
    118–119